MARKET-ORIENTED PRICING

Recent Titles from Quorum Books

MARKET-ORIENTED PRICING

STRATEGIES FOR MANAGEMENT

MICHAEL H. MORRIS *and* GENE MORRIS

Foreword by Stanley Freedman

QUORUM BOOKS

New York • Westport, Connecticut • London

Library of Congress Cataloging-in-Publication Data

Morris, Michael H.
  Market-oriented pricing : strategies for management / Michael H.
Morris and Gene Morris.
    p. cm.
  Includes bibliographical references.
  ISBN 0-89930-402-8 (lib. bdg. : alk. paper)
  1. Pricing. I. Morris, Gene. II. Title.
HF5416.5.M68 1990
658.8′16—dc20   89-10712

British Library Cataloguing in Publication Data is available.

Library of Congress Catalog Card Number: 89-10712
ISBN: 0-89930-402-8

First published in 1990 by Quorum Books

Greenwood Press, Inc.
88 Post Road West, Westport, Connecticut 06881

Printed in the United States of America

The paper used in this book complies with the
Permanent Paper Standard issued by the National
Information Standards Organization (Z39.48-1984).

10 9 8 7 6 5 4 3 2 1

To Carl Stern, pricing scholar and teacher

CONTENTS

ILLUSTRATIONS

TABLES

FIGURES

EXHIBIT

FOREWORD

When a business firm attempts to mold its whole policy to meet the prices of its competitor, that business is entering a labyrinth the center of which is the chamber of despair. Highest quality never can be given nor obtained at the lowest prices. If a price must be sacrificed, quality must be sacrificed. If quality is sacrificed, society is not truly served.

H. T. Garvey

I suspect we agree that business is not a very precise science. And of the many business functions, pricing emerges as one of the least understood. Like most fuzzy areas, it has generated more than its share of books, seminars, and articles. It's sort of a contradiction. Pricing, one of the great Pillars of Marketing, is loaded with vagueness and inconsistency. As practiced by many, pricing is anything but a planned and coordinated business function. An example:

A manufacturer of business and computer forms is trying to get in with a major national bank. The forms company is a division of one of *Fortune's* Fifty and has some of the advantages of a conglomerate's corporate clout. The competition, a medium-sized company, has been selling to the bank for years. The dialogue:

"Hell, the bank's V.P. Purchasing is so fond of them there's no way we can get in."
"How about price?"
"Price? We just might get a piece of it if we went in at cost or even shaded that a bit. After we are in, maybe we could bring the price up. Problem is getting it past our legal people. Predatory pricing ain't pretty words, George."
"Here's another idea. As a conglomerate, we have loads of different division bank

accounts. The bank's got to want additional banking business. Suppose we meet with their national accounts guy, offer them some additional banking action, and have their senior people set us up with the bank's purchasing people for some profitable forms sales."

Price started out as the critical element. It fell by the wayside and the sale was made on the basis of a tie-in with new bank accounts. How did things turn out? The bank's very ticked-off V.P. Purchasing quietly kept book on all quality and delivery problems. He was able to erode the new relationship and bring back his old vendor (at a higher price).

And then you run into something like this. Joe, a V.P. Marketing, has been around a long time. He's got a new president and calls in some chits:

"Hello, George, I need a favor. I'd like to increase our price to you by 5 percent as of the first of the month. I've got a big squeeze from my new boss. I'll make most of it up to you the last half." Legal? Maybe. Proper? You know the answer. Does it happen? You bet. And do managers want to talk about it? No. It becomes part of the enormous mishmash of strange episodes that, along with rational events, comprise the not-so-disciplined business function called pricing.

Michael Morris's *Market-Oriented Pricing* brings a nice degree of order to the pricing scene. It arrives at a time when the pressures on pricing people are at a historical high. Deregulation has shell-shocked a good deal of U.S. business, and competition is international and hard hitting.

Market-Oriented Pricing makes no pretense of being the ultimate answer to all pricing situations. What it does is treat in common-sense terms the bulk of influences impacting pricing and then offer a marketing-planning approach to setting prices. As presented by Morris, pricing assumes an overwhelmingly logical role as a major means of attaining near-term and long-range company objectives. And enjoy. Morris spares us jargon and the too-theoretical. Instead, he shares cases and actual pricing practices.

This is an enjoyable book. It is readable. I suspect it can help managers make more profit for their firms. And it certainly makes room for Albert Einstein's philosophy, "Sometimes one pays most for the things one gets for nothing."

Stanley Freedman

PREFACE

Listening to managers informally discuss their businesses with outsiders reveals much about priorities. Consider the topics emphasized in the typical conversation. The speaker will elaborate extensively on new equipment purchases, products being introduced, expensive promotional programs just underway, difficulties in penetrating particular markets, problems with employees, differences with suppliers, and complaints about competitors, among other job-related topics.

Absent from most such conversations, and rarely noticed by the casual observer, is that managers rarely talk about the prices they charge. Why is this, and why do managers actually seem to avoid any discussion that involves price? A number of possible explanations exist. Many managers take price for granted, assuming the principal function of price is to cover costs. So long as this happens, they really have little interest in actual price levels. Further, they tend to assume that everybody is probably charging the same thing. Others view the company's pricing decisions as proprietary competitive information. They are concerned that any such discussion will tip the company's hand to competitors or raise regulatory concerns about collusion.

Alternatively, some managers may be worried about customers finding out how the company determines prices. They are firmly convinced that customers will react adversely if they were aware of markups, margins, and differences in prices charged to various customers. Correspondingly, they believe that all parties should be kept in the dark.

There is, however, a more fundamental reason for "price avoidance." Namely, many managers do not understand how to price, and are insecure about the adequacy of their current pricing methods. As a result, they rely on overly simplistic rules of thumb and place an exaggerated amount of emphasis on costs.

And yet, pricing represents one of the most underutilized competitive weapons available to the modern manager. Not only is price a means of distinguishing the firm's offerings from those of competitors, it is also a tool for communicating with customers and influencing the way they buy.

This book presents price as a fairly simple but powerful marketing tool. It is a creative variable that managers can manipulate to accomplish a wide variety of ends. Doing so requires a dramatic change in the way companies typically approach price management. They must move away from the traditional short-term, tactical, reactive methods relied upon to set and manage prices and adopt a systematic, strategic, and proactive perspective. Most importantly, they must embrace a market-based perspective.

These ten chapters attempt to provide direction regarding how market-based pricing can be achieved. The central theme throughout each of these ten chapters is that pricing begins and ends with the customer. Further, every pricing action should be part of a larger pricing program built around the realities of customer needs and competitor pressures.

Efforts such as this book do not happen in a vacuum. While we take full responsibility for the limitations of the book, there would have been no finished product without the considerable efforts of a very impressive group of individuals. First and foremost, we wish to express the deepest gratitude to Merrell Mary Bailey, who brought organization to our scatterbrained efforts, provided detailed background research on many of the topics investigated in these pages, and served as the principal person behind chapter 10, on computers and pricing. Second, we thank Ann Houser for her tireless job of word processing and proofreading, and for her patience. Third, the tables and figures that we feel bring life to many of the subjects discussed were prepared by Sean Aten, Roland Dube, and Paul Stephenson. Fourth, we owe much appreciation to Duane Davis, Gordon Paul, and Alvin Burns, colleagues at the University of Central Florida who provided much-needed advice and support. Finally, there would be no book without Lois Morris, wife and sister-in-law, source of inspiration.

MARKET-ORIENTED PRICING

1

INTRODUCTION: PRICE AS A STATEMENT OF VALUE

CREATING CUSTOMER VALUE

Ours is a marketing society. Virtually everything is marketed today, from soap products and computers to religion, social causes, and political candidates. Competitive pressures and changing technology are forcing even the most skeptical of managers to acknowledge the need for effective marketing. Meanwhile, the tools and techniques of the profession are becoming increasingly scientific and sophisticated. A large number of models, programs, and frameworks are now available for use by those engaged in modern marketing.

With this heightened emphasis, many successful companies have come to a fundamental realization: The job of any market-driven organization is not to sell a product, but instead to create value for customers. Value creation, rather than creative slogans, aggressive salesmanship, or expensive media campaigns, is the source of competitive advantage in the marketplace. The fundamental purpose of any business is to create value where there was none before.

Firms create value in many ways. In fact, the possibilities are virtually limitless. Improved quality, faster service, more comprehensive warranties, unique features and options, better delivery, easier ordering, and a convenient location are but a few examples of sources of customer value. Value is created, then, through product or service attributes and benefits. Customers do not purchase a product or service per se. What they are actually buying is a set of need-satisfying benefits.

Consider the company purchasing a new word processing system for its office personnel. The firm is not so much buying hardware and software as it is purchasing such attributes as improved speed in document preparation, more complete editing capability, enhanced document storage capacity, or better record keeping. This value package can be enhanced by the manufacturer who offers complete installation services, or a user-friendly training program on the customer's premises.

PRICE AND VALUE

Once a company has designed the package of benefits it wishes to provide to prospective customers, a price must be determined. Prices are numerical statements of what a customer must pay for an item. But the key to effective pricing is to ensure that the price charged reflects the amount of value a customer is receiving. A fundamental principle in market-based pricing is to recognize that *price is a statement of value, not a statement of costs.*

One of the leading causes of new-product failure is a phenomenon marketers refer to as the "price crunch." This is the situation where the company charges a price that is significantly higher or lower than the amount of value customers associate with a particular purchase. Just as the majority of homeowners were not willing to purchase microwave ovens when they were six hundred dollars a unit, a substantial number of customers might be expected to resist purchasing a one hundred-tablet bottle of aspirin for fifty cents.

The underlying reason for much of today's ineffective pricing is a preoccupation among those who set prices with the need to cover costs. Cost coverage, not customer value, is the single most important factor in the pricing policies of most companies. In fact, the most popular method for determining prices is called cost-plus pricing. Cost per unit is determined, usually based on some allocation scheme, and a profit margin is added. Customer considerations, and especially value to the user, are virtually ignored.

Alternatively, the challenge facing managers who seek to be value-driven is twofold. First, the package of benefits offered for sale must reflect the underlying needs of buyers. Customers vary in how much value they assign to a particular product or service attribute, and are involved in trade-off decisions concerning how much of an attribute is sufficient. For instance, some car buyers place considerable importance on gas mileage, while others are much more concerned with styling. In the final analysis, most buyers make some sort of trade-off between acceptable mileage performance and automobile appearance. This trade-off defines the value for which they are willing to pay.

The second problem involves assigning a dollar price tag to the attribute package that accurately reflects the value being received by a customer. This problem is complicated by the fact that value is perceived in the minds of individual buyers. Different customers are unlikely to perceive product value in quite the same way. Further, the subjective nature of value makes it difficult to quantify and measure. And yet the key to enhanced profitability in today's competitive environment lies in dealing with such complications. The beginning point is to develop a better understanding of the concept of value and its underlying sources.

WHAT IS VALUE?

The concept of value is ever present in the minds of most consumers. Such phrases as "value for the money," "best value," and "you get what you pay for," are fairly commonplace. The word *value* is used in a variety of ways by customers and has a number of interpretations.

An important study on the relationship between price and perceived value (Zeithaml, 1987) argues that consumers have at least four different definitions of value.

Value is low price. Some buyers use the word value to refer to situations where they simply pay a relatively low price, such as when an item is on sale. The focus here is purely on what is given up monetarily. When a product or service is sold at a specially reduced price, such as at an inventory clearance, or when a customer receives a discount for using a coupon or takes advantage of a one-time rebate, there is a sense of getting value.

Value is getting what I want in a product. Other buyers look at value in terms of the benefits they receive from the item. They focus on their own subjective estimate of the usefulness or amount of need satisfaction resulting from the purchase. Buyers typically enter into a purchase decision process with specific choice criteria in mind. The extent to which they perceive that a product or service performs well on those criteria is one way in which value is defined.

Value is the quality I get for the price I pay. An alternative approach is to view value as perceived quality received from a purchase divided by the price paid. The buyer's focus is affordable quality. The best value is not the highest-quality item or the lowest-priced item. Instead, quality is divided by price for each available alternative, and the one producing the highest quotient represents the best value. Such calculations may not be very precise, as quality is subjectively estimated in the mind of the customer.

Value is what I get for what I give. A final perspective is to approach value as a trade-off between what a buyer is going to receive from the purchase and what a buyer is required to give up. The best value is the one that provides the most benefit (in terms of the customer's desired set of attributes) for the least price. The buyer has a set of attributes which vary in terms of their relative importance. A product is evaluated on these attributes. The result is divided by the price of the product to produce an indicator of value.

Given these different perspectives, we can conclude that value roughly represents a buyer's overall evaluation of the utility of a product or service based on perceptions of the net benefits received and what must be given up. From this point of view, what must be given up includes not only the monetary price, but also the time and effort that the buyer must invest. Superior value issues from either offering customers lower prices than competitors for equivalent benefits or providing unique product benefits that more than compensate customers for paying a higher price. Creating and sustaining superior value is crucial for establishing competitive advantage.

This discussion suggests that prices actually serve a dual purpose when it comes to value. The amount that a company charges is both a determinant and a reflection of the amount of value a buyer receives. Price determines value because the customer is comparing the benefits gained to the price given up (e.g., value for the money). Price also reflects or is a statement of value in that higher (or lower) prices should correspond with more (or less) valuable benefit packages.

VALUE IS PERCEPTUAL

A common mistake made by managers is to confuse actual and perceived value. Actual value implies some standardized, objective means of determining that product A offers more value than does product B. This requires objective measures of product performance, product quality, service levels, and any other attributes and benefits. Even if such measures exist, they are not necessarily relied upon by customers. Rather, customers develop their own judgments based on any number of considerations. So even if hard data is available from an independent source that "proves" that Able Company is providing better customer service on its computers than is Baker Company, this can be meaningless. If customers perceive that Baker offers the better service, regardless of why they hold this perception, then Baker does in fact offer better service.

Groocock (1986, p. 42) explains the perceptual nature of value in more definitive terms: "Product value, like product quality, has no clear meaning except in terms of the needs of particular customers. At one extreme, when we say an item has only sentimental value, we mean that it has value to only one or two people. At the other extreme, when we talk about the intrinsic value of an item, we mean that it has at least some minimum value to a very large number of people; we do not mean that it has some value entirely divorced from people."

The reason managers often miss this point is that they are too close to their products and services. They are intimately familiar with their own production, distribution, and service operations. Not only are managers apt to be biased regarding the performance of their own products or services, but they place undue weight on any tangible evidence of superiority, such as conformance to technical specifications. Further, they assume customers have all the facts and make rational judgments.

Buyers can encounter considerable difficulty when trying to assess value. This difficulty may be attributable to the complexity of the product, time constraints, the lack of available substitutes, and market inefficiencies. Further, buyers do not have perfect or complete information, and they ignore and distort much of the available information. Their judgments are often biased and emotional. In addition, customers are usually looking at a combination of factors when judging value, some of which may be different from the factors considered important by managers.

Moreover, to the extent that perception of value is partially determined by price, it is important to note that price is also perceptual. The actual price of a product may differ from the price customers associate with the product. This is because customers often do not pay attention to, or remember, actual prices. Prices are registered in their minds in ways that are easy to remember. They round prices off, recall a range of prices they may have paid over time, remember a price some friend or associate claims to have recently paid, or think in volume terms, such as the price of a dozen units of some item. For many purchases, the customer may recall the price as being nothing more than "fairly cheap" or "pretty expensive."

VALUE AND QUALITY ARE DIFFERENT

Also important is the distinction between quality and value. High or low quality does not necessarily imply high or low value. Buyers develop perceptions of quality based on their evaluation of an item's overall excellence or superiority. They rely on specific cues or signals to signal the level of quality in a product or service. These cues or signals tend to be fairly common among groups of buyers. For instance, such specific attributes as freshness in bread, odor in bleach, and size in stereo speakers are commonplace indicators of quality. These examples also serve to demonstrate that the key quality indicators differ from product to product.

Even where buyers agree on the indicators of quality for a particular product and assign fairly similar ratings to that product in terms of its quality, they may disagree widely on the amount of value offered by the product. This is because of differences in individual definitions of value, as discussed above, as well as differences in how customers perceive price and how much importance they place on price.

While not the same as value, quality has important implications for the ways in which customers react to products or services and their prices. Customers frequently do not purchase the item with the highest quality, but they do tend to consider only those products that meet minimal quality standards. So quality serves as an important screening mechanism in getting a buyer to consider a particular item.

Further, some observers assume that quality is directly associated with price. That is, higher price serves as an indicator of higher quality. If such a relationship exists, it would seem to complicate the ability to determine value. However, the evidence in this area is inconclusive. It appears that price is used by buyers as an indication of quality only in the absence of any other knowledge or information about a particular product or service. Also, where buyers are confused about the attributes and performance capabilities of an item, they will tend to use price as an indicator of quality.

SOURCES OF VALUE

The difficulties that arise when trying to assess value are significant but manageable. Such problems can be simplified by first developing a better understanding of the sources of value. In general terms, value has two basic sources. These are called "value in use" and "value in exchange" (see figure 1.1 for an illustration).

Value in use is concerned with a customer's *subjective* estimate of a product's ability to satisfy a set of goals. It is the estimated gain, satisfaction, or return the buyer believes he or she will receive from an item. The use value of a product is determined by a number of factors, the most important of which tend to be the nature and extent of the buyer's needs in a particular product area, the buyer's awareness of available substitutes, and the buyer's evaluation of the product itself on key attributes.

Value in exchange is an *objective* statement of value that is determined in the open, competitive marketplace. Based on freely interacting sources of supply and demand, a market price is established for most commodities. The market price becomes a statement of exchange value. The value of a product at any point in time is determined by the willingness and ability of a set of customers to buy and the willingness and ability of a set of suppliers to sell. This value can be distorted, however, when the market operates inefficiently. In the absence of sufficient competition, or where regulatory constraints exist, the company may be charging a price which is not reflective of its true market value.

Consider the case of a Broadway play. Assume that tickets for the typical show are about $60. This is the going rate determined in the marketplace based on conditions of supply and demand. Theatre operators apparently believe they will realize the highest profits by charging something close to this rate. The $60 price is a statement of value in exchange.

A tourist visiting New York for the first (and perhaps only) time may in fact be willing to pay much more than $60. This person may have always wanted to see a play and feel that a trip to New York is incomplete without such an experience. Further, these plays are viewed as representing the highest quality, having no acceptable substitutes. Also, the tourist will receive considerable satisfaction from recounting the experience of having seen a play to friends and family upon returning home. As a result of all these considerations, this individual is actually willing to pay as much as $110. This represents value in use.

Next, assume a black market were to develop, perhaps because ticket sales are sold out months in advance for the current shows. A scalper may proceed to ask for and receive a price higher than the going rate, and much closer to the value in use. However, if the scalper asks for $125, the buyer will likely walk away (unless the buyer subsequently reevaluates his or her value in use).

VALUE OVER A PRODUCT'S USEFUL LIFE (EVC)

Some products also derive value from their ability to save customers money over time. Specifically, for many industrial products as well as consumer durables such as automobiles and home appliances, customers often incur costs

Figure 1.1
Illustration of the Sources of Value

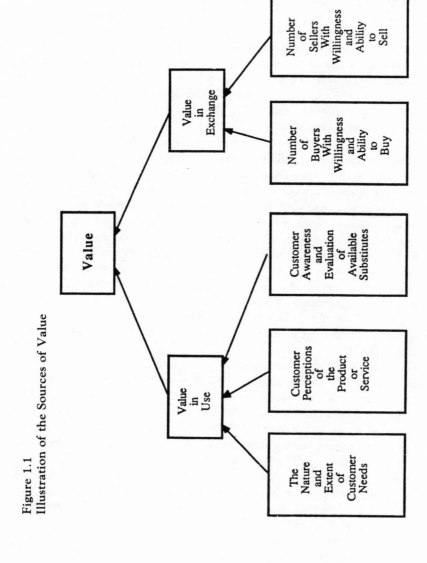

beyond the initial purchase price of an item. These are called life-cycle costs, and include delivery, installation, plant modification, training, maintenance, and servicing, among others. If products A and B both have the same price tag, but product A does not require that the customer spend as much on these subsequent costs compared to B, then A is delivering more value.

There are three categories of life-cycle costs: initial cost (i.e., the purchase price), start-up costs, and postpurchase costs. The purchase price is defined as the total dollar amount paid to a vendor for an item, including freight costs, insurance, and any technical training provided by the supplier for a fee. Start-up costs are initial costs that are not paid to the vendor from whom the product was purchased but must be incurred to make the product operational or usable. These costs are either paid to other suppliers or absorbed by the customer. Examples include the costs of modifying physical facilities, meeting power requirements, or establishing the temperature control necessary to satisfy product requirements, as well as lost production time during installation or any training not provided by the product vendor. Postpurchase costs are generated to keep the product in working condition after it has been put into use. Such ongoing expenditures as repair, servicing, financing costs, power consumption, inventory costs, and space requirements related to the usage of the item represent postpurchase costs. To get a complete picture of a product's total cost over its useful life, the purchaser may also want to subtract any salvage value that can be recovered when the item is disposed of.

The calculation of life-cycle costs can be difficult, requiring technical expertise and insight. The expected life of a product must be estimated and reasonable judgments made regarding expected product performance, wear and tear, and use requirements. Past experience and value analysis studies can be useful here. Costs that are incurred over a number of years must be discounted and expressed in present value terms. To do so, a reasonable discount rate must be determined.

The relationship between life-cycle costs and customer value can be established by introducing another concept, economic value to the customer (EVC). Assume there are two competitors, one of whom manufactures product X, while the other makes product Y. Product X is currently being sold for $100 and has estimated start-up costs of $50 and postpurchase costs of $80 over its useful life of six years. For simplicity, assume there is no salvage value, although this is rarely the case. Total life-cycle costs are $230. Product Y is a new competitor going after the same market as Product X, and is also good for six years. A successful product development effort has resulted in start-up costs for Y of only $30, while its postpurchase costs are estimated at $60. The price of Y has yet to be determined.

Taking the life-cycle costs for the product currently sold (X) and subtracting the start-up and postpurchase costs of the new product (Y), the result is the economic value to the customer (EVC of product Y). In this case, EVC is $140. Another way to arrive at this figure is to take the price of the existing product and add the savings in start-up and postpurchase costs provided by the new product. Also, if product Y had any features not found in product X, these would raise EVC for product Y even higher, for the features are a source of incremental value.

EVC provides a justification for asking a higher price than that currently charged for available substitutes. This can be seen in figure 1.2, which presents an illustration of the EVC for product Y. Subtracting the competitor's price ($100) from this EVC figure ($140) gives us $40, which is product Y's competitive advantage. However, let's say the price for B is set at $120. The difference between EVC and the actual price charged can be thought of as an inducement to the customer ($20, in this case).

HOW TO MANAGE VALUE: FOCUSING INSIDE THE FIRM

Regardless of the product or service in question, companies must carefully manage value to gain maximum competitive advantage. These managerial efforts should focus on both actual and perceived value. Actual value involves concentrating on internal company operations, while perceived value requires efforts directed toward customers.

A useful tool for explaining how companies create value is called the value chain (Porter, 1985). The value chain is based on the principle that value comes from many different places within a company and virtually everyone in the firm has a role to play. So the company is broken down into strategically relevant activities that represent sources of value. The basic components of the value chain are (a) value creating activities and (b) margin. Figure 1.3 provides an illustration.

Value creating activities are subdivided into primary and support activities. Primary activities are those involved in the physical assembly of the product and its subsequent sale and transfer to the buyer as well as any post sale assistance. These are grouped into inbound logistics, operations, outbound logistics, marketing/sales, and service. Support activities provide the supplementary support that enables the primary activities to be accomplished successfully. These include procurement, (e.g., purchasing of all types of inputs), technology development (e.g., methods for improving products and processes), human resource management (e.g., recruiting, training, evaluating), and the firm's infrastructure (e.g., general overhead). As diagrammed in figure 1.3, support activities overlap with primary activities. For instance, procurement overlaps with operations in that the purchasing department buys raw materials and component parts that enable operations to accomplish the production job. Procurement also purchases advertising and marketing research services, which facilitate the ability of those in marketing to do their job. The exception is the firm's infrastructure. This includes general management, planning, finance, accounting, legal, and government regulation–

Figure 1.2
Calculation of Economic Value to the Customer

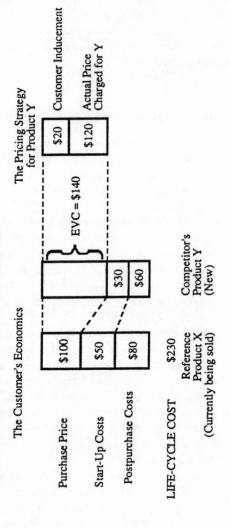

The Customer's Economics		The Pricing Strategy for Product Y

EVC = $140

Purchase Price	$100				
Start-Up Costs	$50		$30		$20 Customer Inducement
Postpurchase Costs	$80		$60		$120 Actual Price Charged for Y

LIFE-CYCLE COST $230

Reference Product X (Currently being sold)

Competitor's Product Y (New)

(Note: If Product B is sold for $120, then life - cycle costs for Product B would equal $210).

10

Figure 1.3
The Value Chain

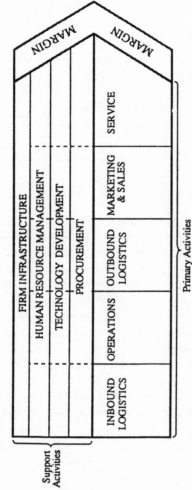

Reprinted with permission of The Free Press, a Division of Macmillan, Inc., from *Competitive Advantage: Creating and Sustaining Superior Performance* by Michael E. Porter. Copyright © 1985 by Michael E. Porter.

11

related activities, each of which supports all of the other functions within the firm. The end result is a matrix of the potential sources of customer value.

Each cell in the matrix can be further broken down into direct, indirect, and quality assurance activities. Direct activities are those that actually involve creating activities for the buyer (e.g., product assembly, sales force activities) while indirect activities make it possible for direct activities to function on an ongoing basis (e.g., equipment maintenance, sales force training). Quality assurance activities ensure the quality of direct and indirect activities (inspecting, monitoring).

Everything a firm does should be captured in a primary or support activity. By taking the time to look at the company from a value chain perspective, the manager is in a better position to determine:

• What are the potential sources of value in my firm?
• Which departments or functional areas should be held accountable for creating value in each of the value chain categories?
• To what extent are the value-creating activities of functional areas coordinated and integrated in a systematic fashion?
• What value-creating opportunities are we missing?

The value chain approach gets everyone in the firm thinking about end users and how their own jobs impact upon the value delivered to the customer. People are rewarded and evaluated not based simply on their functional area efficiency, but instead on their value-creation effectiveness.

Figure 1.4 provides an example of the application of the value chain to a manufacturer of copiers. Viewed in this manner, the firm may discover significant value opportunities that are underdeveloped and that can serve as a source of market differentiation. An example might be the ability to better utilize computer technology in outbound logistics to improve order accuracy or delivery times. Further, management may identify inconsistencies and conflicts in the activities of various parts of the firm that are undermining the ability to maintain competitive advantage in the marketplace. For instance, the raw materials being purchased for production may be of a higher quality than necessary given that the marketing department is trying to position the company as medium quality and medium priced in its promotional efforts.

The other component of the value chain, margin, is pictured on the right-hand side of figures 1.3 and 1.4. Margin is the difference between the total value being provided by the firm and the cost of performing the primary and support activities that create value. It is margin that provides the linkage between value and price.

The wider the margin between total value produced by the firm and total cost incurred, the greater the revenue opportunity. Revenue is equal to the price per unit times the number of units sold. On a per-unit basis, then, value should be roughly equal to the price charged. However, the firm may pass some

Figure 1.4
Value Chain for a Copier Manufacturer

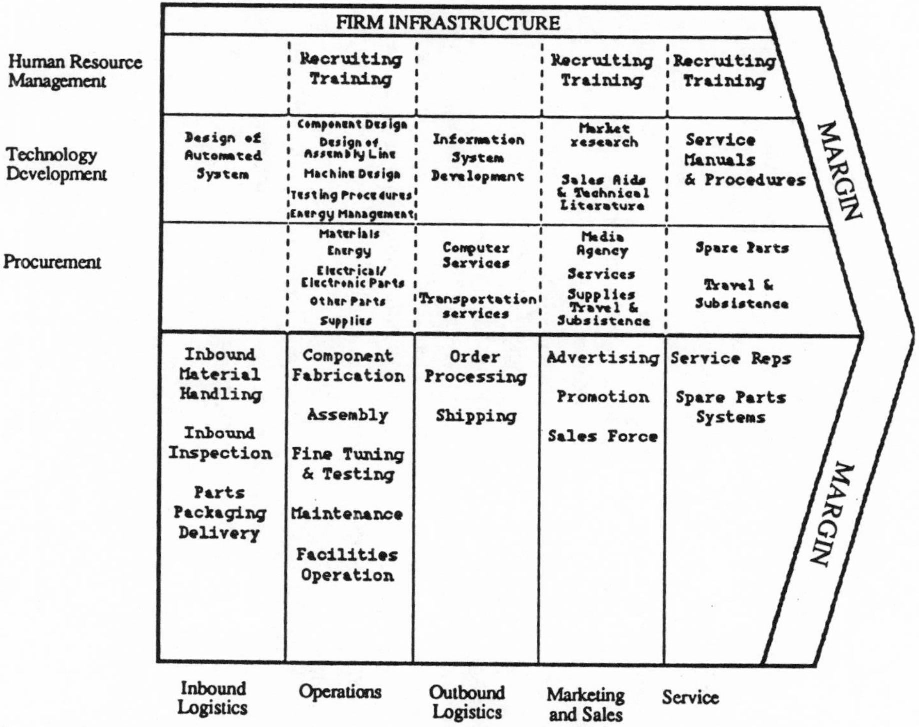

	Inbound Logistics	Operations	Outbound Logistics	Marketing and Sales	Service
Firm Infrastructure					
Human Resource Management		Recruiting Training	Recruiting Training	Recruiting Training	Recruiting Training
Technology Development	Design of Automated System	Component Design Design of Assembly Line Machine Design Testing Procedures Energy Management	Information System Development	Market research Sales Aids & Technical Literature	Service Manuals & Procedures
Procurement		Materials Energy Electrical/ Electronic Parts Other Parts Supplies	Computer Services Transportation services	Media Agency Services Supplies Travel & Subsistence	Spare Parts Travel & Subsistence
	Inbound Material Handling Inbound Inspection Parts Packaging Delivery	Component Fabrication Assembly Fine Tuning & Testing Maintenance Facilities Operation	Order Processing Shipping	Advertising Promotion Sales Force	Service Reps Spare Parts Systems

MARGIN

MARGIN

Reprinted with permission of the Free Press, a Division of Macmillan, Inc. from *Competitive Advantage: Creating and Sustaining Superior Performance* by Michael E. Porter. Copyright © 1985 by Michael E. Porter.

of the value margin on to the customer with a lower price. This decision becomes a function of competitive conditions and the overall pricing strategy of the firm, both of which shall be addressed in subsequent chapters.

HOW TO MANAGE VALUE: FOCUSING ON THE CUSTOMER

Companies must not only systematically manage their value chains, they must also take responsibility for managing the value perceptions of buyers. That is, the superior value created by the firm must also be recognized by customers. All too often, value is present without ever being perceived. The market-oriented firm is in a position to influence both the value in use perceptions of customers and value in exchange.

Customers typically purchase many different products and services, and rarely familiarize themselves with all the precise details of each item's design, production, delivery, and after-sale support. Instead, their value judgments are strongly influenced by an evaluation of basic product or service attributes, such as weight, size, or convenience. These judgments can also be significantly affected by packaging, advertising, sales and service personnel, the sales environment, brand names, price promotions, product literature, and a variety of other vehicles under management's control.

Take as an example the introduction of L'eggs pantyhose. Innovative packaging (a plastic egg shell), a distinct brand name, clean and unique sales display racks (the L'eggs boutique), distribution through supermarkets, and strong advertising support, combined with a moderately low price, all contributed to the perception of high value. The market response has been phenomenal, and the company continues to reinforce customer value perceptions.

Subjective estimates of value are additionally affected by the magnitude and urgency of the customer's needs. Buyers with very strong needs for a particular product are likely to rate the expected benefits quite high, while giving less scrutiny to the price which must be paid. Similarly, a 10 percent price reduction may contribute very little to value perceptions when the customer has less need for an item. Efforts directed at heightening the customer's sense of need for a particular product represent another means of influencing value perceptions. For example, promotional efforts that attempt to convince parents of college students that their children will be at a competitive disadvantage and may perform inadequately unless they own an Apple Computer are seeking to heighten the sense of need. If successful, these efforts are likely to change value perceptions in a positive direction.

Another avenue of attack is to influence how the customer evaluates a product or service relative to available substitutes. When the firm is able to convince customers that there are no *acceptable* substitutes for a particular item, value perceptions are enhanced. Informing customers that "if it doesn't say Hellman's, it's not real mayonnaise" represents a case in point.

While more difficult than influencing value in use, firms are sometimes able to affect value in exchange. This requires an ability to manipulate market conditions. For instance, by constraining the available amount of supply or attracting a significant number of new buyers to the market, the firm can drive up exchange values. An upscale restaurant that limits its operating hours is constraining supply, the end result of which may be an ability to charge higher prices. Similarly, the magazine that aggressively expands circulation may attract so many new advertisers that is can increase advertising rates.

While this discussion has attempted to provide a range of different ways in which customer value perceptions can be managed, the possibilities are virtually limitless. The only real constraint is the manager's own creativity. Value perceptions should be proactively managed, with pricing programs built around customer value. Otherwise, the firm is taking the chance that buyers will make accurate value judgments of their own.

PRICE IS A CREATIVE VARIABLE

Implicit in the argument that price must reflect value is the need for flexibility in the methods used to establish prices. While it may seem obvious to some, a fundamental truism in a market-oriented environment is that "price is a variable." The opposite of a variable is a constant, something that is unchanging. Many managers approach price as a constant. That is, they set prices using a fixed formula, such as determining cost per unit and adding a predetermined margin to arrive at price. Having applied the formula, they give no further thought to the use of price as a marketing tool. Not only is such an approach naive and overly simplistic, but it causes the manager to lose sight of the real purpose of a price and to miss creative opportunities for realizing profits.

Prices can be varied in many ways. The only requirement is creative thinking on the part of the manager. Examples of ten ways to vary a price include the following:

- Keep the same price currently charged but give the customer greater (or lesser) product quality.
- Keep the same price currently charged but give the customer a smaller (or larger) quantity of a particular item.
- Change the time of payment, such as by allowing a customer four months to make payment.
- Offer a rebate or a dollars-off coupon.
- Provide cash, quantity, and/or trade discounts.
- Charge different prices to different types of customers.
- Charge different prices based on the time of day, month, or year.
- Offer to accept a trade-in from the customer.

- Accept partial or full payment in the form of goods and services instead of money.
- Bundle the product or service with other products and services and charge a single price lower than the combined individual prices.

These are but a few of the possibilities. The downside is that price as a variable is a more complicated management task and requires considerably more hard work than does price as a constant or fixed phenomenon. Also, creativity can be dangerous if not properly structured. Pricing decisions should not be made in a piecemeal fashion, but instead should be part of a larger pricing strategy. A strategic framework for pricing will be introduced in the next chapter.

SUMMARY

This opening chapter has attempted to set the tone for the remainder of the book. Our basic orientation is that the job of any business is to create value in the marketplace and the role of price is to reflect value. The costs that a company incurs in producing a product or service have little to do with the amount customers are willing to pay. Customer needs and wants are the key.

The sheer rate of change in the modern business environment is forcing companies to be more aggressive and adaptive in all aspects of business operations. Entrepreneurial management is the order of the day, and pricing is no exception. Prices must be set to reflect continuously changing market conditions. Customers will only become more demanding and competitors less predictable. Successful companies in the years ahead will be those who approach price management as a creative activity, recognizing that profit opportunities lie in developing a better understanding of customer value.

Value refers to a buyer's evaluation of an item's utility based on a comparison of the benefits to be received and the price that must be given up. Importantly, value is perceived by customers. These perceptions can be quite different than the "actual" amount of value that has been engineered into a product or service. Further, value and quality are not the same thing. A product can be of high quality but perceived as a poor value for the money.

Customers frequently have a difficult time assigning values to products. Moreover, different customers will perceive differing amounts of value in a product or service. This complicates the job of the price manager and may explain why so many of them ignore value and focus instead on costs. An emphasis on costs is risky, however, and is likely to place the firm at a competitive disadvantage in the marketing-oriented environment of the 1990s.

Firms must do more than evaluate customer value perceptions. They must carefully manage the amount and sources of value delivered to customers and proactively work to influence value perceptions. Value is often present without being perceived, so the use value of a product or service has to be marketed.

A key aspect of value management is the design and implementation of effective pricing programs. Prices actually serve a dual purpose in this regard.

They are both a determinant and a reflection of value. Further, prices are a variable component of the firm's overall marketing efforts. By identifying and managing the many variable dimensions of an item's price, the firm is in a much better position to charge an amount consistent with the value customers seek.

In the chapters to come we will investigate the major considerations to be taken into account in value-based pricing. We begin with an examination of the components of a strategic pricing program (chapter 2). Following this are three chapters devoted to different aspects of customer evaluation. In chapter 3, the concept of elasticity, or price sensitivity, is introduced. Next, chapter 4 examines psychological aspects of pricing. Chapter 5 focuses on the process of negotiating prices with customers. Cost analysis is then investigated, but again from a market-oriented vantage point. This is the thrust of chapter 6. We then turn to the role of market structure and competitor analysis when determining prices (chapter 7). Given that price decisions are typically made by a company for entire sets of products, chapter 8 provides an assessment of the issues to be considered in product-line pricing. The underlying legal implications of creative pricing programs are reviewed in chapter 9. Finally, chapter 10 presents an evaluation of ways in which computers can serve the pricing manager.

REFERENCES

Groocock, J. M., *The Chain of Quality*. New York: John Wiley and Sons, 1986.

Porter, M. E., *Competitive Advantage*. New York: Free Press, 1985.

Zeithaml, V. A., "Defining and Relating Price, Perceived Quality, and Perceived Value." Report No. 87-101. Cambridge, Mass: Marketing Science Institute, June 1987.

2

DEVELOPING PRICING PROGRAMS

THE NEED FOR STRATEGIC PRICING PROGRAMS

Assume that a company faced with stagnating sales growth decides to temporarily reduce the price of its leading product by 5 percent. Such a move might seem commonplace in today's competitive environment. And yet pricing decisions such as this are frequently made arbitrarily and prove to be costly mistakes in the marketplace. The firm may discover much later that it is giving away margins unnecessarily, alienating middlemen, confusing customers, and inviting aggressive responses from competitors.

Mistakes like this one occur because management has no specific purpose in mind when reducing the price other than increasing sales. To better understand the problem, consider some of the potential underlying reasons for a price cut. A number of possibilities exist, including:

- An attempt to attract new users to the market
- An effort to increase usage rates among existing customers
- A method of taking customers away from competitors
- A means of discouraging current customers from switching to competitors
- An approach for encouraging customers to purchase now instead of later
- A technique for discriminating among different types of buyers
- A means of using the low price of one product to help sell other products in the line

Each of these reasons represents an entirely different rationale for the pricing action. That is, the same price cut could be used for a number of distinct purposes.

To be effective, individual pricing moves such as the one described above must be part of a larger program of action. Management must identify a specific purpose for the price change, together with measurable goals for evaluating the effectiveness of the change. Otherwise, the company is, in effect, blindly taking a chance that a particular move is appropriate. This explains why managers are so frequently unsure as to whether or not they have made the correct pricing decision.

The program of action that should guide pricing has four key components: objectives, strategy, structure, and levels (tactics). Of these, the most important is objectives.

THE ROLE OF PRICE OBJECTIVES

There is no one best price to charge for a given product. Once the need to set or change a price has been recognized, the manager must determine what he or she is trying to accomplish with this particular price. The answer might seem obvious: to sell more products or services. But this response is too general, and may not even be the case. In fact, companies can have a number of different pricing objectives.

Table 2.1 provides examples of some of these objectives. The ones cited are not mutually exclusive, and some could be used in combination. For instance, using price to accomplish a particular image, such as that of premier quality provider, may also serve to maximize long-run profitability. On the other hand, certain of these objectives conflict with one another. An emphasis on long-term profits may come at the expense of short-term profits, and vice versa. Similarly, charging low prices to discourage market entry may serve to irritate middlemen or detract from the desired image of the firm.

Objectives should be measurable, which generally means they must be quantifiable. Otherwise, it becomes difficult to determine how well they are being accomplished and whether or not the pricing program is working. In some cases, quantifying objectives is straightforward, such as with an objective of "increasing market share by two percentage points," or "increasing annual profitability by three percent." Other objectives are more difficult to measure, such as "maintain middleman loyalty" or "be regarded as fair." Primary research may be necessary, such as surveys of middlemen or customers before and after the pricing action.

ESTABLISHING A STRATEGY

If objectives are the performance levels the manager wishes to achieve, then strategies represent comprehensive statements regarding how price will be used to accomplish the objectives. A pricing strategy provides a theme that guides all of the firm's pricing decisions for a particular product line and a particular time period. Thus it serves to coordinate all of the pricing activities related to the

Table 2.1
Examples of Twenty-One Pricing Objectives

1. target return on investment

2. target market share

3. maximize long-run profit

4. maximize short-run profit

5. sales growth

6. stablilize the market

7. convey a particular image

8. desensitize customers to price

9. be the price leader

10. discourage entry by new competitors

11. speed exit of marginal firms

12. avoid government investigation and control

13. maintain loyalty and sales support of middlemen

14. avoid excessive demands from suppliers

15. be regarded as fair by customers

16. create interest and excitement for the item

17. use price of one product to sell other products in line

18. discourage others from lowering prices

19. recover investment in product development quickly

20. encourage quick payment of accounts receivable

21. generate volume so as to drive down costs

product line. By definition the strategy adopts a longer-term time horizon, usually from six months to two years, and is flexible or adaptable to changing environmental conditions.

To illustrate, the Gucci retail shops use a pricing strategy that can be characterized as premium pricing. High prices and margins are charged, with relatively low volume expectations. The central theme is exclusivity. Price is used to reflect the highest quality levels, and the firm is careful not to compromise its image with special deals or discounts.

Pricing strategies generally fall into one of two groups: cost-based and market-based. The market-based approaches tend to focus either on the competition, customer demand, or both. Table 2.2 provides examples of various pricing strategies.

Of these two groups, cost-based approaches are much more prevalent in business than are market-based approaches. This tendency is one of the great ironies of business, and reflects a general level of naivete among managers

Table 2.2
Types of Pricing Strategies

<u>Cost-Based Strategies</u>

a. mark-up pricing - variable and fixed costs per unit are estimated, and a standard mark-up is added. The mark-up is frequently either a percentage of sales or of costs.

b. target return pricing - variable and fixed costs per unit are estimated. A rate of return is then taken times the amount of capital invested in the product, and the result is divided by estimated sales. The resulting return per unit is added to unit costs to arrive at a price.

<u>Market-Based Strategies</u>

a. floor pricing - charging a price that just covers costs. Usually in order to maintain a presence in the market given the competitive environment.

b. penetration pricing - charging a price that is low relative to a) the average price of major competitors, and b) what customers are accustomed to paying.

c. parity pricing (going rate) - charging a price that is roughly equivalent to the average price charged by the major competition.

d. premium pricing (skimming) - the price charged is intended to be high relative to a) the average price of major competitors, and b) and what customers are accustomed to paying.

e. price leadership pricing - usually involves a leading firm in the industry making fairly conservative price moves, which are subsequently followed by other firms in the industry. This limits price wars and leads to fairly stable market shares.

f. stay out pricing - the firm prices lower than demand conditions require, so as to discourage market entry by new competitors.

g. bundle pricing - a set of products or services are combined and a lower single price is charged for the bundle than would be the case if each item were sold separately.

h. value-based pricing (differentials) - different prices are set for different market segments based on the value each segment receives from the product or service.

i. cross-benefit pricing - prices are set at or below costs for one product in a product line, but relatively high for another item in the line which serves as a direct complement. (e.g., certain brands of cameras and film).

responsible for pricing decisions. As was emphasized in chapter 1, price is a reflection of value. It is a statement of what the customer is willing to pay. Value and customer willingness to pay are market-based considerations. Costs, alternatively, are frequently unrelated to the amount customers are willing to pay.

The popularity of cost-based strategies reflects the fact that they are easy to implement and manage. In addition, setting a price that covers costs and generates a fixed profit margin makes intuitive sense to the typical manager. Unfortunately, this price is often too high or low given current market conditions.

The actual strategy chosen should be based on a careful evaluation of a number of key factors, both internal and external to the company. These will be described later in this chapter. Further, the strategy should be driven by pricing objectives, for they reflect what management is ultimately trying to accomplish with the price variable. We will, in this book, devote entire chapters to each of the issues involved in strategy selection. The central theme, however, is that every pricing consideration must be examined from a customer perspective. The perceptions of customers represent the ultimate reality defining company success, mediocrity, or failure in the business world.

DEVELOPING A STRUCTURE

Once a pricing strategy has been selected, the concern becomes implementation. Implementing a strategy requires that the manager develop a pricing structure and then a tactical plan.

The pricing structure is concerned with which aspects of each product or service will be priced, how prices will vary for different customers and products/services, and the time and conditions of payment (Monroe, 1979; Stern, 1986). A number of the managerial questions that should be addressed when establishing the price structure are identified in table 2.3. Unfortunately, most of these issues are ignored entirely by those with price responsibility.

The simplest structure involves charging one standard price, with no discounts or variations, for a product or service. This is relatively simple to administer and easily understood by customers and middlemen. This does not suggest all customers or middlemen prefer such a one-price structure. Either may feel they deserve price breaks or special concessions for a variety of reasons.

The biggest problem with such simple structures concerns their lack of flexibility as markets become more competitive and as new profit opportunities arise for the firm. Consider the case of a family restaurant that charges relatively moderate list prices on its standard menu items. The firm is basically making a trade-off between the customers who perceive high value from dining at the restaurant and those who perceive lower value. That is, high-valuation customers would likely pay more than the restaurant is asking, while lower-

Table 2.3
Some Key Managerial Questions to be Addressed in Developing a Pricing Structure

1. Should a standard list price be charged for the product or service?

2. Should frequent or large customers be charged the same base price?

3. Can and should separate prices be charged for different aspects of the product or service?

4. How should the time of purchase affect the price charged a customer?

5. To what extent should the price charged be varied to reflect the cost of doing business with a particular customer?

6. Should customers who value the product more be charged a higher price than other customers?

7. What is the nature of any discounts to be offered to the buyer?

8. When and where should title be taken by the buyer?

9. Is it realistic to offer a dual-rate structure, where the same customer has a choice between two pricing options for the same product or service?

10. Should the price structure involve a rental or leasing option?

value customers may patronize the restaurant more frequently than would be the case at higher prices. Management may hope, in the process, to maximize revenue.

However, consider the ways in which flexibility could be added by altering the price structure. Revenue might be enhanced by giving senior citizens a 10 percent meal discount, especially if they generally fall into the lower perceived value group of customers. Facilities might be more completely utilized by charging less for certain meals during low peak hours, or a premium during high peak hours. Rather than charge a set price for a meal, items might be sold a la carte. Or, alternatively, special "packages" might be put together for a single price, including a beverage, appetizer, entree, and dessert. To facilitate long-term revenue, frequent patrons might be given a discount card or told they can purchase on credit. The structural possibilities are virtually limitless if the manager is creative and knows his or her customers.

As competition in an industry intensifies, price generally moves in the direction of costs, while demand is increasingly saturated. Both of these developments have implications for price structure. First, any differences in the cost positions take on significance, as the price structure is modified to reflect a competitor's cost advantages or disadvantages. Second, competitors are apt to respond to market saturation with more aggressive market segmentation and targeting. One frequent result is price breaks for certain groups of customers.

Creative price structures are also critical for companies that do not sell a tangible product that can be inventoried indefinitely. This includes most service businesses, as well as those that sell perishable goods or products with short life cycles. Airlines, for example, sell asset usage, not the asset itself. If a particular seat on a flight is not purchased during a particular time period, revenue is lost forever. As a result, an airline may well vary price based on the distance to a destination, the popularity of that destination, the time of day, how long a person plans to stay, whether or not the customer is a regular patron (frequent flyer), how far in advance the reservation is made, and whether or not the customer will accept a "no cancellation" penalty. Many of these structural approaches have proven effective in reducing the number of unfilled seats on specific flights. The trade-offs, however, are the complexity of administering such structures and the potential for confused customers and antagonized middlemen.

DETERMINING PRICE LEVELS AND RELATED TACTICS

Once established, strategies and structures may remain in place for a fairly long period of time. The day-to-day management of prices focuses, alternatively, on setting specific price levels and employing periodic tactical pricing moves.

Price levels refer to the actual price charged for each product or service in the line as well as the specific amount of any types of discounts offered. In determining exact levels, the manager's decisions must not only translate the firm's pricing strategy into specific numbers, but also must reflect a variety of practical considerations. Some of these issues include finding the acceptable range of price levels that convey the desired value perception, determining whether or not to charge odd prices (e.g., $1.95 instead of $2.00), ensuring that price gaps between items within the same line are wide enough to convey meaningful differences in the items, and reflecting tax considerations in setting the final price.

Price levels may require frequent modification in response to changes in production costs, competitor tactics, and evolving market conditions. For instance, costs of a key raw material may increase, a leading competitor may unexpectedly lower prices on a selective basis, supply conditions may change because a competitor has overproduced, or demand sensitivity (elasticity) may change within the current price range.

The ability to manage price levels effectively is heavily dependent on the manager's sense of timing. Price changes must not come across as arbitrary. Customers should sense a degree of consistency and stability in the firm's price levels over time. They must be able to justify, in their own minds, paying prices that are higher or lower than was previously the case. Otherwise, the company winds up sending conflicting signals regarding the value of its products or services, undermining customer confidence.

Beyond levels themselves, periodic tactical moves can include rebates, two-for-one price deals, cents-off coupons, and any other creative means of temporarily varying price. These tactics are generally promotional in nature, and are usually part of special sales campaigns. They should be used with specific short-term objectives in mind, some of which may be communications-related objectives (e.g., creating product awareness, encouraging product trial). The pricing manager must ensure, however, that such tactics are consistent with the firm's overall pricing program.

PUTTING THE FOUR TOGETHER

The four components of an effective pricing program (objectives, strategy, structure, and levels) are not independent and should not be approached in an isolated fashion. Rather, they must be closely coordinated, with each element providing direction to the next. Consider two separate examples.

Assume a new car rental agency has entered the market positioning itself as a no-frills, low-cost provider. Price objectives are set with an emphasis on high volume and revenue, low unit profits, and the use of price to convey a bargain image. To implement these objectives, the company selects a penetration strategy, in which price is set low relative to competitor prices and customer expectations. Structure is designed to include a very low price per day and unlimited mileage for each of three classes of cars, with relatively small differences among each car group. An even lower rate is offered to those who rent for five days or more or over a weekend. Levels for the basic car groups are established at $16.95, $19.75, and $25.75, respectively.

This pricing program may serve the car rental agency for a number of years. Pricing objectives and strategy may remain largely unchanged for an indefinite time period. Structure may require periodic modification, such as the addition of a "frequent traveler" program or special price deals for those who fly a particular airline or work for particular firms. Levels and tactics will require ongoing modification as competitor tactics, production costs, and demand conditions fluctuate.

As a second example, a major manufacturer of quality copiers has found that unit costs have been falling while competition has intensified. At the same time, the product line has proliferated. Product life cycles have been getting shorter, as brief as one year for some models. In response, the firm institutes an entirely new marketing strategy, of which price is a central component.

The pricing objective in this case involves maximizing annual profitability across the product and service line. The strategic focus is on selective demand, where sales result from replacements and additions sold to the existing customer base and from taking accounts away from competitors. The selected pricing strategy is parity pricing, with the firm attempting to charge base prices at or near the average competitive price. Structure is designed to be flexible, where salespeople are given some leeway in arriving at a final price. This is especially the case with mature products and those with the lowest manufacturing costs. The actual intent is to use the structure to place machines but then to sell customers a service contract, for which margins are considerably higher. In addition, significant discounts are provided to customers who purchase multiple machines. Finally, base price levels are established and adjusted monthly to reflect an index of the average prices of the three top-selling machines in each major product category. A discount of 20 percent is provided for each purchase of three or more units.

Again, the four elements of the pricing program are tied intimately to one another. Approached in this manner, price becomes an innovative variable with immense potential for affecting the strategic direction of the firm. Alternatively, if management approaches pricing as an afterthought, concerned only that costs be covered and the firm be reasonably competitive, opportunities are lost and mistakes are much more probable. (For two other examples see exhibit 2.1.)

Exhibit 2.1
Managing the Pricing Function: Two Case Studies

In a detailed study comparing how companies within the chemical and construction industries in South Africa set their prices, Abratt and Pitt (1985) developed some interesting insights. Their investigation covered pricing responsibility, factors considered when setting prices, pricing objectives, approach to cost analysis, specific price policies, and pricing strategy used with new products. The following is a summary of their major findings:

a) In both industries, a high percentage of the people responsible for pricing decisions come from the marketing/sales department, although senior management tends to get more involved in the construction industry;

b) In both industries, the most important factors influencing price setting are costs and the competition; however, the construction industry also regards the economic climate as an important factor; Cost-plus pricing is prevalent in construction and chemicals;

c) When setting objectives, the construction industry places heavy emphasis on target return on investment followed by market share target; Chemical companies emphasize market share target most frequently, followed by target mark-up on cost;

d) One-third of construction companies use full-cost pricing, 17 percent use contribution pricing, and 50 percent use both; In the chemical Industry, one-third use full-costing, one-third use a contribution approach, and one-third use both;

e) When setting prices, the construction industry tends to emphasize uniform prices to different customers, and does not rely heavily on discounts; Chemical companies are more apt to vary price to match competition, and place slightly more importance on discounts; In general, pricing policies are not well-defined;

f) When a new product is launched, both industries initially use a price skimming strategy;

Source: Adapted from R. Abratt and L. F. Pitt (1985), "Pricing Practices in Two Industries," Industrial Marketing Management 14, New York: Elsevier Science, 301-6.

LINKING PRICING STRATEGY TO MARKETING STRATEGY

Up to this point, the need to systematically approach pricing as a strategic variable has been emphasized. Price is, however, only one of the strategic decision areas facing the manager. As such, it is essential that pricing programs be consistent with the decisions made in these other areas.

As discussed in chapter 1, price is a reflection of customer value. Pricing programs should be designed in concert with the other value-related activities of the firm, especially those activities that directly interface with customers. Of primary importance here are product programs, sales and promotion programs, and distribution programs. A high price can help convey a quality product image. A special price deal can be an integral part of the firm's promotional program. A trade discount can be an incentive for distributors to provide stronger support in pushing the company's products.

The focal point of all these activities should be the firm's overall marketing strategy. Marketing strategies attempt to define where the firm wants to be in the marketplace and how it plans to get there. They provide the larger framework within which pricing and other programs are developed. Accordingly, there should be a clear link between the strategies and the individual programs.

A large number of marketing strategies are available to any company. The appropriate choice requires considerable creativity and keen insight regarding current and future marketplace conditions. One example of a fairly common marketing strategy is called differentiation. This is where the company attempts to create unique perceptions in the marketplace of its product offering relative to the offerings of all other competitors in the industry. For instance, IBM differentiates itself on the basis of customer service, while Burger King does so on the basis of its flame-broiled hamburgers; Caterpillar uses its outstanding dealer network as a source of differentiation.

If a company were to pursue a differentiation strategy, how might the pricing program be designed to reinforce this strategy? As a general rule, successful differentiation allows the manager to charge somewhat higher margins than competitors, reflecting the higher value being delivered to customers. In addition, differentiation encourages brand loyalty, frequently making customers less price sensitive. Customers are likely to perceive fewer acceptable substitutes. The more salient the source of differentiation is to customers, the more brand-loyal they are likely to be.

Another marketing strategy is called targeting or niching. This involves focusing on a particular market segment, such as a certain type of user, a specific product application, or a single geographic region. Bic ballpoint pens are targeted to the low-end user, while Porter Paints are positioned solely to the professional painter, and the Bryan brand of hot dogs is marketed only in the southern part of the United States. Using the Bic example, price is set well below that of conventional fountain pens to convey the idea that the buyer is getting a reliable but disposable writing utensil. This represents good value for the money to a large segment consisting of students, office workers, and others.

Inconsistencies between overall marketing strategy and product or service pricing strategy frequently produce failure in the marketplace. The company that has positioned itself as a high-end or premium quality provider but then drops prices when confronted with competitive pressures is undermining its own market position, confusing customers, and giving away margins. Similarly, pricing strategies that focus on quickly recouping the initial investment in a product or service often result in prices that are too high given the firm's desired position in customers' minds.

PRICING STRATEGY OVER THE PRODUCT LIFE CYCLE

Perhaps the most widely known marketing concept is the product life cycle (PLC), which proposes that every product evolves through stages of growth and eventual decline. Put simply, the PLC plots the sales volume and profit curves for an industry (or company brand) over the history of the product. The sales volume curve is generally shown as an S-shaped curve, as found in figure 2.1.

The PLC is a key tool for market planning and strategy development, including pricing strategy. The basic idea is that strategies should be modified to reflect changing market conditions as a product evolves from its initial introductory stage through growth, competitive turbulence, maturity, and decline.

Consider the range of strategic pricing options presented earlier in this chapter. One of the distinctions drawn in table 2.2 was between charging prices significantly lower than competitors (penetration pricing), approximately the same as competitors (parity), or above those of competitors (premium). The question of which to use, or where on this continuum to operate, must be made at the introductory stage of the PLC. The product is unknown at this time and may require significant customer learning. Price is instrumental in the original positioning of the product. Some of the key considerations in selecting among these alternatives are identified in table 2.4.

The initial strategy places constraints on any subsequent pricing decisions. As a case in point, consider the marketer who uses a penetration strategy in anticipation of significant cost savings with large volume production—then does not achieve such economies. Although a price increase may be desirable, the market may strongly resist such a change, for it has come to equate a certain amount of value with a given price. It is, in fact, almost always easier to lower price than to raise price.

Also, the manager does not necessarily set a single price for a product in each stage of its life. Different market segments come into play in each stage, perhaps with differing price sensitivities. Charging a high price initially may be related to an initial target segment that views the product as a necessity with few or no

Figure 2.1
Pricing Over the Product Life Cycle

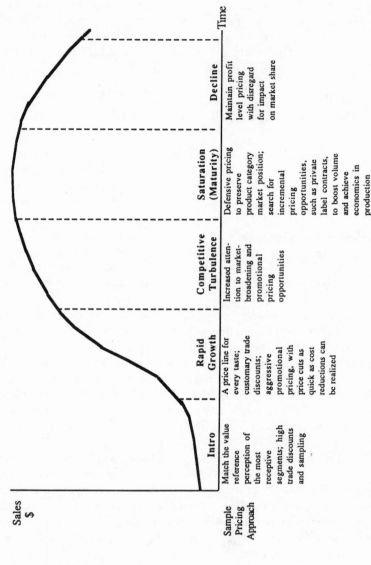

	Intro	Rapid Growth	Competitive Turbulence	Saturation (Maturity)	Decline
Sample Pricing Approach	Match the value reference perception of the most receptive segments; high trade discounts and sampling	A price line for every taste; customary trade discounts; aggressive promotional pricing, with price cuts as quick as cost reductions can be realized	Increased attention to market-broadening and promotional pricing opportunities	Defensive pricing to preserve product category market position; search for incremental pricing opportunities, such as private label contracts, to boost volume and achieve economics in production	Maintain profit level pricing with disregard for impact on market share

Source: Adapted from C. R. Wasson (1978), *Dynamic Competitive Strategy and Product Life Cycle,* 3rd edition, (Austin Press), 256-57.

Table 2.4
Considerations in Evaluating Initial Pricing Strategy Options

Factors Favoring Penetration Price	Factors Favoring Parity Price	Factors Favoring Premium Price
possibility of significant cost reductions with volume production	well entrenched competition or presence of a price leader	no cost savings from increased production volume
sizeable segments with highly elastic demand	desire to be regarded as "fair" by distributors and customers	sizeable segments with highly inelastic demand
low barriers to competitive entry	moderate barriers to competitive entry	high barriers to competitive entry
low customer switching costs	need exists to stabilize the market	high customer switching costs
ability to use price to convey bargain image	product or service does not lend itself to non-price differentiation	ability to use price to convey unique quality benefits or exclusivity
ability to use low price of one product to sell other products in the line	no differences in cost structures among the various competitors	clear-cut cost advantage which competitors cannot duplicate

substitutes. As other segments enter the market, separate pricing strategies can be tailored to reflect the distinct needs of each.

One danger in introductory stage pricing is attempting to recoup too quickly any research and development or related start-up expenditures incurred prior to actual product introduction. These expenditures can be significant, and place an undue burden on the new product. Their recovery, together with an acceptable rate of return on the required investment, should be achieved over a product's life cycle.

A product in the growth stage typically is confronting new competitive entries. The benefits of large-scale production economies and the learning curve, if any, are beginning to surface, bringing down costs. A common market price emerges in this stage, with the range of acceptable prices narrowing. The marketer is encountering downward pressure on prices, although this depends on the extent of product differentiation among competitors and the rate at which technological improvements are being made to the product.

Also, in the growth stage individual need or benefit segments may surface. A benefit segment is a sizable group of buyers that places heavy emphasis on a specific product attribute or particular mix of attributes. These segments will often differ in their willingness to pay for specific attributes (e.g., faster delivery, smaller inventories, better service, a special feature). There may, at this stage, still be a substantial amount of untapped market potential, suggesting the firm need not focus solely on competition-based pricing.

The competitive turbulence stage is the most competitively intense. Aggressive pricing actions result not only because the market leaders are experiencing significant cost reductions, but because new customers are becoming increasingly scarce. Price is pushed further in the direction of costs as firms attempt to run the less efficient producers out of the market. Correspondingly, this period is also referred to as the "shakeout" stage.

With maturity comes an increasingly saturated market and fairly well-entrenched competition. The manager focuses largely on repeat sales to established customers and on ways to achieve internal cost efficiencies. Customers are increasingly apt to see little real difference among competitive offerings. Competition is more heavily price-based, although head-to-head price wars are likely to be dysfunctional. Frequently, the pricing orientation is to maximize short-term direct product contribution to profit. The manager may use the product as a cash generator, the proceeds of which are used to support newer, growth-stage products.

Market decline presents a number of pricing opportunities. For instance, the firm may raise price to take advantage of any remaining market segments that are very price insensitive. The spare parts business for most products provides a good example of these segments. Alternatively, the strategy might be to cut support expenditures and leave price alone, letting the product die a natural death. Another approach might be to cut the price to the break-even level or lower and use the product as a loss leader to help sell complementary products in the line.

PRICING FOR PRODUCTS VERSUS SERVICES

The design of pricing programs is also likely to be fundamentally different when selling products compared to services. This is primarily true in terms of pricing structure as opposed to objectives, strategy, or levels.

Differences in pricing opportunities exist because of the unique characteristics of services compared to products. Services are intangible and are usually consumed at the time of purchase. Because they cannot be inventoried and sold at a later time, revenue is lost forever if they are not sold during the particular time periods in which they are made available. Since they lack physical qualities, customers may have a tendency to take services for granted, and frequently have a more difficult time assigning values to them. In fact, the customer is often using price as an indicator of service quality.

While some services can be produced efficiently in large volumes, they generally are not as conducive to mass production as are products. In fact, services frequently require a degree of customization when delivered. Further, many services are not transportable, requiring the customer to come to the vendor's place of business.

Managers often encounter difficulties in estimating the actual costs of providing a service to a particular customer. This is due to a number of factors. Two of the principal costs in service delivery are direct labor and depreciation of any machinery or equipment involved. Differing amounts of time and effort may be required to deliver the same service to two different customers. In addition, services are consumed in irregular patterns, often with wide demand fluctuations over time.

Given these characteristics, pricing programs for services permit considerable flexibility and creativity. Pricing for a health spa's services represents a case in point. When purchasing a membership, a customer is paying for an intangible. There are tangible features, primarily the equipment and facilities at the spa, but the customer is paying for use of these assets.

One of the goals of service pricing is to manage demand relative to supply. Assume the health spa charged on a per visit basis. Any time the facilities are open but not being used by customers, revenue is being lost while expense is being incurred. Similarly, any time more customers visit the spa than can be comfortably handled and subsequently leave, revenue is lost.

The need to effectively manage demand has led many spas to charge flat fees for memberships ranging in duration from six months to a number of years. Different fee structures can be charged for customers who agree to use the facilities only during limited (low peak) hours. If the health spa has multiple locations, the fee structure can be designed to encourage more traffic at a particular location by a particular patron or group of patrons, or instead to encourage a patron to frequent all locations. In addition, to counter high turnover, renewal rates can differ from initial membership rates.

The services can also be "unbundled," with separate fees charged for individual services. One fee might be charged to use all services, with separate rates for those who want to use only exercise machines or the sauna and pool. Or a flat membership fee might be charged for use of most of the facilities, with a per-use charge for high demand facilities such as racquetball courts.

Service pricing also lends itself to charging price differentials, where two customers pay a different price for the same service. With the health spa, assume a prospective customer visited the club in search of information regarding fees and facilities. The manager can consult with the prospect and glean the nature of his or her needs. Based on responses to questions regarding the prospect's exercise goals, workout habits, weight training experience, type of employment and work schedule, plans to relocate in the foreseeable future, and so forth, the manager can propose a particular "membership plan." The actual fee charged may be somewhat negotiable. The company could have an inventory of twelve to fifteen so-called standard plans, with a fee range for each.

Finally, note the difficulty management would have in attempting to determine the cost of delivering the service to a particular client. Customers come in when they want, for as long as they choose. Many engage in different activities on each visit. While costs are important, the prime concern should be determining (a) the break-even level of revenue and (b) the incremental costs incurred if one more customer uses the facility at key time periods. These issues shall be revisited in chapter 7. The key point here, however, concerns the need to focus on demand-based pricing, not cost-based pricing, and to capitalize on the innovative opportunities made possible by the unique characteristics of services.

THE UNDERLYING DETERMINANTS OF PRICE

When putting together the firm's pricing program and subsequently managing the program over the stages of product or service life, the manager must continually evaluate a number of critical price determinants. These determinants fall into five categories: overall company objectives and strategies, costs, demand, competition, and legal issues. Figure 2.2 provides an illustration.

Two of these determinants, overall objectives/strategies and costs, can be classified as internal company factors. The remaining three, demand, competition, and legal issues, are external to the company.

Company objectives and strategies constitute a framework within which pricing decisions can be made. They effectively serve to define a role for the price variable. Costs indicate to the manager a minimum level for setting price in order to break even, and so represent a beginning point in pricing. Demand analysis seeks to determine customer perceptions of value, the relative importance of price when customers make purchase decisions, the size of the market, and the different quantities that are likely to be purchased at different price levels. Competitor assessments focus on evaluating market structure, estimating competitors' cost structures, identifying their current pricing strategy, determining their relative market advantages, and anticipating how they will respond to the various pricing moves of other companies. Lastly, many pricing actions raise serious legal questions and must be evaluated in this context. Unfortunately, jurisprudence is often quite vague in terms of the legality of specific price tactics. The manager's prime concern is to estimate how the use of a particular pricing method will affect the firm's competitive market position and whether it will create an unfair competitive advantage.

Each of these price determinants are discussed in detail in the chapters that follow. Importantly, the ability to decipher them involves both art and science. For instance, certain skills are required to properly calculate unit costs or to estimate customer price sensitivity (i.e., elasticity). These analyses can sometimes become quite sophisticated. At the same time, creativity is required in developing realistic estimates of figures for which no data is available, while both insight and experience are invaluable when making hard judgments regarding competitor actions and reactions or assessing customer value perceptions.

The real challenge lies in putting these factors together and drawing

Figure 2.2
Company Pricing Program and Its Determinants

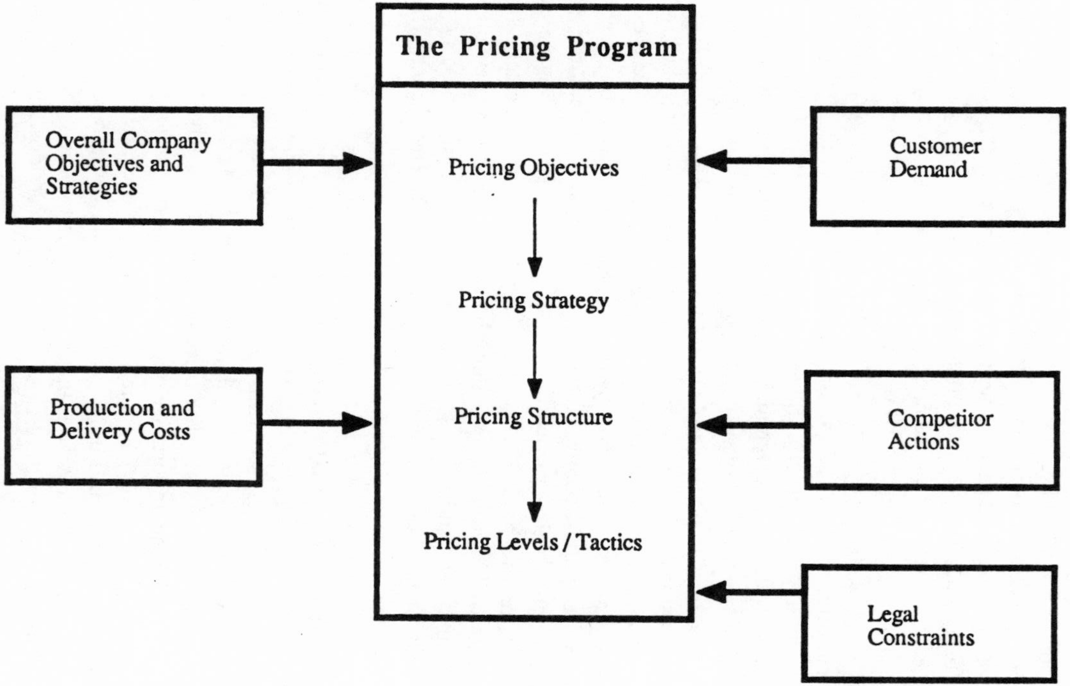

| Customer Demand | | Competitor Actions | | Legal Constraints |

The Pricing Program

Pricing Objectives → Pricing Strategy → Pricing Structure → Pricing Levels / Tactics

Overall Company Objectives and Strategies

Production and Delivery Costs

implications for price decisions. Consider the case of the Jefferson Chemical Company, a producer of specialty and commodity chemicals for industrial use, including muriatic acid.

Based on a decline in profits and market share the past year, the product line manager has proposed that the firm either cut the price of its acid by 10 percent or increase sales and promotional support by $50,000. How would one go about evaluating the price component of this manager's suggestions?

The first step would concern product and company objectives. What are the implications of the price reduction for the image of the product? How will the price cut affect other products in the line? What is the profit goal associated with such a price cut and how does it relate to overall company profit objectives? Much of the remaining analysis follows from objectives in these areas. Assume that the goal is a 5 percent increase in profit and that this increase is the sole objective of concern.

The next step would involve examining costs. A logical approach would be to cover the lost unit revenue from the price cut (i.e. to break even on the price cut) plus the sales necessary to increase total contribution by 5 percent. This could be accomplished by determining how many dollars the product is currently contributing to overhead and profits after covering its own direct costs (before the price cut) and adding to this a 10 percent increase in contribution. This total figure would then be divided by the new profit margin (price-unit cost) resulting after the price cut. The result would be a required sales figure from which current sales would be subtracted, leaving the required sales increase.

The required increase would next be expressed as a percentage of current sales. Assume it to be 20 percent. This brings us to demand analysis. The company requires a 20 percent increase in sales in response to a 10 percent price reduction, which suggests demand must be fairly elastic. Is this likely to happen? Based on experience and knowledge of the market, management must determine if customers are that price sensitive. The analysis here should raise questions about the importance of price compared to other product attributes, the strength of existing customer loyalties, and the extent to which market potential (both users and usage rates) has already been reached.

Finally, even if the research up to this point indicates the price cut makes sense, management must anticipate competitor reactions. How does the firm's cost structure compare to theirs? How dependent on cash flows from this product are they? How well-established are their customer ties in this product area? Do they view this market as growing, mature, or declining? The answers to these questions will provide insight into whether or not competitors will match the price cut.

SUMMARY

This chapter has described the development of pricing programs. An effective pricing program consists of four key components: objectives, strategy, structure, and levels (tactics). Managers need to determine specific price objectives as opposed to general objectives (i.e., increased sales). The strategy must be a comprehensive statement regarding how price will be used to accomplish the objectives. Implementation of the strategy requires managers to develop a pricing structure that details what aspects of each product or service will be priced. The last component, levels, concerns the daily management of prices and the tactical moves required to achieve the objectives within the strategy and structure. Most important, all four elements must be closely coordinated, with objectives guiding strategy and strategy guiding structure and tactics.

This chapter has also discussed the importance of combining pricing strategy with marketing strategy. The pricing strategy must be consistent with the objectives of the firm's overall market strategy. Considerable thought should be given to the pricing strategy and its implications when combined with product programs, promotion programs, and distribution programs. Also critical is the need to adapt pricing programs to reflect changes in these other areas over the product life cycle.

Attention has also been devoted to the pricing of services, which frequently require programs that differ from those for products. Services offer distinctive pricing opportunities due to their unique characteristics. Because services are intangible, consumed at the time of purchase, often customized to the user, and not able to be inventoried, price plays an instrumental role in managing service demand and supply and in conveying service quality.

Finally, the chapter examined the five key considerations that go into formulating a pricing program: overall company objectives and strategies, costs, demand, competition, and legal issues. Company objectives and strategies provide the underlying basis and direction for all pricing decisions.

Costs establish a minimum level from which to begin the evaluation of possible price alternatives. Demand analysis attempts to ensure that final price decisions are consistent with customer perceptions of value. Competitive considerations serve to assess the realism of pricing actions given market structures and the resources of firms offering similar or substitute products. Finally, pricing strategies must be decided upon within the context of current legal and regulatory constraints. Given their importance, each of these major determinants of pricing programs will be addressed in detail in subsequent chapters.

REFERENCES

Monroe, K. B., *Pricing: Making Profitable Decisions.* New York: McGraw-Hill, 1979.
Stern, A. A., "The Strategic Value of Price Structure." *The Journal of Business Strategy* 7 (1986): 22-31.

3

UNDERSTANDING AND USING ELASTICITY

THE NATURE OF DEMAND

Customers buy products and services for many different reasons. Their purchases reflect a diverse set of needs and motivations. The way in which they arrive at a particular buyer decision sometimes appears convoluted or irrational. In fact, researchers have developed highly complex models that attempt to describe the nature of buyer behavior.

When a customer considers making a purchase, he or she is effectively buying a "bundle of attributes" (see chapter 1). For instance, a person who buys a new car is not so much purchasing the metal, glass, component parts, or technical design specifications. Rather, he or she is buying a set of need-satisfying attributes, such as dependability, gas mileage, acceleration, handling, comfort, or even sex appeal. Similarly, when a business purchases a computer, it is buying storage capacity, processing speed, data security, software capability, and service availability, among other attributes. Customers differ in which attributes they emphasize and in how they make trade-off decisions among attributes, which complicates the job of the product or service marketer.

Price represents one of the attributes customers are evaluating when they buy. It is often a highly visible attribute, and frequently defines the customer's ability to pay for a given product or service. Every customer approaches evaluation of price in a unique manner, both in terms of the amount of importance placed on a product's price and the extent to which their purchases are sensitive to different price levels.

In addition, price plays a dual role in the purchase decision process. It is generally assumed that customers buy more of a product at lower prices and less at higher prices, all other things being equal. To the extent that this is true,

Figure 3.1
Examples of Demand Curves

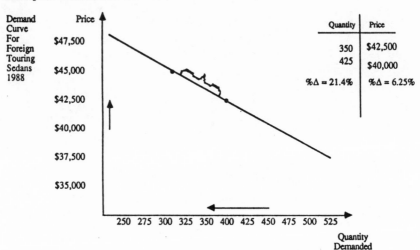

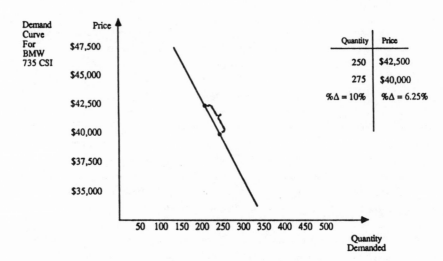

price serves as a disincentive to buy. Alternatively, customers often use price as a measure of product quality. If more quality is associated with higher prices, then price can become an incentive to buy.

Of these two roles, the more prevalent is price as a disincentive. Traditional demand theory assumes an inverse relationship between quantity demanded and price, as illustrated with the demand curves pictured in figure 3.1. Curves are included for both industry and a particular brand. The illustrated relationships assume that all other determinants of demand are held constant. These other determinants include all of the nonprice attributes of the product or service as well as the buyer's needs, income, wealth, and future expectations, the prices of substitute and complementary goods, and seasonability, among others.

The demand curve is also based on the assumption that buyers are perfectly rational and behave so as to maximize their return per dollar spent. This is not always the case, as will be discussed in chapter 4. However, demand curves are fairly accurate descriptions of the basic ways in which customers behave and can be quite useful tools for price managers.

Demand curves have different shapes depending on how sensitive customer demand tends to be at different price levels. This brings us to the concept of price sensitivity, also called price elasticity, which is the focus of this chapter.

DEFINING ELASTICITY AND ITS CHARACTERISTICS

The most basic economic concept for understanding customer price behavior is price elasticity of demand, which measures the percentage change in a product's unit sales resulting from a 1 percent change in its price. That is, if price is raised (or lowered) by a certain percentage, elasticity is a measure of the percentage decrease (or increase) in quantity demanded. Since price times quantity demanded equals total revenue, our actual concern is with the impact of changes in price on sales revenue. As such, elasticity is a measure of sensitivity.

If price were changed by a certain percentage and quantity demanded changes by a smaller percentage, demand is said to be inelastic (insensitive). Alternatively, if a percentage change in price produces a larger percentage change in quantity demanded, demand is elastic (sensitive). So if a 5 percent price cut leads to a 2 percent increase in unit sales, demand is inelastic, but if it results in a 10 percent increase in unit sales, demand is elastic. It does not matter whether we are dealing with an increase in price and reduction in quantity demanded or a decrease in price and increase in quantity demanded. The concern is with *percentage changes.*

Earlier, in figure 3.1, industry and brand demand curves were presented for foreign touring sedan automobiles. Over one illustrated portion of the industry demand curve, it is noted that a 6.25 percent increase in price is met with a 21.4 percent decrease in quantity demanded, suggesting that demand is elastic (i.e., the percentage change in quantity demanded exceeded the percentage change in price). For the brand demand curve, the example suggests that a 6.25 percent price increase results in a 10 percent decrease in quantity demanded, indicating that demand is more inelastic. In general, the steeper (more vertical) the demand curve, the more inelastic, while the flatter the demand curve (more horizontal), the more elastic.

Elasticities will tend to differ over the range of prices for a given product, across different market segments, for individual companies compared to the overall industry, and over time. In addition, customers may have different elasticities for a price increase compared to a decrease over the same price range. Consider the price for security alarm systems sold to businesses. Demand is likely to be more inelastic at lower prices, and become more elastic when price is relatively high. Certain market segments, such as companies located in areas with high crime rates, or those with valuable inventory and equipment, will tend to be more price inelastic when compared to other segments. Further, demand for products of the security alarm industry as a whole may tend to be somewhat elastic, while demand for a particular company's alarm system may be fairly inelastic, reflecting the reputation and perceived product quality of that particular vendor. At the same time, demand frequently becomes more elastic over time, as buyers become more aware of possible alternatives and perceive less real differentiation among available security systems. Also, a particular firm may find demand for a particular system is more inelastic when price is lowered from $500 to $450 than when price was earlier raised from $450 to $500.

DETERMINANTS OF ELASTICITY

What makes demand for a product more, or less, price sensitive? There are at least eight key factors which combine to determine demand elasticity. These include the availability of acceptable substitutes, the degree to which the customer perceives the product to be a necessity, the extent to which the product has unique and salient attributes, the ability of the customer to compare the product to those of competitors, the percentage of the customer's budget spent on the item, the portion of the price actually paid by the buyer, the existence of brand switching costs, and the presence of a price-quality relationship. These determinants are illustrated in table 3.1.

The leading determinant of a product's demand elasticity is the availability of substitutes from other sources. The fewer substitutes from which the customer can select, the more inelastic will be the demand for any one alternative. More substitutes generally mean customers will be more apt to resist higher prices. Importantly, the issue here is the number of substitutes of which customers are aware. Customers often have incomplete information and may not know of all the acceptable alternatives.

Even if there are no substitutes, demand could be fairly elastic if the product is not an important purchase. Specifically, the more an item is perceived to be a necessity, the more inelastic demand becomes. This is why demand for many industrial goods tends to be inelastic. Products that are nonessential purchases, or viewed as luxury items, will tend to have more elastic demand.

When products contain unique and salient features that differentiate them from those of competitors, demand will be more inelastic. In other words, price becomes a less important attribute, with the customer more willing to pay for the unique feature. Also, the more unique the product, the less customers will view competitive offerings as acceptable substitutes. On the other hand, demand for undifferentiated, commodity-like products will be more elastic.

Table 3.1
The Determinants of Elasticity and How They Work

	Determinant	Demand Will Be More: Elastic	Inelastic
a.	many substitutes are available	X	
b.	item is perceived by customer to be a necessity		X
c.	item has unique features which are important to the customer		X
d.	customer can easily compare item with products of competitors	X	
e.	item's price represents a substantial percentage of the customer's budget	X	
f.	customer is paying only a portion of the total price		X
g.	product has low switching costs	X	
h.	price is used by customer as an indicator of quality		X

Products that are more complex and that have qualities and features not easily understood usually are difficult for customers to evaluate and compare. Because of the difficulties in comparing brands, demand is more inelastic. Conversely, simple products that customers have no difficulties in comparing to those of competitors will have more elastic demand.

If a product's price represents a small percentage of the customer's budget or income, then demand will be more inelastic. Customers become more sensitive to price when the purchase requires a larger proportion of their budgets. This is somewhat modified, however, depending on the time of payment. Allowing customers to pay for high-ticket items in installments over time may make them somewhat less price sensitive.

In addition, customers sometimes only pay a part of the price, with a third party covering the difference. For instance, health insurance companies will pay for a proportion of a customer's medical expenses, a business may pay part of an employee's college tuition, and the government may subsidize some purchases through either direct payment or tax breaks. The smaller the proportion of the total price that buyers must pay, the more inelastic their demand is likely to be.

Switching costs refer to the amount a customer must spend beyond the purchase price when changing from one brand to another. Any additional equipment, materials, employee training, or related expenditures required to make the change are included. Switching from one brand of computer to another may necessitate the purchase of new software, peripherals, office furniture, electrical outlets and wiring, and retraining of employees. Buyers will be less price sensitive to the brand they are currently using if switching costs are high, and more sensitive to price when they can easily switch to another brand.

The final determinant of elasticity is the existence of strong price-quality relationships. Generally speaking, demand is more inelastic for products that rely heavily on price to convey a high-quality image. The higher price indicates that the product is of high quality. It may signal exclusivity, prestige, or a premium image. Customers may actually expect the price to be somewhat steep.

MANAGERIAL IMPLICATIONS OF ELASTICITY

Managers are concerned with elasticity because it has implications for bottom-line profitability. Changes in price or quantity demanded produce changes in total revenue. Depending on whether demand is elastic or inelastic, a given price change could actually serve to lower revenue.

As illustrated in table 3.2, lowering price causes a loss in revenue when demand is inelastic, because the percentage reduction in price is greater than the percentage increase in quantity demanded. Similarly, raising price when demand is elastic also serves to reduce revenue, now because the percentage

Table 3.2
The Relationship between Elasticity and Revenue

Nature of Demand \ Pricing Action	Raise Price	Reduce Price
Elastic Demand	Total Revenue Decreases	Total Revenue Increase
Inelastic Demand	Total Revenue Increases	Total Revenue Decrease
Unitarily Elastic Demand	No Change in Revenue	No Change in Revenue

increase in price is more than offset by a larger percentage reduction in quantity demanded.

The message might seem clear. Managers should only raise price when demand is inelastic and lower price when confronted with elastic demand. However, this is not always the case, for two reasons. First, the manager may be willing to sacrifice revenue for strategic reasons. For instance, the goal may be to maintain a presence in the market, take customers from competitors, or use the product to help sell other products in the line, even at a revenue loss.

Secondly, increases in revenue do not necessarily translate into increases in profits. Changes in quantity demanded lead to changes in production volume. As the company finds itself producing larger or smaller volumes, it may also find the unit production costs change. Assume quantity demanded increases significantly in response to a price cut, and the company must produce more. However, due to capacity constraints, labor shortages, or unavailable raw materials, the cost per unit of producing the extra volume goes up. As a result, revenue may have increased, but higher costs lead to an actual reduction in profit. This is referred to as cost-volume-profit relationships, a topic discussed in more detail in chapter 6.

Companies should not only be aware of the revenue and profit implications of elasticity. The proactive manager will recognize the potential to influence customer elasticities through creative marketing programs.

A number of opportunities exist for a company to make customers less price sensitive toward its own products or more price sensitive toward the products of competitors. This can be accomplished by working with the underlying determinants of elasticity. Examples include influencing customers to feel that there are no substitutes for a brand, that the brand is a necessity, that the product has unique benefits more important than price, or that the price is a smaller percentage of the customer's budget than they might think.

Consider the line of tools sold by Sears under the Craftsmen brand name. By stressing product quality, Sears lessens customer price sensitivity. This is reinforced with a strong product warranty, where defective tools are replaced without questions. Also, the company will finance all tool purchases with its Sears and Discover credit cards, effectively making it easier for customers to buy any time they want. Sears is, in effect, differentiating its product offerings so that customers will not perceive other brands as effective substitutes, but instead feel that Craftsmen tools are somehow unique. Promotional programs reinforce this differentiation, all of which enables the firm to charge higher margins.

ELASTICITY AND MARKET SEGMENTATION: CHANGING DIFFERENTIALS

Because customers differ in the amount of value they attach to a product or service and in their ability to pay for an item, their elasticities also differ. One customer may respond very little to fairly large changes in price while another reacts strongly to a relatively minor price change for the same product. Such behavior is regularly demonstrated in the wide range of prices asked for and received by ticket scalpers just before major sporting or other entertainment events.

In an ideal sense, a firm would charge each customer a different price based on the value that customer received (and correspondingly, his or her elasticity). Unfortunately, it is difficult to make precise assessments of the differential worth a product holds for every user. It is possible, however, to make such assessments for larger classes or segments of users. Even here, though, the manager may be hesitant to charge different prices for the same item, or price differentials, due to legal or ethical concerns. Or the manager may be unaware of the opportunities and means for taking advantage of price differentials.

The legal term for charging price differentials is price discrimination. It refers to the practice of selling units of the same commodity at price differences not directly related, or proportional, to differences in the costs of manufacture, sale, and delivery, with due allowance for risk and uncertainty (Posner, 1976; Stern and Eovaldi, 1984).

A useful classification of approaches to price differentials involves distinguishing between unsystematic and systematic discrimination. Unsystematic discrimination is usually evident in price bargaining, or haggling, such as where the salesperson who is paid a commission equal to some percentage of gross margin attempts to negotiate the most favorable price. Here, no consistent or systematic basis for price differentials is evident except the voracity of the buyer.

Systematic discrimination exists when there is some underlying basis for separating market segments and subsequently charging differential prices in one or more of those segments. Systematic discrimination is fairly prevalent in our "one-price" policy society, especially in mass consumer markets. Such factors as age (children's discounts, senior citizen discounts), sex (ladies' days and nights, club membership), locations of buyers (in-state versus out-of-state), buyer's income or earning power (professional association dues, doctor's fees), to name a few, have all been utilized as bases for price differentials.

The primary reason for a firm to use price differentials in its marketing program is to increase sales and profits. However, the key to the successful application of a differential price structure is elasticity. For systematic price differentials to be effective, and thereby have a positive impact on profitability, it is necessary that there be two or more identifiable groups of buyers whose price elasticities for the product differ appreciably, and that can be separated at a reasonable cost. The groups of segments themselves must be fairly homogeneous in terms of their elasticities. Further, the buyer of the product with the lower price must not be able to resell the item to the buyer facing a higher price. This is called arbitrage.

Let's apply these requirements to a case example. A nightclub decides to sell drinks to females at half the price charged males in an attempt to generate more revenue. Management is assuming that there are meaningful differences in price sensitivity based on gender. Females may be less likely than males to frequent nightclubs, including this one, and their presence may serve to attract more males. However, if there are no significant differences in the price elasticity of females versus males toward this particular establishment, management is only giving away margins. Similarly, if there are wide differences among females in terms of their elasticity, such that many of them have elasticities more similar to those of males than to other females, the price differentials may not make sense. Also, if the price differences are not significant enough to reflect the degree of price insensitivity demonstrated by females, money is being lost. Stated differently, price may not be a salient attribute in the female's decision to frequent a nightclub, such that any pricing action must be fairly dramatic to alter their perceptions. Moreover, the strategy will be less successful if there are no controls over the ability of females to purchase half-price drinks and give them to males.

Beyond their ability to improve company profitability by taking better advantage of elasticities, price differentials can serve a variety of other managerial needs. They can be used to modify demand patterns, as in discouraging certain types of customers from buying or encouraging customers to purchase at off-peak hours. Or differentials could be used to support sales of other products or services in the company's line. They can also help move goods that are obsolete or for which the firm has excess inventories. Another use could be to fill or utilize excess production capacity in the manufacturer's plant or encourage volume purchases, which reflect lower production costs. Further, differentials represent a means by which to selectively respond to competitor forays into particular markets.

There are, however, some ethical and legal considerations affecting the use of differentials. The major ethical concerns include the possibility that differentials may take advantage of customers who are more vulnerable, and that some customers may be given a price break for seemingly noneconomic or arbitrary reasons. It would appear, further, that those who raise ethical questions do so on an egalitarian impulse. That is, all buyers should pay the same price for a good regardless of any other considerations, except perhaps cost differences.

Discriminatory prices, on the other hand, lie at the heart of price competition. The idea that customers pay in accord with the value received is part and parcel of an efficient free enterprise system. So the larger ethical question may concern free enterprise itself, except where price differentials actually serve to lessen competition.

The legal aspects of price discrimination are addressed in the Clayton Act (1914) and, primarily, the Robinson-Patman Act (1936), albeit vaguely (see chapter 9). Neither piece of legislation prohibits price differentials per se. Instead, the legislation deals with situations in which it may be legal and those in which it may be illegal to charge price differentials.

The Robinson-Patman Act has been labeled confusing, complex, anticompetitive, and anachronistic (Johnson and Schneider, 1984; Posch, 1984). It generally encourages price uniformity, but has been subject to lax enforcement in recent years. The intent of the act is to prohibit preferential pricing, allowances, or services that result in a significant economic disadvantage to the marketer's customers or competitors. Price discrimination is illegal if it can be shown to (a) substantially lessen competition, (b) result in a tendency toward monopoly, or (c) injure, destroy, or prevent competition at the primary, secondary, or tertiary level of distribution.

For illegal price discrimination to be alleged, the products for which there are different prices must be of like grade and quality, the sales must be reasonably close in time, the buyers must be in competition, and the transaction must involve interstate commerce. Also, the legislation does not apply to services. If any of these conditions are not met, or if the seller can demonstrate that no competitive injury resulted from the differentials, then a defendant can argue that the Robinson-Patman Act has no jurisdiction over the case. While the burden of proof has traditionally been with the seller (defendant), recent court decisions have moved this responsibility more in the direction of the private litigant, requiring that the litigant prove specific injury.

As the regulatory climate has become more permissive in the area of antitrust, the logic of price differentials as a segmentation tool has become more persuasive. Stern and Eovaldi (1984) argue "it is only rational to charge different prices to different customers if those customers are typified by different demand elasticities, even if the prices cannot be cost justified or are not set to meet competitors' prices." Further, research on managers' attitudes and behaviors in this area suggests that they attach substantial importance to the use of price differentials, are fairly informed regarding the associated economic and legal issues, and feel differentials are an effective business tactic that they use on a somewhat regular basis (Morris, 1987; see also table 3.3).

THE CALCULATION OF PRICE ELASTICITIES

Some years ago, Alfred Oxenfeldt, a leading pricing expert, argued that no one had yet developed a completely reliable method to measure the price elasticity of demand for a particular brand. This finding remains true today, nearly two decades later, largely because price behavior is so heavily rooted in customer perceptions regarding their needs and requirements, available substitutes, current financial constraints, and so forth. Also, price is but one of many influences on demand and hence on the revenue generated by a product.

In spite of these problems, there are approaches to measuring elasticity. To understand how to calculate the degree of customer price sensitivity, it is

Table 3.3
Results of a Cross-Sectional Attitudinal Survey of Industrial Marketing
Managers Regarding the Use of Price Differentials

		Percent of Managers Responding Favorably
1.	Price Differentials Are:	
	a. An effective business tactic	61%
	b. An unethical business tactic	24%
	c. Difficult to administer	62%
	d. Usually profitable	51%
	e. Widely accepted in your industry	73%
	f. A source of flexibility in pricing	69%
	g. A tactic that should be made illegal	15%

		Percent of Managers Agreeing
2.	Price Differentials Are:	
	Very essential	31%
	Somewhat essential	33%
	Not very essential	17%
	Not at all essential	13%
	No opinion	6%
		100%

		Percent of Managers Agreeing
3.	If possible, prices should be tailored to the individual customer	
	Yes, very definitely	21.5%
	Yes, sometimes	42.5%
	Rarely	22.0%
	No, not at all	14.0%
		100.0%

Source: M. H. Morris, (1987), "Separate Prices as a Marketing Tool," *Industrial Marketing Management* 16, 78-86.

necessary to understand the elasticity formula. The result is an elasticity coefficient (E), which is determined as follows:

$$(1)\ E = \frac{\%\ \text{change in quantity}}{\%\ \text{change in price}} =$$

$$(2)\quad \frac{\dfrac{\text{change in quantity}}{\text{original quantity}}}{\dfrac{\text{change in price}}{\text{original price}}} =$$

$$(3)\quad \frac{\text{change in quantity}}{\text{original quantity}} \times \frac{\text{original price}}{\text{change in price}}$$

The formula begins with what has already been noted, that elasticity is the percentage change in quantity demanded that results from a percentage change in price. Note that the former is being divided by the latter. The percentage change in quantity (or price) is equal to the absolute amount of the change in quantity (or price) divided by the original level of quantity (or price). This is reflected in step 2 of the derivation. When a fraction is divided into another fraction, the solution is to invert the fraction in the denominator and multiply it by the fraction in the numerator. This is accomplished in step 3.

Using the demand curve in figure 3.2, it can be seen that, calculated in this manner, elasticity (E) is equal to 1¼. However, a different coefficient will result if we perform the calculation over the same area of the demand curve, only with the price increasing and quantity demanded increasing. Now, elasticity (E) is equal to ½. This is because the original quantity and price in the equation are changing. To ensure that the same coefficient results when measuring percentage changes in quantity and price over the same range of the demand curve, the formula is adjusted. Instead of the original price and quantity, the

Figure 3.2
Calculating Elasticity Using a Hypothetical Demand Curve

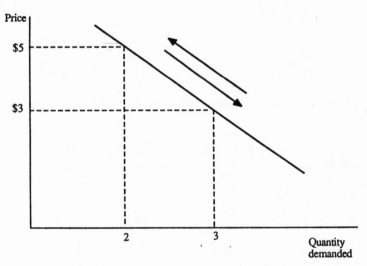

$$E_1 = \frac{1}{2} \times \frac{5}{-2} = \frac{-5}{4} = -1\frac{1}{4} \text{ (when price is decreased)}$$

$$E_2 = \frac{-1}{3} \times \frac{3}{2} = \frac{-3}{6} = \frac{-1}{2} \text{ (when price is increased)}$$

$$E_3 = \frac{1}{.5(2+3)} \cdot \frac{.5(5+3)}{2} = \frac{-4}{5} \text{ (when price is increased or decreased using revised formula)}$$

midpoint between what price (or quantity) was and what price (or quantity) becomes is used. The formula now becomes:

$$E = \frac{\text{change in quantity}}{.5 \text{ (original quantity + new quantity)}} \times \frac{.5 \text{ (original price + new price)}}{\text{change in price}}$$

In the example from figure 3.2, this produces an elasticity coefficient (E) of 4/5.

What exactly do these coefficients mean? Note that they have all been negative. This is because of the inverse relationship between price and quantity demanded. There are occasional exceptions, where an increase in price actually increases quantity demanded. These are usually luxury, exclusive, or fad types of purchases. In general, however, an inverse relationship is assumed. Thus in interpreting the coefficient, the absolute value is taken, eliminating the negative.

If the absolute value of the coefficient is greater than 1.0, demand is elastic. This makes sense, because to produce a coefficient greater than 1.0, the percentage change in quantity demanded (numerator) would have to exceed the percentage change in price (denominator). If the absolute value of the coefficient is less than one, demand is inelastic. Finally, where the coefficient equals one, demand is uniformly elastic. This is where the percentage change in quantity demanded equals the percentage change in price, and there is no net effect on revenue.

APPROACHES TO ELASTICITY MEASUREMENT

The methods that are used to measure price elasticity fall into two broad groups. The first group includes qualitative approaches, which tend to be highly subjective in nature, while the second group consists of quantitative approaches.

Qualitative approaches rely on the intuition and experience of managers and other key company personnel (e.g., salespeople) regarding customer responsiveness to various pricing actions. The accuracy of these estimates will vary depending on how well managers understand the needs and buying behavior of their current customer base and the dynamics of their current competitive situation. For instance, past experience with customers might suggest that they perceive few acceptable substitutes or that switching costs are felt to be high, leading managers to reasonably conclude that demand is fairly inelastic. However, changes in the makeup of the customer base, in the experience of buyers, or in competitor tactics can quickly undermine these conclusions. It is easy for managers to rapidly lose touch with their markets. A related problem is that market judgments may provide conflicting signals, such as where few substitutes are acceptable for a moderately priced product but the customer views the item as a low priority purchase (i.e., a nonnecessity).

Quantitative approaches produce estimates of elasticity coefficients based on actual data. The information is typically obtained either from historical sales records, test markets, or survey research.

When historical sales records are used, the marketer is evaluating statistical relationships between changes in prices and product sales over factors affecting sales, determining the appropriate lag between price changes and sales, and disaggregating company sales data to enable an assessment of individual products or product lines. Where different prices are paid by various customers at a given point in time, the marketer must rely on an average price estimate. The analysis is further limited by the tendency to rely on statistical techniques that assume a linear relationship between price and sales, although a nonlinear relationship is more likely to exist. Also, estimates of elasticity based on past trends may not accurately convey future demand behavior.

Test markets involve selecting a representative sample of customers, or perhaps a single territory, and offering an experimental price to these buyers. Sales response at the experimental price is compared to sales made to those customers paying the regular price. To the extent that market conditions are the same for both groups of buyers, this approach effectively isolates the impact of the price variable. However, the ability to draw such comparisons assumes a single price is charged to each group, and becomes problematic where prices are negotiated or a schedule of discounts is relied upon. In addition, difficulties can arise when customers paying the higher price are aware of those receiving a lower price.

Surveys directed at key buying influences or decision makers represent the most commonly used objective technique for estimating price sensitivity. Questionnaires are designed to measure customer preferences and willingness to *buy over a range of prices and discount structures.* While surveys can provide valuable insights, they are limited by the respondents' ability to accurately recall actual prices and related terms for competing products and the tendency for respondents to favorably or unfavorably bias their responses. Reasons for such bias often include a desire to appear shrewd or informed, or alternatively, a desire not to appear overly negative toward the researcher's company and products.

In addition, a customer's sensitivity to price will frequently vary depending on the presence or absence of other stimuli and cues. Survey research is limited in its ability to manipulate or control for interactions between price sensitivity and various product, vendor, and buying situation characteristics. A survey technique that addresses this problem is conjoint, or trade-off, analysis. Respondents indicate their preferences among pairs of hypothetical products, where each of the available choices is a composite of different levels of product-related attributes. For instance, option A might consist of average quality, medium product compatibility and a low price, while option B specifies a higher quality level, is highly compatible, and has a moderate price. The marketer can then assess changes in buyer price sensitivity when different combinations of other product attributes are present.

Table 3.4
Importance Ratings of Various Approaches to Estimating Customer Price Sensitivity

	very important	important	neither important nor unimportant	unimportant	very unimportant
Qualitative Approaches					
a. managerial judgement	41.5%	52.4%	3.7%	2.4%	0%
b. informed customer feedback	42.2%	49.4%	8.4%	0%	0%
Quantitative Approaches					
c. assessments of past sales data	32.9%	53.7%	9.8%	3.7%	0%
d. surveys of customers	22.9%	54.2%	21.7%	0%	1.2%

Source: M. H. Morris and M. Joyce (1988), "How Marketers Evaluate Price Sensitivity," *Industrial Marketing Management* 17, 169-76.

A major difficulty with any type of survey is the possibility that buying decisions are not made by a single person. Many consumer purchases are made jointly by a number of family members or others, while most industrial purchases involve multiple decision makers. For instance, both husband and wife might be involved in the decision to buy a new dishwasher, and a company's purchase of new production machinery could involve purchasing agents, design engineers, and production managers. Individual participants are likely to differ in their perceptions of price and their different price levels.

The limited research that has addressed elasticity measurement suggests that companies do not approach demand elasticity in a systematic, strategic fashion (Morris and Joyce, 1988; see also table 3.4). Qualitative approaches are relied upon more heavily in demand measurement than are quantitative approaches. Firms typically do not maintain detailed price data bases, nor do most regularly make efforts to estimate demand sensitivity. However, there is a growing awareness among managers of the potential for improved demand measurement practices to result in more effective pricing programs.

SUMMARY

Customer response to price changes is the largest source of uncertainty confronting managers when making pricing decisions (Nagle, 1987). Modern buyers tend not only to be well-informed, but also more sophisticated in their buying decisions than in times past. Moreover, competitive pressures are continually intensifying in most product and service markets. The result is a heightened level of price consciousness among buyers.

A key implication is that managers with pricing responsibility must focus greater attention on developing more exact measures of price elasticity and translating the results of demand analysis into managerial action. Decisions regarding initial price levels, the nature of price changes, and the use of price discrimination hinge on the skill and insight of the price manager in these areas.

In addition to monitoring actual price and market performance variables over time, managers would be well-advised to focus on the underlying determinants of elasticity as they apply to the existing customer base. For instance, data should be periodically collected on buyer awareness of effective substitutes, perceived switching costs, the extent to which an item is felt to be a necessity, the size of customer budgets, and so on.

REFERENCES

Johnson, J. C., and K. C. Schneider, "'Those Who Can, Do—Those Can't . . . ' Marketing Professors and the Robinson-Patman Act." *Journal of the Academy of Marketing Science* 12 (1984): 123-38.

Koch, J. V., *Industrial Organization and Prices*. Englewood Cliffs, N.J.: Prentice-Hall, 1974.

Morris, M. H., "Separate Prices as an Industrial Marketing Tool." *Industrial Marketing Management* 16 (1987): 79-86.

Morris, M. H., and M. Joyce, "How Marketers Evaluate Price Sensitivity." *Industrial Marketing Management* 17 (1988): 1-8.

Nagle, T. T., *The Strategy and Tactics of Pricing*. Englewood Cliffs, N.J.: Prentice-Hall, 1987.

Posch, R. J., *What Every Manager Needs to Know about Marketing and the Law*. New York: McGraw-Hill, 1984.

Posner, R. A., *The Robinson-Patman Act: Federal Regulation of Price Differences*. Washington, D.C.: American Enterprise Institute for Public Policy Research, 1976.

Stern, L. W., and T. L. Eovaldi, *Legal Aspects of Marketing Strategy*. Englewood Cliffs, N.J.: Prentice-Hall, 1984.

4

THE PSYCHOLOGY OF PRICING

Contrary to the assumptions made by economists, buyers are not perfectly rational and do not have perfect information when they purchase products and services. In fact, buyers of both consumer and industrial goods are sometimes fairly irrational in the way they go about making purchase decisions. Perfect rationality implies that these decisions are made in a way that maximizes the gain on every dollar spent. This rarely happens in the real world.

Buyers typically make dozens of purchase-related decisions on an almost daily basis. They do so within the context of the many other decisions and activities that make up their lives. In the marketplace, they encounter a wide array of vendors and product offerings with a complex variety of benefits, prices, terms, and promotional messages.

If not perfectly rational, then what? Research findings suggest that much of what people do when they buy products and services follows a certain logic. They look for cues to help simplify decision making, and often rely on simple rules of thumb. Correspondingly, it is possible to identify patterns of behavior in the way buyers go about satisfying their needs.

The purpose of this chapter is to identify some of the more prevalent behaviors customers rely upon when evaluating the prices of goods and services. Because much of this behavior is a function of mental and emotional processes that take place inside the individual, it is referred to as the psychology of pricing.

Our discussion will begin with a reassessment of the basic law of demand first presented in chapter 3. Following this, the difficulties customers have in recalling actual prices are assessed and the concept of a reference price is introduced. The tendency for buyers to establish upper and lower threshold levels for prices is then explained, together with a theory regarding how customers adapt their reference prices and threshold levels. A related perspective involves assimilation and contrast effects, which are used to explain how buyers form perceptions regarding the legitimacy of a particular price range for a product or service. Next, attention is devoted to the issue of price-quality relationships. The chapter closes with an evaluation of the effectiveness of odd prices, such as $1.95 instead of $2.00.

DEMAND REVISITED: HOW DO BUYERS ACTUALLY RESPOND TO PRICE?

The law of demand assumes that price is the principal determinant of the quantity of an item sold. Correspondingly, demand is defined as a schedule that demonstrates the various amounts of a product that customers are willing and able to purchase at each specific price during a specific period of time. Further, the law of demand states that customers will buy more at lower prices and less at higher prices, all other things being equal. The inverse relationship can be plotted as a downward sloping curve, as illustrated in figure 4.1, graph a.

Changes in prices result in movements along the curve. The curve itself will shift to the left or right if any of the nonprice determinants of demand change. These other determinants include the prices of competing and complementary

Figure 4.1
Some Alternative Versions of the Demand Curve for a Particular Buyer

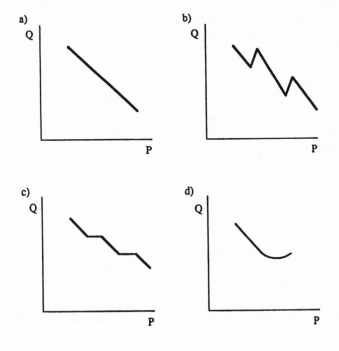

goods, the buyer's income or budget, the buyer's tastes or preferences, the buyer's expectations regarding prices and incomes in the future, seasonality, and the firm's advertising efforts, among others.

Assuming, however, that the nonprice determinants of demand are relatively constant, the demand curve suggests an incremental relationship between price and quantity demanded. For instance, if a customer buys five units at $2.00 apiece, he or she may buy four units at $2.20 apiece and three units at $2.40 apiece. In fact, this is not really how buyers normally behave. The psychology of price behavior indicates that the traditional demand curve may need modification.

In figure 4.1, graphs b, c, and d provide alternative views regarding the shape of the demand curve. In graph b, as price is increased, quantity demanded drops to a point, then rises, then drops to a point, then rises, and so forth. This might happen in response to odd pricing. The customer does not incrementally buy less at higher prices. Rather, at the odd price (e.g., $1.95) more is bought than at the round figures (e.g., $2.00) or at lower figures (e.g., $1.90). As will be discussed later in this chapter, the evidence is mixed regarding the extent of this effect.

The demand curve in figure 4.1, graph c suggests a different psychological phenomenon. In this instance quantity demanded rises as price is dropped, but there is a range of prices over which no real change in quantity demanded occurs. For example, as long as price is between $1.80 and $2.05, customer X will buy two units. This indicates that customers do not change their levels of demand in direct proportion to price, but instead buy a certain quantity over one price range and a different quantity over another price range.

Graph d presents another price behavior that is not at all uncommon. In this case the traditional demand curve relationship holds at low and medium price levels but not at higher levels. Instead, it appears that customers actually buy more at the higher prices. This may occur because there are market segments that associate high prices with prestige and an enhanced image for the buyer. Such "conspicuous consumption" occurs in both consumer markets (e.g., the purchase of expensive jewelry) and industrial markets (e.g., the purchase of a corporate jet).

These examples do not represent an exhaustive list of the different ways in which the demand curve can be portrayed. Moreover, they represent conjectures regarding what probably happens much of the time, not empirically based laws regarding what happens all of the time. The key point to keep in mind is that the way in which customers behave toward prices is more complex and less informed than is assumed in traditional economics.

THE CONCEPT OF REFERENCE PRICES

Ask people to name the price of a gallon of milk, a color television, a pair of jogging shoes, a news magazine, or virtually any other everyday product, and they will most likely provide a response. That is, most will not say "I really don't know" regardless of how aware they actually are of these prices. The price provided is an indication of what they would expect to pay or what they believe the product is worth.

When customers go to buy a product or service, they bring with them an expected price. This is called a reference price, and represents an amount the customer regards as fair or appropriate for the value received. It may or may not be anywhere near the price the customer actually encounters. It is critical, however, because reference prices have a significant impact on whether or not the customer ultimately buys the product or service. They serve as an internal standard for evaluating other prices.

A buyer's internal reference price for any item is probably the result of a combination of influential factors. Some of these include:

Last price paid. The price the buyer last paid for an item becomes a benchmark in evaluating prices subsequently encountered.

Going price. The buyer evaluates his or her historical experience in buying an item and estimates a modal price (the amount paid most frequently) as the reference.

Fair or just price. A fair or just price implies that there is a normative price that reflects what the buyer "ought" to pay. The buyer interprets this price from the perspective of his or her own individual means.

Favorite brand price. The price of the brand usually purchased by the buyer serves as a frame of reference in evaluating other prices.

Average prices of similar goods. A variation of the price most frequently charged; may be an average of competing brand prices.

Absolute price limit. The highest price the buyer would consider, given his or her current need for an item.

Expected future price. A buyer's expectation of future prices may influence present purchasing behavior. An anticipated price increase may encourage a present purchase, while an expected price decline may lead one to defer purchasing. In prolonged periods of inflation, reference prices are less stable.

There is a reference price for each unique quality level within a product line or category. However, the reference price for an item is also influenced by the context within which it is purchased. For instance, the price one would be ready to pay for a soft drink might be quite different if purchasing it at a college football game, a corner gas station, a fast food restaurant, or from room service in a hotel. This occurs despite the fact that it is the same size and brand and may have come from the same beverage distributing company at the same unit cost, in all four cases.

There is some evidence regarding the impact of current marketing programs on a customer's reference price. Figure 4.2 summarizes a study of customer perceptions regarding what the ordinary price of a home stereo unit should be.

Figure 4.2
Customer Price Perceptions and Actual Prices for Home Stereo Equipment

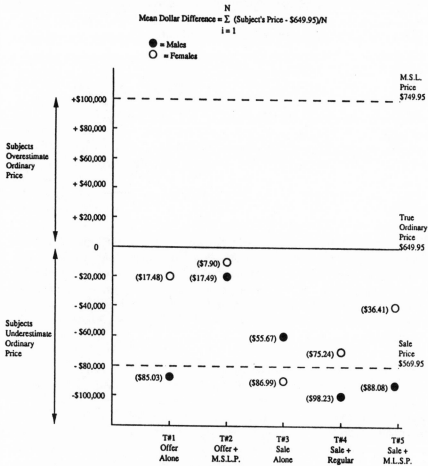

$$\text{Mean Dollar Difference} = \sum_{i=1}^{N} (\text{Subject's Price} - \$649.95)/N$$

● = Males
O = Females

M.S.L. Price $749.95

+$100,000

+ $80,000

Subjects Overestimate Ordinary Price

+ $60,000

+ $40,000

+ $20,000

True Ordinary Price $649.95

0

($7.90) O

- $20,000 ($17.48) O ($17.49) ●

- $40,000 ($36.41) O

Subjects Underestimate Ordinary Price

- $60,000 ($55.67) ●

($75.24) O

- $80,000 Sale Price $569.95

($85.03) ● ($86.99) O ($88.08) ●

-$100,000 ($98.23) ●

| T#1 Offer Alone | T#2 Offer + M.S.L.P. | T#3 Sale Alone | T#4 Sale + Regular | T#5 Sale + M.L.S.P. |

Source: J. Liefeld and L. Heslop (1985), "Reference Prices and Perception in Newspaper Advertising," *Journal of Consumer Research* 11 (March), 873.

The study sought to determine if the customers' reference prices would be higher when encountering (a) the current store price or offer by itself, (b) the current store price with the manufacturer's suggested list price, (c) a sale price alone, (d) a sale price with the regular price, and (e) a sale price with the manufacturer's suggested list price. The manufacturer's suggested list price was $749.95, the true ordinary price was $649.95, and the sale price was $569.95.

Figure 4.2 identifies the amounts by which customer estimates were over (or under) the true ordinary price for each of the five scenarios, and for men and women. As can be seen, the mention of a manufacturer's suggested list price had little impact, but the advertisement of a sale and sales price tended to significantly lower buyers' estimates of the ordinary selling price.

CAN CUSTOMERS ACCURATELY RECALL PRICES?

Related to the concept of a reference price is the price awareness of buyers, or their ability to accurately identify the prices currently being charged for goods and services. Buyers do not have perfect information regarding available products and their prices. Even if such information were available, people are not perfect information processors. In reality, customers ignore much of the information they receive. They distort informational inputs and selectively decide which facts to assimilate. As a result, buyers are not always very price aware.

The research with respect to price awareness remains sketchy. Awareness tends to be inversely related to income levels, although those with very low incomes tend not to be especially aware. Awareness is also lower for brand name products. Alternatively, buyers tend to be fairly accurate in estimating price ranges for items purchased recurrently and at short intervals, as might be expected. For significant dollar purchases, buyers tend to be more aware of down payment and monthly payment amounts than of the total price paid for an item.

One measure of price awareness is price recall, or the ability of buyers to correctly name the price they paid the last time a particular item was purchased. In a series of studies by Gabor and others (1961, 1971, 1988), a number of interesting findings regarding price recall were identified. The percentage of respondents correctly identifying the prices of tea, coffee, sugar, and flour tended to be quite high in research conducted over a twenty-five-year time span. For these four products, the percentage of prices correctly identified averaged 68.1 percent, 65.1 percent, 66.9 percent, and 50.5 percent respectively. Other studies of thirty-six frequently advertised and price-competitive brands found between one-fourth and one-third of the respondents identifying prices within 5 percent of the correct price. As a generalization for most of the research to date, the ability of customers to accurately recall prices seems to have declined in the past few decades.

The pricing manager must keep in mind that recalled prices are significant, regardless of their accuracy. They are a key determinant of reference prices and an indicator of the price image customers have toward a product or service. At the same time, the relevance of the price last paid for current purchase behavior varies widely by product category (e.g., consumer durables versus nondurables) and depends heavily on the rate of inflation, the rate of technological change in a product area, and the dynamics of fashion trends.

PRICE THRESHOLDS AND WEBER'S LAW

Customers bring not only a reference price with them to the market. In addition, they have two price limits in hand. One is an upper limit beyond which the price is perceived as too high relative to perceived value. The other is a lower limit below which the quality of the item becomes suspect. These are called price thresholds, and they determine an acceptable range within which a given item's price should fall. If price is looked upon as a stimulus directed at customers, it would seem logical to assume that a given response from a buyer will occur over some range of this stimulus. The upper and lower price thresholds represent points at which the buyers will change their responsiveness to the stimuli. This means if prices are too high, customers may buy a lower quantity than desired or none at all. If prices are too low, customers may not only restrain from buying more, but may resist making a purchase altogether.

Approached in this manner, the impact of prices can be better understood by applying two laws rooted in psychology, Weber's law and the Weber-Fechner law (Monroe, 1973; Gabor, Granger and Sowter, 1971). Applied to pricing, Weber's law indicates that buyer reactions to price differences for an item are directly proportional to price levels. That is, the psychological perception of differences between two prices is relative, not absolute. Assume that the decision to increase a product's price from $5 to $5.50 represented just enough of a difference to dissuade a buyer from buying. This is a 10 percent difference. Weber's law would then indicate that the price of some other product currently priced at $10.00 would have to be raised not to $10.50, but instead to $11.00 (again 10 percent), to discourage the buyer from buying. The focal point is not a constant dollar amount of difference, but instead a proportionate difference. Related to price thresholds, Weber's law serves to define the amount of difference that must exist between the lower and upper thresholds for an item.

As another example of the application of Weber's law, consider a firm that is going to have a special sale featuring its major product. To attract customers, the management is reducing price. The real problem involves determining how much of a price cut is required. Weber's law is useful here, as it would suggest the need for an amount below the customer's lower threshold. For example, there is some evidence that a price reduction of at least 15 percent is necessary in this situation for customers to perceive any noticeable difference (Loudon and Della Bitta, 1988).

The Weber-Fechner law is a more specific statement of the psychological relationships involved in pricing, and can be portrayed as follows:

$$R = k \log s + a$$

Where: R = magnitude of buyer response
      s = magnitude of the price
      k = constant of proportionality
      a = constant of integration

This indicates that buyer responsiveness to a price change is primarily a function of the degree of the change. Further, the relationship between price and the quantity purchased by a buyer is logarithmic. That is, the amount of the differential among prices should increase at a logarithmic rate to convey equivalent differences. In addition, the value of k will be different for every product. This means that the distance between the lower and upper thresholds differs among products for most buyers, and so their sensitivity to a given price change depends on the product in question.

ADAPTATION THEORY AND PRICING

Greater insights regarding reference prices and thresholds can be gained by considering adaptation theory. This is a body of thought with implications for how buyers develop and adjust their price expectations. Adaptation theory suggests that buyers have a reference price or adaptation level that acts as an anchor for judgments of other prices and that determines the buyer's ultimate behavior. This adaptation level is subject to change over time, however, based on focal and background stimuli.

Focal stimuli represent the phenomena to which the buyer is most directly responding. These are the actual set of prices a buyer encounters in the marketplace. Background stimuli are factors related to the purchasing situation or context, such as the physical surroundings within which the purchase is made, the buyer's budget, the buyer's motivation for making the purchase, the tactics of salespeople, and the time pressure under which the buyer is operating. Buyers tend to adjust their adaptation levels to be consistent with these stimuli. In the final analysis, price perceptions are the result of the present situation, past experiences, and the buyer's physical and psychological state.

Adaptation theory can be useful in price management. For example, consider the customer who is in the market for a set of stereo speakers and encounters a wide selection of brands and prices from which to choose. The customer has a reference price or adaptation level of $130 for a speaker. Now, consider two scenarios. In the first, the salesperson exposes the customer to speakers priced at $850, $590, $400, $250, $170, and $120, in that order. In the second, the customer is exposed to the same speakers, but in reverse order, starting with the $120 unit. Adaptation theory suggests the customer will adapt his or her reference price upward by a greater amount in the first scenario. The likelihood is that the customer will walk out having purchased a more expensive speaker if initially exposed to the higher prices.

Proactive managers will attempt to determine customer adaptation levels and then work to move these levels in the direction of the firm's desired customer expenditure level. This requires a focus on both focal and background stimuli, as well as patience in allowing buyers time to adapt their reference prices. The example above involved manipulating the focal stimuli. This could also be accomplished by stressing price per ounce or per application instead of the total list price, by creative use of the quantity discount structure, or by allowing the customer to pay the price over time. Background stimuli provide even greater opportunity. In a retail context, customers might be induced to adjust their reference prices by a store layout policy in which cheaper items are placed as far away from the entrance as possible. The customer is forced to pass a number of higher ticket items in attempting to locate the desired item. Similarly, a sales program that stresses limited supply availability can lead buyers to raise the reference price. Reference prices might also be raised when the seller attempts to compare his price with a higher suggested manufacturer's price, a higher price previously charged (Was $____, Now $____) or with a competitors's price (Their price $____, Our price $____).

ASSIMILATION AND CONTRAST EFFECTS

The discussion to this point has indicated that once an adaptation level or reference price is established, there is a range of new prices around it that are acceptable. These new prices will in turn be assimilated, and buyers will be drawn toward them. As a result, the reference price may periodically change. At the same time, prices that vary significantly (higher or lower) from the reference standard will be rejected and assigned to some other product category. These prices are contrasted from the reference standard.

Given this, the price behavior of customers can be characterized as a process of assimilating and contrasting the price levels encountered in the marketplace. Customers effectively classify new price stimuli as consistent or inconsistent.

Assimilation and contrast effects also have managerial implications. For instance, assume a customer in the market for a personal computer walks past a store window in which there is a computer with the sign Was $1900, Now $1300. Alternatively, assume the same customer encountered the same computer, but now with the message Was $1900, Now $1775. How will the buyer respond? Economic theory would suggest the $1300 offer would be the most appealing to customers. However, there is reason to think that this may not be the case.

Customers may have difficulty associating $1900 worth of value with a $1300 price. They assume the product was not really worth $1900 in the first place, and was artificially marked up, and then down. Or, they assume the product is defective or obsolete. Such suspicion or disbelief leads the buyer to contrast $1900 and $1300 and probably to not make a purchase. In the case of $1900 and $1775, customers are apt to perceive they are simply getting a good deal. It seems more probable that a company would be willing and able to offer $1900 worth of value for $1775. In this case, they assimilate the two prices and are more likely to make a purchase. One implication is that the firm can not only charge too high a price for this computer, but also too low a price.

To be assimilated, pricing actions must be systematic and consistent. While dramatic price changes can be assimilated over time, especially where demand is highly inelastic, the greater likelihood is that they will be contrasted. Alternatively, small changes in the high and low end prices in a product line are more easily assimilated. For instance, an incremental increase in the high end price, which is one of the more highly visible prices and serves as an anchor, will tend to be assimilated. This may lead, in turn, to an adjustment in the customer's reference price for other items in the line.

IS THERE A PRICE-QUALITY RELATIONSHIP?

Price is not only used as an indicator of the cost that a buyer must incur. It also serves as a signal of the quality of a product (see chapter 1 for a discussion of quality and value). In fact, for some buyers the most salient aspect of price is the connotation of quality. What is not clear is the extent to which customers directly associate higher prices with higher quality and vice versa.

Consider the buyer who, in need of a last minute birthday gift for a relative, decides to purchase a radio/clock alarm unit such as those often found on bedside tables. This buyer goes to a local department store, and encounters five different versions of the product, priced respectively at $20, $24, $27.50, $32, and $41. Will the buyer naturally assume the $24 unit is of higher quality than the $20 unit, and so forth across the range of available prices? The answer, unfortunately, is a qualified maybe.

If this customer has no real knowledge of the product category, is unfamiliar with brand names, and has not been exposed to any advertising or other information sources (e.g., word of mouth, a salesperson) then the answer is probably yes. This assumes that the buyer fundamentally believes there are likely to be quality differences among the available brands and not that "one brand is as good as another." That is, under these circumstances, the customer is virtually forced to rely on price to differentiate the product offerings. He or she has no other cues or signals on which to base an evaluation.

The price-quality relationship becomes much less clear when other cues and information are available. Such factors as store information, an established brand image, advertising, and customer purchase experience tend to modify, and in some cases discount altogether, the relationship. For instance, perceptions of product quality may result from the interaction of store information with available prices. Alternatively, factors such as brand image may have such an overriding impact on quality perceptions as to make price an insignificant factor insofar as quality goes.

It appears, then, that the interaction between price and quality is somewhat complicated. To the extent that price does reflect quality, the relationship is probably not linear. This means the perceptions of quality differences between two radio/clock alarm units selling for $20 and $25 are not equal to the perceived quality differences of units priced at $25 and $30. Instead, it may take large price differences to convey equal quality differences in moving up the range of prices.

Alternatively, the price-quality relationships may only be significant over certain ranges of price and quality. For instance, there is a tendency for some buyers actually to buy more as price increases, but only at the very high end of the price scale (e.g., see graph d in figure 4.1). This suggests they directly associate price and quality only at premium levels of both.

A related issue concerns how customers go about matching quality to price. As suggested in chapter 1, customers have perceptions of both price and quality. These perceptions, or subjective evaluations, may differ from actual or objective levels of price and quality. A mental picture of the process customers go through is pictured in figure 4.3.

This figure suggests that buyers first categorize an item's price by judging the price levels actually encountered on some subjective rating scale (e.g., extremely high–too cheap). At the same time, they rate the quality encountered in an item on a subjective scale (e.g., outstanding–poor). Once price and quality are categorized, buyers attempt to match them. They are effectively drawing a line from where the item rates on the price scale to where the item rates on the quality scale. If the line is flat, such as a straight line from 'cheap' price to 'just

Figure 4.3
The Subjective Aspects of Relating Quality to Price

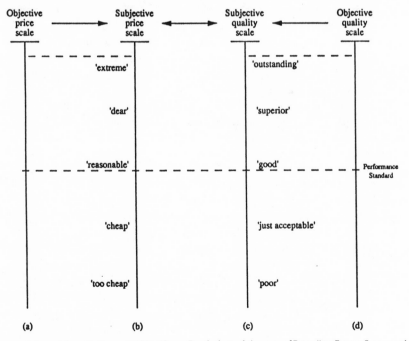

Source: Adapted from F. Emery (1970), "Some Psychological Aspects of Price," in *Pricing Strategy* ed. B. Taylor and G. Wills. (Princeton, N.J.: Brandon/System Press,), 104.

acceptable' quality, the buyer has found a consistent price-quality relationship. If the slope of the line is negative or positive, then price and quality are judged as inconsistent.

Buyers also bring to the process a performance standard for price and quality. This standard is based on their previous purchasing experience. The willingness of buyers to compare their performance standards to the price-quality relationship that comes out of this matching process depends on the slope of the line. Where the slope is fairly large, buyers will be hesitant to pursue the evaluation, opting instead not to buy.

THE EFFECTIVENESS OF ODD PRICING

Try to find an automobile priced at $15,000, a television priced at $500, or a paperback novel priced at $5, and the results will be disappointing. As a rule, none of these products will be available at the stated prices. However, there will probably be quite a few cars for $14,993, televisions for $497.75, and paperbacks for $4.99.

These are called odd prices, because they end in an odd amount, usually just below the nearest round number (ending in zeros). Most prices end in either a nine or a five, not in a zero.

The explanation usually put forward for this practice is that buyers perceive a price just below an even denomination as being lower than it actually is. Buyers are said to substantially exaggerate what is only a marginal difference downward rather than simply rounding the price upward to the nearest denomination. However, there are serious doubts regarding the extent to which odd pricing actually affects buyer behavior.

The research findings in this area have produced mixed results. There are instances where odd prices create lower price illusions, but such cases do not occur consistently. A number of factors are likely to affect how buyers respond to odd prices. Some of these include their elasticity of demand toward the product or service, their reasons for patronizing a particular vendor or store, their knowledge of the prices of competitive goods, and the extent of the shopping effort.

Memory effects have been observed in odd pricing (table 4.1). In one study (Schindler, 1984), pictures of products with odd and even prices were displayed. Two hours later, participants were again shown the same products, but for half the products prices were raised. Subjects were less likely to remember the price increases for odd-priced items. On the other hand, respondents were more likely to perceive price increases where there were no increases when products ended in zeroes (even). These findings imply that odd pricing may be effective prior to raising prices, but when lowering odd-priced products, a reference price should be included to help buyers more easily perceive the change.

Table 4.1
Results of a Study Regarding Effectiveness of Odd Pricing

		First session price	Prices which increased for second session	
			Version 1	Version 2
1.	Digital watch	$ 55.00		$ 65.00
2.	Director's chair	24.98	31.98	
3.	Binoculars	59.99		69.99
4.	Television	400.00	500.00	
5.	High intensity lamp	14.98		17.98
6.	Food processor	39.99	49.99	
7.	35mm camera	299.98		399.98
8.	Automatic coffee maker	19.99		29.99
9.	Stereo	279.99	329.99	
10.	10-speed bicycle	124.98	149.98	
11.	Luggage	29.98		39.98
12.	Video cassette recorder	499.98		599.98
13.	Table lamp	34.98	44.98	
14.	Sneakers	22.00		26.00
15.	Indoor exerciser	75.00	90.00	
16.	Typewriter	225.00		275.00
17.	Popcorn popper	28.00	35.00	
18.	9-piece cookware set	64.99	74.99	
19.	Carousel projector	149.99		174.99
20.	Hooded sweatshirt	12.00	15.00	

PERCENT OF "INCREASE" AND "NO INCREASE"
RESPONSES FOR PRICES WHICH DID INCREASE

Responses	$.00	Price Ending $.99	$.98
No increase	30	47	43
Increase	70	53	57

PERCENT OF "INCREASE" AND "NO INCREASE"
RESPONSES FOR PRICES WHICH REMAINED UNCHANGED

Responses	$.00	Price Ending $.99	$.98
No increase	72	80	77
Increase	28	20	23

Source: R. M. Schindler (1984), "Consumer Recognition of Increases in Odd and Even Prices," Advances in Consumer Research 10, pp. 459-61.

Despite its questionable effectiveness, there are some specific aspects of odd prices which make them appealing. These include the following:

1. Buyers tend to focus on the respective digit positions of the numbers in prices when making a comparison. For example, consider the following pairs of prices.

First set–$.99 $.85
Second set–$.91 $.77

People will generally perceive the second set of prices as being the better bargain. Apparently, buyers focus on the relationship of the first digits of each set. In the first set nine is only one more than eight but in the second set nine is two more than seven. The buyer notes this difference and despite an identical absolute differential ($.14), regards the second set in a more favorable light.

2. The circles in double nine (99) attract attention, eight (8) is symmetrical and soothing, seven (7) is angular and jarring, and five (5) is the happy mean.

3. Odd numbers give the impression that the seller is setting his price as low as possible.

4. Odd endings suggest that the product is unique.

5. Odd endings provide the customer with change—he is making a saving and thus foregoing an additional expense.

6. Odd prices connote savings whereas even pricing connotes prestige.

Beyond this, odd prices may serve another purpose. Even if they do not lead a buyer to make a purchase, they may draw the customer. That is, the odd price may be enough to arouse interest and get the customer to take a look. At this point, other marketing variables (e.g., a salesperson, a display, literature) must take over.

SUMMARY

This chapter has attempted to demonstrate that customers do not respond to prices in a perfectly logical or rational manner. Rather, there is a psychology involved in price behavior. As a result, price behavior can be better understood by applying some basic psychological concepts.

Buyers usually enter the market with a reference price in mind. Reference prices are determined by a combination of influences and tend to change over time. They differ significantly from the actual prices customers encounter in the marketplace. Surrounding a customer's reference prices are upper and lower thresholds. These thresholds define an acceptable price range within which a given quantity of an item will be purchased.

Customers also tend to adapt their reference prices, based in part on the marketing efforts of the firm. Adaptation theory and assimilation and contrast effects have been presented as frameworks that can be helpful to managers in achieving the desired customer response to pricing programs. Examples of specific tactics that rely on these frameworks have also been included.

The role of price in conveying product quality and the effectiveness of odd pricing were also investigated in this chapter. In both instances, the evidence is unclear. However, there do appear to be conditions under which buyers use price as an indicator of quality and respond more favorably to an odd price.

Although it is an area of few hard facts or findings, managers can find it profitable to focus more attention on customer price psychology. This is a fairly new area about which much is currently being learned. The limited findings to date suggest that the time has come to disregard the simplistic assumptions of traditional economic thinking.

REFERENCES

Gabor, A., *Pricing Concepts and Methods for Effective Marketing.* Cambridge, England: University Press, 1988.

Gabor, A., and C. W. J. Granger, "On the Price Consciousness of Consumers." *Applied Statistics* 10 (November 1961): 170-88.

Gabor, A., C. W. J. Granger, and A. Sowter, "Comments on Psychophysics of Pricing." *Journal of Marketing Research* 8 (May 1971): 251-52.

Liefeld, J., and L. A. Helsop, "Reference Prices and Deception in Newspaper Advertising." *Journal of Consumer Research* 11 (March 1985): 868-76.

Loudon, D., and A. J. Della Bitta, *Consumer Behavior.* New York: McGraw-Hill, 1988.

Monroe, K. B., "Psychophysics of Pricing: A Reappraisal." *Journal of Marketing Research* 8 (May 1971): 248-50.

———. "Buyers' Subjective Perceptions of Price." *Journal of Marketing Research* 10 (February 1973): 70-80.

Schindler, R. M., "Consumer Recognition of Increases in Odd and Even Prices." *Advances in Consumer Research* 10: 459-61.

5

NEGOTIATING PRICES WITH CUSTOMERS

In many instances, customers do not pay a standard list price. Instead, the final price is determined through a process of negotiation between buyer and seller. Commercial negotiation is defined as the efforts made by two (or more) parties to complete a transaction through the use of bargaining. It represents a form of decision making in which parties seek to achieve mutual interests and resolve differences.

The negotiation process becomes necessary when neither of the parties to a transaction has the power to impose its own will over the other(s). Implicit in negotiation is the assumption that the respective parties desire to obtain an agreement with which all can live. Such an accommodation is a learning experience wherein the parties may well define their relationship for the future.

This chapter will focus on price negotiation from a marketing perspective. A strategic approach for planning and conducting successful negotiations is presented. Attention is devoted to the underlying analysis necessary to accurately define the firm's negotiation position and to develop effective negotiation tactics.

NEGOTIATIONS BEGIN INTERNALLY

Before examining the nature of the negotiation process between buyers and sellers, it is worth considering what is happening inside the selling organization. For sellers to achieve a competitive advantage in the marketplace, a number of key activities must be well-coordinated. Research and development, production, finance, distribution, and marketing departments must collaborate in offering product value to customers. This collaboration is usually achieved through a process of *internal negotiation*. For example, the research department

...ay develop a product, but the production department must determine its ...easibility. The finance department must ensure that the funds are available for development, and the marketing department must assess demand and competition. From the drawing board to the shipping dock, the firm engages in an interactive accommodation and coordination among its members.

A common breakdown in this cooperative relationship occurs because of the competitive pressures salespeople encounter in striking a deal. Members of the sales force are under great pressure to achieve both their personal goals and the goals of the sales department, to satisfy the customer's objectives, and to maintain a competitive posture with respect to the opposition. Often a salesperson will "get out front" not only of the production or financial capacity of his firm but of the preexisting sales commitments of his or her own department. Not uncommonly, the salesperson makes the deal, leaving the details (qualifying the customer's credit worthiness or ensuring production or delivery capability) to the relevant departments. As a result, the firm finds the cart has been placed before the horse. The prospective buyer may have an uneven credit history, may demand costly product changes, or may insist on impractical production or delivery schedules. These and other conditions may result in this sale or future sales unraveling because of poor communication with the other internal players in the firm.

The salesperson must understand the ongoing operational commitments of his or her own firm when formulating sales objectives. By recognizing the firm's limitations, the salesperson can initiate discussions with a buyer that focus on determining what is possible, and in the process define what is negotiable. Problems can be minimized if the sales department follows a few simple guidelines (Keller, 1988):

- Allot time for negotiations with other functional areas of the firm.
- Develop and maintain cooperative relationships with other departments.
- Determine the relationship between specific items in the sales agreement and areas that typically require internal negotiation.
- Verify assumptions regarding the firm's ability to fulfill terms of the sales agreement.
- Recognize issues in the sales agreement that pose internal credibility problems.
- Manage salesforce enthusiasm in a disciplined and productive manner.
- Stay abreast of internal changes that may affect relationships with customers.
- Keep superiors current on developments in major sales agreements as they occur.
- Be knowledgeable of customer histories as they relate to issues requiring internal negotiation.
- Help customers and internal people find creative alternatives when roadblocks develop.

The salesperson who is an effective internal negotiator is also apt to have more success in customer negotiations. He or she is likely to have more leverage in bargaining with customers and may well be able to go further in satisfying their needs. With this in mind, let us turn to a more detailed discussion of the customer negotiation process.

THE NATURE OF CUSTOMER NEGOTIATIONS

Negotiation is concerned with needs of buyers and sellers. Both parties gain from a transaction. The customer acquires a product or service that meets needs, and the vendor makes a sale. The possibility of mutual gain is what brings the buyer and seller together. The amount of gain realized by either party creates the conflicts that must be negotiated. Conflict occurs because the parties find themselves competing for some of the same gains.

In all cases, negotiation involves both science and art. The scientific aspect involves systematic approaches for resolving conflicts between two parties. The artisitic side concerns interpersonal skills, the ability to convince and be convinced, and judgment regarding which tactics to use and when to use them.

There is no typical negotiation. A particular negotiation can involve any number of people and focus on any number of issues. It can be formal or informal, lasting hours, weeks, or months. Most important, the process involved is dynamic, not static or fixed. The positions assumed by each party at the outset can differ significantly from those held at the close of the process.

These dynamics are strongly influenced by a number of structural and situational characteristics. A primary consideration is the extent to which the buying and selling representatives have the formal authority to negotiate. How much clout do these representative have in terms of the issues under negotiation? Are there conflicts within the seller organization (or buyer organization in industrial markets) on some of these issues?

Another consideration is the degree of interdependence between the buyer and seller. Both parties need each other, so the real issue concerns where the balance of power lies. Power is a function of dependency. That is, the more the seller is dependent on the buyer, the more power the buyer has. Dependency is determined by how much one party needs the resources (i.e., products, services, or revenue) controlled by the other party and the availability of those resources from alternative sources. If the buyer is purchasing a critical item from a vendor who is the only available source of supply, the buyer's heavy dependency enhances the seller's negotiating power.

Negotiation can be further characterized by the number of issues involved. The willingness to pay or receive a certain price may interact with other issues. The existence of multiple issues to be jointly resolved through negotiation permits the parties to enlarge the size of the total pie before determining how much each side is to receive. However, it is a real challenge to determine which trade-offs the other party will be inclined to make when multiple issues are involved.

Also, the existence of time constraints should be noted. By optimally using the time frame available, the disadvantages of hasty negotiation by one party can be averted. In addition, the degree to which the negotiation is public is important. If different terms are worked out with various customer accounts, the ability to negotiate flexibly with any one account is affected by how much other customers learn of the tactics used and final terms agreed upon. Competitors are also in a position to benefit from learning a firm's negotiation strategy.

Further, negotiations can be repetitive or nonrepetitive. That is, will this be a one-time sale, or might there be frequent negotiations in the future? Repetitive bargaining usually finds the parties adopting a more cooperative stance. Separately, the marketer should evaluate the presence of any linkage effects, that is, circumstances in which a particular negotiation and its outcome are linked to other negotiations. Obstacles can sometimes be overcome by using linkages creatively.

Finally, the location of the negotiation is a factor. There may be a psychological benefit, as well as an ability to control the agenda of the proceedings, when the party negotiates on its home turf. One side can enhance its own bargaining position by negotiating in an environment in which support people are readily available. Alternatively, negotiating on the other side's turf allows one to learn firsthand about the needs and capabilities of the other party.

NEGOTIATION OBJECTIVES

In preparing to negotiate, the marketer needs to consider some fundamental questions. Of these, the most important are

- What do I want to achieve through negotiation, and why?
- What does the buyer want to achieve, and why?

The answers to these questions will define the negotiation atmosphere. If they cannot be answered satisfactorily, it may be that one or the other of the parties does not understand their own needs. Failure to understand needs may suggest that the necessary time and commitments have not been expended in preparing to negotiate. However, it may be impossible to answer these questions prior to substantive discussions between the parties. Needs often emerge in the discovery process of give-and-take during preliminary discussions.

Clearly defining needs allows a negotiator to establish meaningful aspirations. Aspirations are defined by their level and limit. In a best-case scenario, the level of aspiration is the level of benefit sought, the specific goal the negotiator professes to seek. An aspiration limit is the ultimate fallback position of a negotiator. It is the irreducible minimum below which he is unwilling to go.

In price negotiations, the needs of buyer and seller are a function of value derived and value imparted (see chapter 1). While negotiations may ostensibly revolve around price, the other components of the product offering (quality, volume of purchases, service delivery financing, return policies, etc.) may be on the agenda of the vendor or the customer (see also table 5.1). While buyers will tend to verbally emphasize price throughout the bargaining, any of these product aspects can serve as a negotiable issue while price remains firm. In fact, market studies have demonstrated that among industrial buyers, premium price differentials of as much as 20 percent are acceptable if accompanied by superior product attributes. Further, the more issues there are in a negotiation, the greater the opportunities for compromise and creative bargaining. If price is the sole issue, flexibility may be limited to the various dimensions of price (e.g., volume discounts, time of payment, inflation clauses). Clearly, then, the negotiator needs to view the bargaining process from a broader perspective.

Table 5.1
Examples of Factors That Are Negotiable

delivery time and mode	software provided
form of payment	manuals and training
warranty	cancellation clauses
transportation costs	technical support
spare parts	price of features
tooling	options
cost analysis	back-order charges
price protection	warehousing
stocked parts	consigned stocks
progress payments	penalty clauses
drawing aid	factory assembly
product additions	systems analysis
inventory controls	returns policies
discount policies	trade-in allowances
preinstallation sitework and installation	ongoing service after the sale

Figure 5.1
A Strategic Framework for Managing Price Negotiations

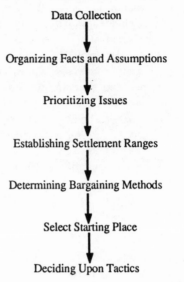

Data Collection

↓

Organizing Facts and Assumptions

↓

Prioritizing Issues

↓

Establishing Settlement Ranges

↓

Determining Bargaining Methods

↓

Select Starting Place

↓

Deciding Upon Tactics

A STRATEGIC APPROACH TO NEGOTIATION

The large number of factors that impact on bargaining outcomes suggest that every negotiation is unique. The most effective approaches tend to be tailored to the particular buying situation at hand. Correspondingly, the marketer is well served to develop a strategic perspective on the negotiation process. Figure 5.1 presents a step-by-step framework for approaching negotiations strategically.

Collecting Background Information

The beginning point in preparing for any negotiation is to gather critical intelligence regarding the needs and motives of the other party. Each side possesses information about the other that is complete in some areas and incomplete in others. Assumptions must be made where data resources are inadequate, a frequent situation. Examples of ten key information needs of the seller include

- Customer familiarity with available alternatives
- Previous purchase behavior in product category and likely points of customer resistance that will be encountered
- Size and flexibility of customer budget
- Identity of actual price decision maker

- Product modification required by customer
- Volume requirements and economies
- Customer financing requirements
- Urgency of customer need and latest acceptable delivery time
- Customer service and maintenance capabilities
- Application or use to be made of product and likelihood of follow-up business

Organizing Facts and Assumptions

Negotiators often confuse facts with assumptions. The two must be separated, with the negotiator attempting to validate assumptions as the bargaining process unfolds. Facts themselves should be organized into categories, including those related to customer price sensitivity, product or service requirements, and personal characteristics of the negotiator(s) on the buying side. Categories such as these have direct implications for the selection of negotiating tactics.

Prioritizing Issues

Next, the negotiator needs to assign a priority to the issues subject to negotiation. Some will be more important than others. For instance, holding the line on price may be critical. Alternatively, price may be flexible if the customer will permit a product alteration or agree to a seller-specified delivery schedule or packaging proposal.

The establishment of priorities should maximize seller profit consistent with buyer value, keeping in mind that customer value is determined by a composite of product attributes. From a strategic standpoint, critical issues should be intermingled with flexible issues so that the negotiation is taken as a whole. This suggests that the priorities of buyer and seller are likely to emerge only in the advanced stages of bargaining. It serves little purpose for the parties to signal in advance their priorities or desired negotiation outcome. Some negotiation authorities believe that efficiency requires that major points be settled early, allowing the flexible issues to be used as seller concessions—pacifiers to make the deal easier to swallow. However, by viewing negotiation as a whole, the seller can organize issues so that the buyer obtains a concession while agreeing to a seller proposal, thus maximizing profit. The more complex the negotiation, the more issue interplay occurs. The important thing in negotiation is not efficiency but effectiveness.

Establishing Settlement Ranges

Focusing on price itself, the seller should next seek to determine settlement ranges for both parties. A settlement range is the distance between a party's reservation, or walkaway, price and its initial offer (see figure 5.2). For the seller the reservation price is the minimum acceptable price, while for the buyer it is the maximum acceptable price. These should reflect each side's assessment of the consequences of not coming to any agreement. As illustrated in figure 5.2, if the seller's minimum is compared to the buyer's maximum, the difference is called the bargaining zone, or zone of agreement. The final price should fall in this zone. Also illustrated in figure 5.2 are the buyer and seller aspiration levels, which often fall in between the opening offer and the reservation price.

In attempting to determine the buyer's opening position, it is important to recognize that these positions may be deliberately exaggerated for tactical purposes. If either the buyer or the seller position is too extreme, the negotiation may degenerate into a purely adversarial contest. Assuming both parties have performed sufficient background research, opening positions will be realistic, if not immediately optimal. There is an inherent dynamic in negotiation that impels each party to desire that movement in position come from the other side. Sellers may tend to aim high and then switch discussions of price to other aspects, such as volume discounts.

Determining Bargaining Methods

The actual approach relied upon by the seller when bargaining depends upon his or her particular negotiation philosophy. There is a tendency to approach the process as a *zero sum* (or win-lose) game, in which the seller's gains come completely at the expense of the buyer, in exact proportion. For example, if the seller gains revenue by negotiating 5 percent more in terms of the price charged, then the buyer experiences an expense to his or her budget in the same amount.

It is frequently possible to turn negotiation into a *positive sum* (or win-win) game. Creative thinking is the key. The seller focuses on finding options that hold merit for both parties. An example might be standing firm on the price increase, but giving the customer a favorable delivery schedule or adding to the provisions of the warranty. Another possibility is a longer-term contract with a customer, guaranteeing that the price will not be raised during the period of the contract. The goal, then, is to increase the size of the pie, rather than competing for existing pieces of a fixed pie.

A third alternative involves approaching negotiation from a future investment point of view. The *negative sum* (or lose-win) game finds the seller knowingly giving up more than he or she gains so that the buyer might benefit. Such an accommodating bargaining method can make sense if the seller is attempting to establish a profitable future relationship or if the seller wants to make a goodwill gesture to help the buyer out of some present difficulty.

People bring unique assumptions and objectives to a negotiation. Each party's perception of the other's approach toward negotiation may be quite different. One study asked negotiators to evaluate their own approaches and

Figure 5.2
Defining the Bargaining Zone for Price Negotiation

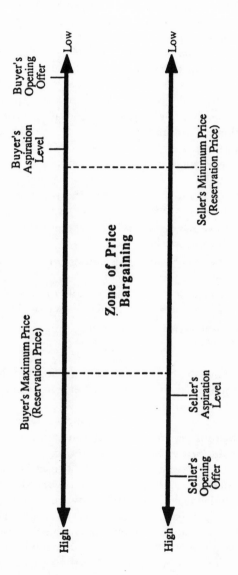

those of their opposite numbers. The sample tended to perceive themselves as cooperative, collaborative, and willing to compromise while viewing the other side as uncooperative, hostile, or hard-nosed. When asked to characterize their own behavior, they described themselves as informing, suggesting, and reminding while the other side was perceived as being unreasonable, demanding, and refusing. It is important to remember that since perceptions differ, the negotiator should always pursue his objectives with the overall negotiation process in mind. By keeping the goal of mutual satisfaction as the target, discussions evolve from a "position" orientation to a "process" orientation.

The perception an individual brings to a negotiation may lead to a behavioral predisposition or a tendency to behave consistently across different conflict situations. This consistency has been termed a dominant style of behavior. One recent study (Perdue, Day and Michaels, 1986) noted five dominant styles of negotiation among organizational buyers:

Collaborative: Buyers seek to achieve both their own goals and those of the seller. This is a problem-solving approach in which joint gains are sought.

Competitive: Buyers seek their own gains at the expense of the seller's interests. This approach can be termed "zero-sum."

Sharing: Buyers try to achieve partial gains for their own concerns in an attempt to satisfy the goals of the seller.

Accommodative: The buyer attempts to fully satisfy the concerns of the seller at the expense of his/her own concerns and seeks a peaceful coexistance with the seller.

Avoidant: Buyers are indifferent to the concerns of either party and avoid confrontation with the seller.

The authors found the collaborative and sharing approaches most common among their sample. On an intuitive level, it seems these results are consistent with a win-win negotiating strategy.

Buyers and sellers have objectives that include what they must have, what they would like to have, and what they can give or concede. Only the latter two objectives are negotiable. With respect to wants and concessions, both parties may attach different significance to a given item's value and its actual cost. In industrial markets, buyers have wants or needs that are organizational, job-related, or individual. Similarly, in consumer markets, buyers' needs could be family-related or personal, among other categories. Thus the context of a need may be as important as the substance of the need itself. A given item may serve one or the other of these needs. The manner in which a particular issue is approached or presented should appeal to the actual context of the need. For instance, a buyer's need to obtain a lower price may be less a concern with saving his company some money and more a question of personal pride. The seller who uses company-based appeals is likely to make little headway in getting the buyer to pay a higher price.

Correspondingly effective bargaining methods are those that anticipate buyer objections to seller musts and provide a defense to them, determine sellers' costs and the perceived buyer value of a negotiable item, and classify issues relative to satisfying organizational, job, family, or personal needs.

Selecting a Starting Place

To open any negotiation it is helpful to have an agenda. The negotiator might choose a topic common to the agendas of both parties. The choice of such issues does not necessarily imply mutual agreement on their perceived importance, only that they are the concerns of both. Agreeing to open discussions on a common agenda item provides the mutual advantage of not signaling in advance issues important to one or the other side. Subsequently, issues emerge as the two sides attempt to match their needs and the limits of their negotiating flexibility become clear.

In terms of the opening price, a common reference point is the firm's list or officially stated price to the public, if one exists, absent any stated discount policy. While it is generally argued that the initial price should be high enough to permit some leeway that can be subsequently conceded, the seller must exercise caution. Loading the price early on may prevent the parties from engaging in legitimate bargaining. Rather, the seller should determine in the planning stage how far down price can be negotiated and what the buyer must give up for each incremental reduction in price. An alternative but more risky approach is to start with a reasonable or fair price and then hold firm. This is risky because it can antagonize buyers by forcing them to make all the concessions.

Deciding Upon Tactical Moves

The types of tactics that can be employed during the negotiation process are virtually limitless. The effectiveness of any single tactic is entirely situational. Most important is the need to recognize both the risks and potential gains from a particular tactic. Tactics should not be used haphazardly, but instead should be part of a larger program of action. While contingencies that require the bargainer to adapt will arise during bargaining, these should be anticipated in advance and the response planned.

A key tactical consideration in any negotiation is time. Buyers and sellers commonly employ a variety of tactics to create anxiety on the other side with respect to time passing. For instance, sellers identify deadlines, including a date after which a particular price offer will not be honored. The customer might be told that orders not placed immediately will take much longer to produce or deliver, or that the person that can approve a particular price range will be unavailable in so many days. Time tactics can also be used to delay a decision, possibly because the seller needs more information or is trying to wear down the buyer. He or she might offer to get back with the buyer in a few days.

Other tactics focus on the dynamics and terms of the negotiation itself. Some specific examples include the following:

Make me an offer. While sellers typically state an initial price, this maneuver represents an attempt to get the buyer to go first. In so doing, the buyer reveals part of his bargaining strategy, giving the seller greater maneuverability.

This is all I've got. One party identifies fixed constraints within which the bargaining must take place. The buyer might claim he or she can spend no more than a certain amount, while the seller might claim no deal can be made at a given price unless a minimum sized order is placed.

Take it or leave it. A party sets a fixed price and is resolute about not compromising. This may make sense if the seller knows the buyer cannot walk away, if the buyer would just as soon avoid bargaining, or if the price is near the seller's cost.

I don't really understand. One of the parties feigns ignorance or is slow to comprehend the other's position. Not only does it provide the pretending party with more time, but it can keep the other side from pursuing questions in a particular area and may make the party less insistent on their positions in that area.

*Here's a price you're not going to beat . . . but—*The seller offers a very low price but then adds all sorts of extra charges and conditions when the deal is being finalized. Called "lowballing," the offer turns out to be much less attractive than it first appeared, but by now the buyer is tired and ready to get the transaction completed.

Agreed, but now there is an additional problem. This tactic is called escalation. An issue that has been settled is reopened, or one party stipulates additional demands before he or she will honor a position previously agreed upon.

I'll have to confer with my boss. One party claims limited authority, indicating that approval for anything other than the offer on the table must come from elsewhere. This often puts the other party in the position of having to come up with solutions that work around these authority limitations; it also discourages the other party from emphasizing issues outside this scope of authority, unless he or she wishes to start over again with a person in higher authority.

I guess we're at an impasse. Deliberate deadlocks represent a means of testing the other side's firmness or willpower. Deadlocks also serve to increase both parties' willingness to subsequently compromise. While this tactic may seem risky for sellers, it can be effective in cases where buyers tend to equate deadlock with personal failure.

My last and final offer. This tactic is an indication that the seller or buyer has negotiated as far as possible. Credibility is the key here, for if the other party sees this as a mere ploy, one's ongoing bargaining position is undermined.

Good guy and bad guy. Negotiators on one side work in tandem. One (the bad guy) will niggle over trivial positions, make unreasonable demands, or seek to undo already agreed-upon positions. The other (the good guy) adopts the role of conciliator, seeking to elicit some concession that, if granted, will persuade his or her partner to come on board and accept the deal.

In selecting tactics, one must try not to become preoccupied with the stated positions adopted by the other side. Fisher and Ury (1981), in a landmark book on negotiation, urge that bargainers focus on interests, not positions. The stated positions serve to constrain the situation, while the underlying interests or needs of each actually define the problem. A solution that addresses interests may look quite different from the solutions represented by the formal positions each side puts forth. For instance, a purchasing agent may be adamant about a certain price, when in fact his or her real need is to reduce the buying organization's expenditures in a particular product category by a certain percentage.

ASPIRATIONS AND CONCESSIONS

The aspiration levels, or goals, of bargainers should generally be high but realistic. All other things being equal, parties with high aspiration levels walk away with a better deal than those with low aspiration levels almost every time. This happens as long as the aspiration level is not so high as to alienate the other party, causing them to walk away.

When aspiration levels are either too low or too vague, the likelihood of a positive sum (win-win) outcome diminishes significantly. When goals are easy, negotiators may prematurely compromise or unilaterally concede unnecessarily to reach quick agreement. When goals are too vague, negotiators tend to single-mindedly seek individual rather than joint profit outcomes.

The strategies and tactics of buyer and seller are often aimed at reducing each other's aspiration levels. For instance, negotiators will sometimes create straw issues in addition to the salient issues with which they are actually concerned. By increasing the overall scope of the negotiations, they hope to distract the other party from a particular salient issue, influencing them to lower their expectation levels.

Reductions in aspiration levels often come in the form of concessions. A concession is a change in an offer in the perceived direction of the other party's interest that reduces the benefit sought. Ordinarily, concessions are made to hasten agreement, keep the negotiation going, or encourage reciprocal concession by the other party. The speed with which concessions are made is termed the "concession rate."

Studies on business negotiation tend to emphasize the need to make high initial demands while giving concessions slowly, if at all. This emphasis is often driven by a fear of either position loss or image loss. Position loss is the surrender of part or all of one's negotiation stance or options on a particular issue. Image loss entails giving the appearance of bargaining weakness, that is, the appearance that the bargainer will readily make concessions. Position loss is important because once a concession is made, it cannot ordinarily be rescinded. A concession given represents a potential demand the other side may have and, once accepted, is no longer available to trade for a reciprocal concession. Image loss is to be avoided because it both undermines a bargainer's future demand credibility and encourages the other party to elicit yet more concessions. The other party's perceptions regarding a negotiator's position loss may affect only the negotiation at hand, but an image loss may linger and influence future negotiations as a reference point for the advantaged party.

In a nutshell, the object when giving concessions is to make the concessions more apparent than real, to create a perception that something of value is being conceded that is actually of little real cost. There are, in addition, some general guidelines to be kept in mind regarding the use of concessions. First and foremost, a good negotiator will avoid making the first concession on priority issues. In fact, if the seller makes the initial concession, but on a minor issue, the buyer may be more apt to follow with a major concession. Second, it is a good idea to avoid conceding anything until all of the other side's demands are known. Third, concessions made by the other side do not have to be matched one-for-one. Fourth, concessions should be made in relatively small increments and should be clearly communicated. Large concessions, and those poorly made, can serve to raise the aspiration level of the other party. Fifth, bargainers should ensure that something is gained for every concession given up. At the same time, good negotiators avoid "splitting the difference" on key points, because an even split may not be necessary given the respective power positions of the parties. Finally, a record should be kept regarding the number and size of concessions made, since it is easy to forget how much has been given up by either side.

BUILDING A LONG-TERM RELATIONSHIP

The most successful marketers tend to recognize that their job is not to sell products or services, but instead to create relationships. Developing long-term relationships with customers not only provides a source of competitive advantage, but can be much more profitable than a hit-and-run approach in which the only goal is to make a sale at a point in time. Negotiation strategy plays a critical role in the establishment of such relationships. Specifically, there is a direct connection between a positive sum or win-win negotiating strategy and the seller's ability to foster customer loyalty.

Customers who perceive a negotiation to be one-sided have little incentive to give the seller any future business. Even if the deal seemed fair at the time, dissatisfaction can develop during implementation, especially after a customer has had some time to reflect. Sellers must recognize that the relationship is as important as the literal provisions of the negotiated contract.

Negotiation involves two-way interaction in which *both* parties seek attributes. Either side can walk away if their needs are not being minimally satisfied by those on the other side. Investments are being made by both sides, and each party must perceive the give-and-take to be equitable. Relationships also tend to get more personal over time. If an atmosphere of trust is not created early on, with benefits and burdens mutually shared, the job of the seller becomes more difficult with each new negotiation involving a particular customer.

The uncertainty that surrounds businesses today also affects ongoing negotiations. Rapid changes in technology, the economy, production costs, competition, government regulation, and market size are increasingly commonplace. In fact, the only constant in modern business would seem to be change. Such turmoil can alter the fundamental relationship between a seller and buyer in a very short amount of time. The seller who takes too much advantage of his or her organization's negotiating position today will most likely pay for such shortsightedness in the not-too-distant future.

SUMMARY

This chapter has attempted to provide a systematic method for arriving at prices when they are determined through negotiation. Negotiation was examined as a dynamic, two-way process in which both buyer and seller seek gains and make investments. The value of approaching negotiation as a positive sum or win-win game was emphasized. The effective negotiator seeks creative solutions that accomplish mutual goals.

A seven-step process for strategically managing negotiation was presented. The process begins with research on the customer and his or her requirements. Next, facts and assumptions are organized and implications are drawn for negotiation strategy and tactics. The bargainer then establishes settlement ranges and the zone of negotiation. Following this, a bargaining method is chosen and a starting place is selected. Finally, the tactics that appear most appropriate for the situation are identified.

Suggestions are also made regarding how the process of giving concessions should be managed. The negotiator is encouraged to monitor both position loss and image loss, while making concessions that are more apparent than real. Items that are of apparent value but entail little real cost represent ideal candidates for concessions.

The long-term implications of negotiation strategy for buyer-seller relationships are also stressed. The modern business environment is increasingly one in which buyer-seller relationships are less adversarial, and terms such as "cooperative marketing" or "partnership marketing" have become popular. In addition, extreme turbulence in the competitive environment is continuously affecting the relative bargaining positions of buyers and sellers in many markets. These developments suggest that negotiations be pursued with an eye toward both present and future needs of the parties.

REFERENCES

Fisher, R., and W. Ury, *Getting to YES: Negotiating Agreement Without Giving In.* Boston: Houghton Mifflin, 1981.

Karrass, C. L., *Give and Take: The Complete Guide to Negotiating Strategies and Tactics.* New York: Thomas Y. Corwell, 1974.

Keller, R. E., *Sales Negotiating Handbook.* Englewood Cliffs, N.J.: Prentice-Hall, 1988.

Perdue, B.C.D., R. Day, and R. L. Michaels, "Negotiation Strategies of Industrial Buyers," *Industrial Marketing Management,* 15 (August 1986): 171-76.

6

EXAMINING COSTS FROM
A MARKET PERSPECTIVE

THE LOGIC OF COST-BASED PRICING: SIMPLICITY

The most common method for establishing prices is cost-based, typically relying either on a cost-plus or target-return formula. The popularity of cost-based approaches reflects a risk avoidance mentality on the part of managers. Many believe that the principal function of price is to cover the expenditures that have been incurred by the firm. Further, cost-based approaches assume profit is the sole objective in any pricing scheme, and managers have a tendency to be profit-driven. Also, because they rely on rules of thumb or mathematical formulas, cost-based approaches are easy to use.

Most cost-based pricing methods rely on a full-cost procedure for determining how many dollars are being used to produce, sell, and distribute a product. Full costing operates on the assumption that all costs incurred by a business must be absorbed by the units of output. While this would seem logical, many of the costs of running a business have little to do with the production of a particular unit of output. As a result, some type of cost allocation scheme must be developed. Many possibilities exist in this regard, such as allocating costs based on dollar sales of different products, on the amount of labor or some key raw material used by products, or on the percentage of total production volume accounted for by the particular product.

With full costing, the firm first develops an estimate of variable costs per unit. Variable costs are those that directly vary with the number of units produced or sold, and primarily consist of direct labor and direct materials (see figure 6.1). Next, a percentage of the fixed costs of operating the firm, including overhead, are allocated to the product using a scheme such as those cited above. Fixed costs are those that do not vary directly with the number of units produced,

Figure 6.1
The Assumed Behavior of Variable and Fixed Costs

a. Total Variable Costs (Variable Cost Per Unit x Quantity)

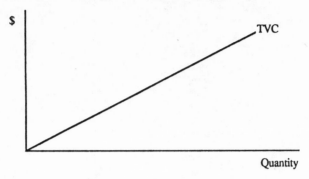

Examples:
direct labor
direct material
unit transportation
 charges
sales commission

b. Total Fixed Costs

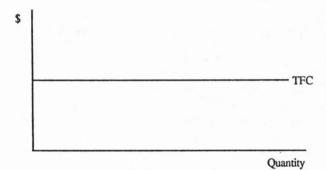

Examples:
rent
depreciation
insurance
salaries
advertising

c. Total Costs (Variable + Fixed)

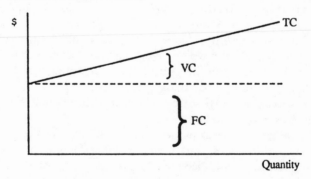

including rent, insurance, depreciation of equipment, maintenance, salaries of management, and advertising, among others (see figure 6.1). Fixed costs are constant within some relevant range of production or operations. The allocation scheme is used to arrive at an estimate of fixed cost per unit. To this is added a markup, to reflect the unit profit margin. The result is a price.

This procedure is illustrated with a line of three lawn mowers in table 6.1. Overhead is allocated as a percentage of the amount of labor expense incurred for each of the products. The focus on labor could be due to its high hourly cost, relative scarcity, or tendency to vary most directly with units produced.

An alternative approach would be to project the total number of units of all three products the company expects to produce and divide this into total projected fixed costs. The result would be a fixed cost per unit charge, which would be added to the unit variable costs to obtain total unit costs. A variation of this method would be to project the percentage of total production volume to be accounted for by each of the three products and use these percentages in allocating overhead.

The target-return approach to price setting is also cost based, but focuses on ensuring that an acceptable rate of return is earned on the capital invested in

Table 6.1
Calculating Price Using a Full-Costing, Cost-Plus Approach

	Product: Lawnmowers		
	Model A	Model B	Model C
Variable Costs:			
Direct Labor	$25.00	$42.00	$51.00
Direct Material	$40.00	$45.00	$60.00
Fixed Costs:			
Manufacturing overhead (allocated 75% of direct labor costs)	$18.75	$31.50	$38.25
Administrative, selling and distribution overhead (allocated at 50% of direct labor costs)	$12.50	$21.00	$25.50
Total Cost	$96.25	$139.50	$174.75
Profit Margin:			
20% markup on total unit cost	$19.25	$27.90	$34.95
Selling Price	$115.50	$167.40	$209.70

the product. Some variation of the following formula is generally relied upon to determine price.

$$P = VC/unit + \frac{TFC}{Q_s} + \frac{rK}{Q_s}$$

where: P = price to be charged
VC/unit = variable cost per unit
TFC = total fixed costs
Qs = standard volume
r = desired rate of return (profit)
K = capital employed

The beginning point is to estimate standard volume, which is the expected level of volume to be produced in the next operating period, usually a year. Alternatively, to deal with cyclical trends in sales, average volume per year over the next five or so years could be used. Once standard volume is estimated, the manager determines what variable cost per unit would likely be at that level of production. Then, total fixed costs incurred when operating at this level are projected and then divided by standard unit volume, to arrive at fixed cost per unit. Next, the manager arrives at a desired profit rate and multiplies this by the investment value of the operating assets employed in the production and distribution of the product to get total desired profit. Total profit is then divided by standard volume to obtain profit per unit. Finally, variable cost per unit, fixed cost per unit, and profit per unit are summed to arrive at price. Table 6.2 provides an illustration, again using a line of lawn mowers.

While the cost-plus and target-return methods can become considerably more complex in practice, both are relatively straightforward. Unfortunately, the simplicity of cost-based approaches is offset by a severe loss of flexibility and realism in the firm's pricing program.

THE DANGER OF COST-BASED PRICING: LOST PROFITS

To appreciate the limitations of cost-based prices, consider the case of a firm that manufactures two types of telephones. One is a standard, black, rotary dial (sbrd) telephone, while the other is a designer push-button (dpb) telephone in the shape of a famous cartoon character.

The costs of producing and distributing the two telephones are fairly similar. The totals are $10 per unit for the sbrd telephone and $15 for the dpb telephone. The lower unit cost for the sbrd telephone reflects higher unit volume and thus economies of scale. In addition, a special licensing fee must be paid for each unit of the dpb telephone produced. The company desires a 200 percent markup on cost for each of the products. This would mean a price of $30 for the sbrd and $45 for the dpb.

Table 6.2
Calculating Price Using Target Return Approach

| | Product: Lawnmowers | | |
	Model A	Model B	Model C
Standard Volume	49,000	33,000	22,000
Variable Costs:			
Direct Labor	$25.00	$42.00	$51.00
Direct Material	$40.00	$45.00	$60.00
Total Variable Costs	$65.00	$87.00	$111.00
Fixed Costs (in thousands)			
Direct	$450	$590	$820
Indirect (allocated as %	705	941	1,294
of direct fixed costs)			
Total Fixed Costs	$1,155	$1,531	$2,114
Desired Profit Rate	20%	20%	20%
Investment Value of Operating Assets Employed	$5,000,000	$7,000,000	$11,000,000
Price	$109.00	$162.00	$307.00

The company may well meet its sales goals for each of the two products and achieve the desired rate of return. However, the strategic potential of the price variable is being ignored. Not only does this approach fail to establish a strategy for pricing, it ignores competitor activities and changing market conditions. Most important, cost-based approaches ignore demand and customer value perceptions. This is where real profit opportunities can be missed.

As an example, assume research is conducted that suggests the demand curve for the dpb telephone approximates that pictured in figure 6.2. Here, demand at the $45 price is somewhat elastic, given the flatter shape of the curve at this point. However, above a price of about $60, demand becomes very inelastic. This suggests there is a sizable group of buyers whose demand is insensitive to price anywhere between $60 and $160. These buyers apparently attach a premium value to the product, viewing it as an exclusive or very unique type of purchase. If a price of $120 were charged, the company would not only make significantly more revenue than at $45, but price would be reinforcing the image of the product.

Cost-based pricing can also produce prices that are higher than competitive conditions and customer value perceptions warrant. Companies frequently

Figure 6.2
Demand Curve for the Designer Push-Button (DPB) Telephone

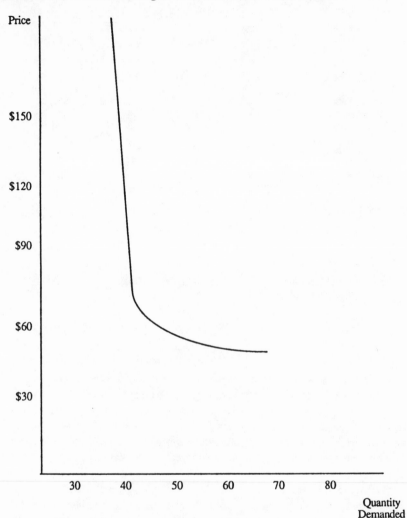

Quantity
Demanded

overprice their products in an attempt to quickly recover the large amounts of money spent in initially developing and then launching the product. In addition, as products mature, there is a tendency to allocate to them significant amounts of overhead that are completely unrelated to their actual costs. Meanwhile, competitors are cutting prices and customers increasingly see little difference between one brand and the next.

This last issue points up another fundamental problem with cost-based pricing. Because cost-based approaches require that fixed costs be allocated to units of a product, there is an arbitrariness to this type of pricing. The actual price charged can vary widely depending on how overhead is allocated to units of a product or service. Similarly, a given product or service can be made to look more or less profitable depending on fixed costs, or the allocation scheme used. This allocation problem is especially apparent where a company produces a number of products with shared fixed costs, and these products vary in terms of how labor- or capital-intensive each is. Of greatest concern, however, is the fact that many fixed costs, such as general administrative costs, have little or nothing to do with the number of units produced or the nature of the production process. No matter how seemingly logical or equitable the allocation scheme, the process of allocating these costs is likely to distort the picture management has of a particular product or service.

Cost-based approaches suffer from one further limitation. They generally assume that some basic level of volume will be achieved, and so establish a price that will generate a certain overall markup or rate of return at that level of volume. This is backward logic. Price should determine how much is sold, not the other way around. In fairly captive or stable markets, this does not pose a problem. However, in markets with wide or unpredictable fluctuations in demand, the widely fluctuating rates of return will be realized. The firm may earn 20 percent per unit, but the overall profit rate could be significantly lower. This is especially true to the extent that unit costs fluctuate with volume.

THE CONTRIBUTION APPROACH

An alternative procedure for analyzing costs, and one which is very compatible with market-oriented pricing methods, is called the contribution approach. The underlying logic of contribution analysis is that a product or service should be held accountable only for those costs directly traceable to its production, sales, and distribution. To understand how contribution analysis works, it is first necessary to introduce the concept of the contribution margin.

If the variable costs of a product are subtracted from the product's price, the result is the contribution margin. This is the amount the product is *contributing* to the firm's fixed costs and profitability each time a unit is sold. The contribution margin can then be divided by price to arrive at the contribution margin ratio, also called the profit-volume (PV) ratio:

$$PV = \frac{P - VC}{P}$$

The PV ratio indicates the percentage of another dollar of revenue that is available to cover fixed costs and profitability.

While the focus of contribution analysis is that products or services should first cover their own variable costs, managers are concerned that all costs be covered. Minimally, then, they want to know if the price charged will allow the firm to break even. The break even point is where enough is being sold to

Figure 6.3
Calculating the Break-Even Level of Sales Using Contribution Analysis

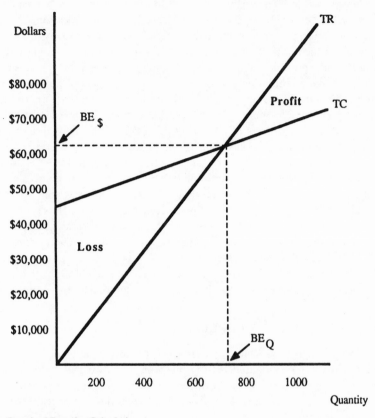

Required Data for Calculations

Q = quantity
P = price = $95
TFC = total fixed costs = $45,000 + $25(Q)
VC = variable cost per unit = $25 per unit
TVC = total variable costs = $25(Q)
TC = total costs = TFC + TVC = $45,000 + $25(Q)
TR = total revenue = P x Q = $95(Q)
CM = contribution margin = P-VC = $95 - $25 = $70
PV = P-V ratio = P-VC/P = $95 - $25/ $95 = .737
BE_Q: breakeven quantity = FC/CM = $45,000/ $70 = 643
$BE_\$$: breakeven in dollars = FC/PV = $45,000/ .737 = $61058

recoup total variable and fixed costs. It is the point at which total revenue (price times quantity) is equal to total costs (fixed costs + variable costs), as illustrated in figure 6.3.

The manager can use the contribution margin to find the level of sales required to break even or to achieve a desired level of profitability. Break even can be expressed in dollars or units, both of which can be arrived at using the contribution margin. The break-even formulas for units and dollars are as follows:

$$BE_Q = \frac{TFC}{P-VC} = \frac{TFC}{CM}$$

$$BE_\$ = \frac{TFC}{\frac{P-VC}{P}} = \frac{TFC}{PV}$$

where: BE_Q = number of units that must be sold to achieve break even

$BE_\$$ = dollar level of sales that must be achieved to break even

TFC = total fixed costs

VC = variable costs

P = price

CM = amount each unit contributes to firm's fixed costs and profitability

PV = profit-volume ratio

In figure 6.3, hypothetical data have been provided to demonstrate the calculation of break even. At a price of $95, the firm must sell close to 640 units and achieve revenue of just over $61,000 in order to break even. These figures can vary slightly depending on rounding. Note that the break-even level of sales is equal to the price times the break-even level of units.

The analysis is valuable in assessing the cost implications of different price levels. For example, if the firm were considering raising or lowering the price of the product illustrated in figure 6.3, the manager could quickly calculate the required change in dollars and units necessary for break even. At a price of $100, breakeven in units becomes

$$\frac{\$45,000}{\$100-\$25} = 600 \text{ units}$$

While at a price of $85, breakeven increases to

$$\frac{\$45,000}{\$85-\$25} = 750 \text{ units}$$

This type of sensitivity analysis is invaluable when establishing prices. Moreover, adjustments can be made to determine the required level of sales to achieve a certain level of profit. This is accomplished by adding desired profit (DP) to the numerator of the break-even formulas, as follows:

$$\text{Required unit sales} = \frac{FC + DP}{CM}$$

$$\text{Required dollar sales} = \frac{FC + DP}{PV}$$

Again, using the product from figure 6.3, assume a desired profit level of $10,000. The required level of sales now becomes 786 units or $74,627 in revenue.

APPLYING CONTRIBUTION ANALYSIS: AN INITIAL PRICING DECISION

Everlight Corporation, a manufacturer of lighting equipment, has developed a standard 72-inch-long fluorescent lamp that burns 50 usage hours longer and uses 10 percent less energy than available lamps. The product would be the company's first foray into the light bulb market. Primary customers would be factories, packing houses, assembly operations, and similar types of production and warehousing facilities.

The variable manufacturing costs incurred in producing the new lamp are estimated to average $6 per unit. A plant to manufacture the lamp would have to be built and equipped at a cost of about $7,000,000 and depreciated over seven years. Administrative overhead is projected to be $200,000 annually, while sales and distribution expenses are estimated at $300,000 per year. This produces total fixed costs of $1,500,000.

Assume that annual sales of fluorescent lamps of this particular type are 5 million units. Further, these sales are primarily accounted for by ten major manufacturers, the largest three having 70 percent market share among them. The market leader currently charges its distributors $8 for lamps of this standard variety.

Management at Everlight wants to evaluate the feasibility of various prices, initially assessing the implications of charging $9.00, $8.00, $7.50, or $7.00. These prices have been selected because of their proximity to competitor prices and to provide management with a starting point from which to assess costs using the contribution approach. If the contribution margin is calculated for each of the pricing alternatives, the result is

SP	$9.00	$8.00	$7.50	$7.00
−VC	−6.00	−6.00	−6.00	−6.00
CM	$3.00	$2.00	$1.50	$1.00

The units and market share required to break even at each price can now be calculated.

Price	Break-even Units	Break-even Market Share
$9.00	$\dfrac{\$1,500,000}{\$3.00} = 500,000$ units	$\dfrac{500,000}{5,000,000} = 10\%$
$8.00	$\dfrac{\$1,500,000}{\$2.00} = 750,000$ units	$\dfrac{750,000}{5,000,000} = 15\%$

Price	Break-even Units	Break-even Market Share
$7.50	$\dfrac{\$1,500,000}{\$1.50} = 1,000,000$ units	$\dfrac{1,000,000}{5,000,000} = 20\%$
$7.00	$\dfrac{\$1,500,000}{\$1.00} = 1,500,000$ units	$\dfrac{1,500,000}{5,000,000} = 30\%$

As can be seen, the new manufacturer will need to capture 15 percent of this market if the leading competitor's price is matched simply to break even. If a penetration pricing strategy is pursued, where the manufacturer attempts to attract attention and market share by going in below the current market price, a reduction of only $.50 would necessitate a 20 percent share, while setting price $1.00 lower than competitors would require a 30 percent share.

Given the competitive structure of this market, such market share goals might seem overly ambitious, especially if the competition is able to duplicate this innovation. It might be argued, though, that 30 percent is achievable given the superiority of the new lamp and that at such a bargain price, that customers would be lining up to make purchases. However, if the lamp is that much better, then it is providing the customer with more value. A higher price might be in order to convey the superior value.

At a price of $9, only 10 percent of the market must be captured to break even. Such an approach approximates a skimming or premium pricing strategy. The manager selecting a price in this range could be trying to achieve a high quality image or go after a particular segment that is less price sensitive. Or the manager could be using the concept of economic value to the customer (see chapter 1) to argue that customers are actually saving money over the product's useful life when paying a price of nine dollars.

The key point is that cost analysis does not tell the manager what price to charge. Rather, costs provide a good starting point and some important insights regarding feasible ranges for setting price. Cost analysis must be considered, however, within the context of the objectives management is trying to achieve (e.g., market share, image, or profit). The ultimate pricing decision depends, further, on a detailed analysis of demand and competitive reaction.

APPLYING CONTRIBUTION ANALYSIS: A PRICE CHANGE

The product manager for the Bronze Samoan line of suntan oils was faced with a dilemma. Sales and profitability for the company's leading oil had been stagnant for the past two quarters, and new competition was aggressively entering the market. In response, the manager was leaning heavily toward one of two possible alternatives: either increase advertising by $200,000, or cut price by 10 percent. If price were cut, however, the manager was concerned that the lower unit margins could negatively impact on bottom-line profits, making the situation even worse. Specifically, how much must unit and dollar sales increase to offset the lower margins resulting from the price cut? This is equivalent to asking what must happen to break even on the price cut.

Presently, contribution analysis begins to provide some answers. Assume the oil was currently priced at $5.00, with variable costs per unit of $2.10. Total volume for the past twelve months is 1,200,000 units. As a result, the contribution margin is $2.90, and total contribution (contribution margin times unit volume) is $3,480,000. The question becomes, then, by how much must sales increase to maintain a total contribution of $3,480,000 if price is reduced?

The first step is to calculate the new contribution margin.

	Currently	With 10 Percent Price Cut
Unit Price	$5.00	$4.50
Variable costs per unit	−2.10	−2.10
Contribution margin	$2.90	$2.40

Next, the level of sales required to achieve the current level of total contribution at the new price is calculated as follows:

$$\$2.40 \ (Q) = \$3,480,000$$
$$Q = \frac{\$3,480,000}{\$2.40}$$
$$Q = 1,450,000$$

Since sales volume is currently 1,200,000 units, the price cut would necessitate an increase of 250,000 units, or 20.8 percent, to maintain the current status quo. The dollar sales increase would be $1,125,000, which is 250,000 units times the new price.

There is an alternative method for determining the required volume change necessary to maintain a given level of profitability. This involves relying on one of the two formulas below, depending on whether price is being reduced or increased:

$$\text{Volume increase (\%) necessary with a given price reduction} = \frac{\% \text{ change in price}}{PV \ - \ \% \text{ change in price}} \times 100$$

$$\text{Volume decrease (\%) acceptable with a given price increase} = \frac{\% \text{ change in price}}{PV \ + \ \% \text{ change in price}} \times 100$$

In this example, the first formula would apply. Note that the calculation involves the use of current PV ratio before the price cut.

$$\frac{10\%}{\dfrac{\$5-2.10}{\$5} - 10\%} \times 100 = 20.8\%$$

With this information the manager could proceed to evaluate customer elasticity (see chapter 3). The cost analysis is indicating that a 20.8 percent volume increase must accompany a 10 percent price decrease. This means that demand must be fairly elastic, or the firm will lose money on the price cut. Next, competitor reactions would have to be projected together with those of middlemen. Again, the cost analysis has not indicated what must be done, but rather has provided a valuable starting point.

THE CONTRIBUTION INCOME STATEMENT

While the contribution margin is measured on a per-unit basis, it is also possible to examine the total contribution of a product or service. This is illustrated with the "contribution income statement" found in table 6.3. The first

Table 6.3
Contribution Format Income Statement for Line of Lawn Mowers
(expressed in thousands)

	Model A	Model B	Model C	Total
Sales Revenue	$5,390	$5,115	$4,598	$15,103
Variable Costs:				
Manufacturing	980	1,155	880	3,015
Selling	147	165	154	466
Distribution	98	66	88	252
Total Variable Costs	1,225	1,386	1,122	3,733
Total Variable Contribution	4,165	3,729	3,476	11,370
Direct Fixed Costs	450	590	820	1,860
Total Product Contribution	3,715	3,139	2,656	9,510
Indirect Fixed Costs				2,940
Profit				$6,570
				=====

Where:	Model A	Model B	Model C
Price	$110	$155	$209
Units	49,000	33,000	22,000

step is to determine total variable contribution. Here the price per unit is taken times the number of units sold, and then total variable costs are subtracted. Total variable costs are equal to variable cost per unit times the number of units sold. Alternatively, the contribution margin could be taken times the number of units sold to get the same total. Total variable contribution is the amount the product is contributing, overall, to the fixed costs and profitability of the firm.

From this total, fixed costs are then subtracted. Note, however, that fixed costs are broken down into direct and indirect categories. A direct fixed cost is directly traceable to the product (or service) itself, such that if the product were eliminated, the cost would not need to be incurred. Examples include depreciation on equipment used only to produce the product in question, advertising spent solely on the product, and salaries for personnel who work solely on the product. All remaining costs are indirect fixed costs, so called because they cannot be directly tied to a particular product or service. An example would be the costs of general management and staff personnel not specifically assigned to a product or service.

In table 6.3 direct fixed costs are subtracted from total variable contribution to produce total product contribution, also simply called total contribution. The logic is that a product should not only cover simply its own variable costs, but also all costs directly related to its production, sale, and distribution. Indirect fixed costs are subtracted next, but note that they are not allocated to individual products. Instead, they are subtracted from the total column. The manager now has a picture of how much each product is contributing to indirect fixed costs and profitability.

The contribution income statement can be useful in pricing analysis. By varying price levels and estimating the likely response in terms of quantity demanded (i.e., elasticity), the manager can see how different prices translate into bottom-line contribution and profitability.

COST-VOLUME-PROFIT RELATIONSHIPS

Up to this point, we have made a critical assumption that does not always hold true. This is that unit costs do not vary with volume. Thus, if price is reduced and volume correspondingly increases, the assumption has been that the cost per unit is the same at the old and new volume levels. What if, alternatively, unit costs were higher at the new volume level? If so, and this cost change is not reflected in the contribution analysis, then management will erroneously conclude that profits at the new volume level will be higher than is actually the case.

The process of evaluating the implications of underlying changes in cost behavior is generally referred to as "cost-volume-profit analysis." This analysis actually has two parts: assessing how volume changes will impact upon unit costs, and then assessing how the combined effect of volume and cost changes will impact upon profitability.

There are a number of reasons why unit costs might increase or decrease with a given change in production volume. First, consider the case of production volume increasing (ostensibly in response to an increase in sales). Unit costs might be higher at the new volume level because the firm was already operating at or near capacity. To produce the additional volume, workers may have to be paid overtime wages, driving up unit costs. Raw materials to produce the extra volume may cost more because of general supply shortages under the new demand conditions or because the extra volume involves smaller raw material lot purchases. Alternatively, unit costs could fall because the firm produces more efficiently at the higher volume level. This could be due to two key cost concepts, the experience curve and economies of scale. Both are discussed in the next section.

Second, with volume decreases, unit costs could also rise or fall. For instance, costs could rise reflecting less efficient use of resources or less economical raw material purchases. They could, alternatively, fall as a reflection of better quality control and a lower defect rate when operating at less than full capacity.

Consider the application of cost-volume-profit analysis to the Bronze Samoan suntan oil problem presented earlier. When price was reduced from $5.00 to $4.50, the contribution analysis indicated that volume needed to increase by 20.8 percent. However, assume variable cost per unit falls from $2.10 to $2.00 at the higher level of production. This increases the contribution margin to $2.50. If required sales are recalculated using this revised contribution margin, the required volume increase is only 16 percent. This level of sales may seem more achievable, leading management to look more favorably on the price cut.

ECONOMIES OF SCALE AND THE EXPERIENCE CURVE

Cost-volume-profit relationships are directly affected, sometimes significantly, by two efficiency-oriented concepts, economies of scale and the experience curve. The first is largely a fixed-cost phenomenon, while the second is primarily concerned with variable costs.

Investing in the capital equipment necessary to operate on a larger scale of operation (e.g., 6000 units per day versus 60) enables unit costs to be lowered. This might seem a confusing point, since total costs are initially increasing due to the capital investment (i.e., depreciation expense). However, this is a fixed total. As more and more units can now be produced, the fixed total is spread over this output, resulting in a lower fixed cost per unit.

Consider a firm which sold direct marketing services and performed frequent mass mailings. A mailing can be broken down into a number of tasks, including letter signing, folding, envelope stuffing, sealing, stamping, labeling, and bundling. Assume the firm employs three hourly employees, each performing all of these tasks. Output is initially 300 letters per hour. At a wage rate of $5 per hour, the labor cost per completed letter is $.05. To take advantage of economies of scale, management subsequently decides to purchase two machines to perform all these tasks. The total investment is $20,000, depreciated over five years. One employee is paid $10 per hour to run the equipment and load materials from machine to machine. The machines are operated about 1,600 hours per year. There is also a cost of about $2 per hour to run the machines (i.e., for electricity, lubricants, maintenance). However, output per hour is now 9,000 letters. Unit costs per letter (excluding materials) fall to $.0016, due to the economies brought on by large-scale production. The fixed costs are higher, but they are being spread over many more units.

Turning to the experience curve, further reduction in unit costs is possible through smarter use of production techniques. The basic idea is that the more times a person performs an activity, the better the performance. More specifically, using the example above, assume that the three workers learn their jobs more thoroughly over time. They become more dextrous and develop systems and techniques for breaking the job down and getting tasks done more efficiently. Output per worker increases appreciably. This is called the experience effect. Not only is labor time per letter reduced, but so too is wastage of materials (letters, envelopes, and stamps). At the same time, finished letter quality improves. This set of events happens, of course, only in a work environment that encourages and rewards learning.

The experience curve is a plot of the relationship between unit costs and *cumulative* volume over time (as opposed to absolute volume in a given time period, which would produce an average cost curve). Numerous studies have shown that unit costs tend to fall a fixed percentage each time cumulative volume doubles (see figure 6.4). This percentage can range as high as 20 to 35 percent for many industrial products. The cost savings come primarily from lower variable production costs, but can also take the form of lower selling and distribution costs. Purchasing and inventory costs can also be reduced if managed from a learning perspective.

A STRATEGIC PERSPECTIVE ON COSTS

To benefit from the experience curve and economies of scale, both concepts must be carefully managed over a product's life cycle. This means a never-ending search for new and better ways to get a job done. In addition, strategies must be designed that generate the requisite volume necessary to achieve a specific cost objective. Moreover, the manager must be able to accurately project cost behavior as a product moves through its life cycle, and adapt strategies accordingly. For companies involved in bidding projects, anticipating unit costs at the volume levels to be achieved if a bid is won can be critical for determining a competitive price. This may well be a price that would not be profitable at current volume levels.

To demonstrate the relationship between cost behavior and strategy, consider the two curves diagrammed in figure 6.5. The cost curve is steadily falling with accumulated volume, reflecting the experience effect. The price

Figure 6.4
Illustration of a 75 Percent Experience Curve

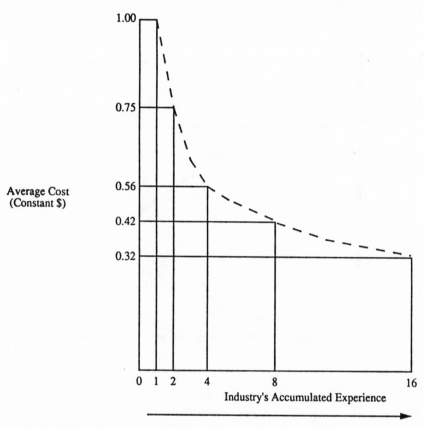

(Note: Cost per unit is falling 25 Percent with each doubling of accumulated output.)

curve, alternatively, reflects a strategy explicitly meant to take competitive advantage of this effect. The initial price level is actually below cost, producing a loss. The firm is pursuing a market penetration strategy in an attempt to capture market share. A significant market share will, in turn, generate significant volume, allowing the firm to move out on the experience curve. As this begins to occur, unit costs drop steadily and significantly. Price is held stable, eventually resulting in large profit margins. However, as competition is attracted to the market, the firm cuts price dramatically. In fact, price is reduced at a faster rate than costs are falling. The firm can afford these price cuts more than can competitors because it is further out on the experience curve. Finally, price and cost relationships stabilize, with further reductions in price closely paralleling cost reductions.

Figure 6.5
Pricing to Take Advantage of the Experience Curve

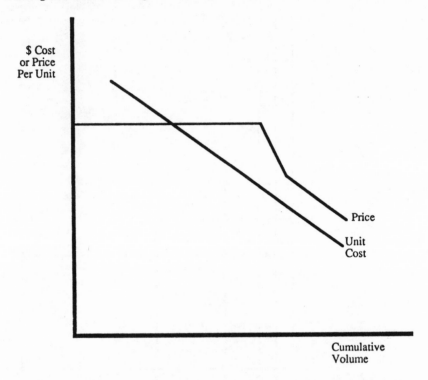

One lesson of the experience curve is that industry price tends to follow costs down. As the price drop occurs, it often becomes possible to find new applications for the product that were previously not economical. This leads to further proliferation. The integrated circuit, a product whose costs dropped about 28 percent with each doubling of volume, is a good case in point.

SUMMARY

Costs represent one of the key considerations in establishing and managing prices. However, the thrust of this chapter has been that costs receive far too much emphasis from price managers, and that market-related factors should be the priority. There is a need to move away from simplistic cost-plus or target-return formulas and their underlying full costing philosophy.

Instead, firms should adopt a contribution approach when examining costs for pricing decisions. Products and services should be held directly accountable only for those costs related to their production, sale, and distribution. The contribution margin can be used to determine the level of sales that must be reached to achieve a desired level of profitability and the extent to which products are contributing to indirect costs and profitability at different price levels. With this information in hand, the manager can then incorporate the demand and competitive considerations emphasized throughout this book. That is, costs represent the beginning point in pricing, not the ending point.

The result is an opportunity for much greater flexibility and creativity in pricing decisions. The arbitrariness inherent in cost allocation schemes is removed, and price becomes a marketing tool. Of course, the simplicity inherent in cost-based pricing also disappears, placing much greater responsibility on the manager for realizing the true profit potential of products and services.

7

INDUSTRY AND COMPETITOR ANALYSIS

Prices in any market are the result of the forces of both demand and supply. Demand considerations include the number of customers willing and able to buy at different prices, their value perceptions, and their psychology. Supply considerations include the number of competing firms willing and able to sell at different prices, their profit and market share objectives, and their current strategies for achieving these objectives. Up to this point, we have focused almost exclusively on demand considerations. And yet, considerable strategic insight can be gained by examining the supply side of the equation.

In all too many firms, competitor analysis is limited to periodically taking note of the prices charged by major competitors and ensuring that the firm's current prices are not too far out of line. Some firms go so far as to limit their entire pricing strategy by simply matching the prices of competitors. Such approaches are shortsighted, and may be costing the firm money.

As a rule, the firms that compete in any industry differ in terms of their goals, opportunities, market positions, resources, cost structures, target markets, and overall marketing strategy. Correspondingly, competitor analysis should focus on identifying these differences, and a firm's prices should reflect these differences.

In this chapter, competitive conditions are first investigated by examining some of the more common industry structures and drawing implications for pricing. Following this is a description of specific types of competitive price behaviors, with suggestions regarding how to anticipate and interpret the pricing moves of competitors. Next, major considerations in evaluating the positions of different competitors are identified. The chapter closes with a discussion of competitive bidding. A method is presented for improving a firm's chances of underpricing its competitors when prices are set on a bid basis.

EVALUATING INDUSTRY STRUCTURES

The most significant supply-related factor influencing the prices charged for an item is the economic structure of an industry. In this context, structure is defined in terms of the number of competing firms within the industry, the power of individual firms to influence market prices, the barriers to market entry, and the extent of product differentiation. The two most prevalent forms of industry structure are oligopoly and monopolistic competition. In addition, because of the tremendous amount of change occurring in today's business environment, some new hybrid structures are emerging.

Oligopolistic Industries

Oligopoly refers to an industry in which relatively few competitors hold a disproportionate share of the market. Fewness is the dominant characteristic; four or five companies may account for 80 to 90 percent of a given market. Each has some influence on overall market prices, the barriers to entry are high, and products can be standardized or differentiated. The oil and airline industries in the United States are examples of fairly undifferentiated oligopolies, while automobiles and computers represent fairly differentiated oligopolies. Of course, differentiation is in the mind of the customer.

The economic concentration found in these industries has a major impact on pricing practices of firms. Where markets are oligopolistic, the strategies pursued by companies are heavily interdependent. That is, whatever one firm does with its prices is dependent upon what the other firms do, and its pricing actions also affect the decisions of those firms. Further, since a relatively small number of competitors controls most of the market, competitors focus much effort toward capturing market share.

Interdependency among competitors is illustrated in the two-firm example found in figure 7.1. Here, the profitability of both the Abel Company and the Baker Company is determined by the price each charges, and four possible prices are considered. The triangular cells indicate the profit to be made by each firm at a particular combination of competitor prices. So, if Abel charges $7 for its product and Baker charges $8 for a competitive product, it is estimated that Abel will make $12.8 million in profits, while Baker makes $13.8 million.

Assume, however, that Abel charged $7 and Baker matched that by also charging $7. A difference still exists in the profits earned by each firm, due to a disparity in their underlying cost structures. Abel appears to be operating more efficiently at this level of price and corresponding volume. After further study, Baker may see that its profits would be improved if it raised its price to $8. If Baker does so, Abel may then conclude that its profits would improve if it now charged $10. Prices may well stabilize at this level, for neither party can gain from a change to another price within this range.

Figure 7.1
A Price-Payoff Table for a Two-Firm Oligopoly

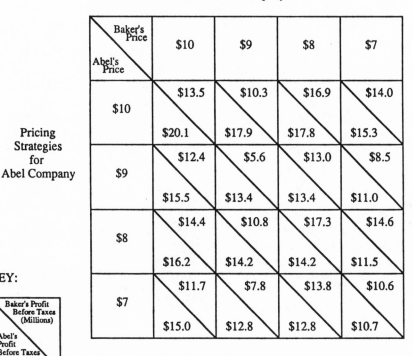

Pricing Strategies for
Baker Company

Baker's Price / Abel's Price	$10	$9	$8	$7
$10	$13.5 / $20.1	$10.3 / $17.9	$16.9 / $17.8	$14.0 / $15.3
$9	$12.4 / $15.5	$5.6 / $13.4	$13.0 / $13.4	$8.5 / $11.0
$8	$14.4 / $16.2	$10.8 / $14.2	$17.3 / $14.2	$14.6 / $11.5
$7	$11.7 / $15.0	$7.8 / $12.8	$13.8 / $12.8	$10.6 / $10.7

Pricing Strategies for Abel Company

KEY:
Baker's Profit Before Taxes (Millions)
Abel's Profit Before Taxes (Millions)

There is a general tendency for prices to be somewhat stable in oligopolistic industries. To understand why, consider the case of three competing steel manufacturers selling a fairly undifferentiated product. Assume Firm A has a 40 percent market share while Firms B and C have between 20 and 25 percent apiece. All three firms currently charge approximately $10 for their competing products. Now, what would happen if Firm B cut its price to $9 per unit? In this instance, Firms A and C have no choice but to follow B down, or they will lose share to B. If all three lower prices, and correspondingly their margins, then no one is any better off unless the size of the entire market expands (i.e., market demand is elastic).

Using the same example, assume Firm A decides to raise price to $11. Now Firms B and C are likely to hold the line and not follow. Since A does not want to lose share, there will be no incentive to maintain the increase. Again, then, price stability tends to prevail.

An alternative development in many oligopolistic industries is price leadership. Here, one firm sets the tone initiating price changes, and the others follow suit. The price leader is usually the firm with the dominant market share position and/or the most favorable cost position (i.e., the lowest cost producer). Price leaders can also be the firm with the greatest technological prowess, a superior distribution network, a preferred image among buyers, or some other competitive advantage. In the example above, Firm A decides to raise price, and the other firms find it in their interest to cooperate, so they follow suit. Alternatively, if B and C attempted to underprice A, they would find A can afford to match them and reduce price even more. Such cooperative relationships serve to maintain status quo, with price increases made on an incremental basis. At the same time, the competitors may find it makes more sense to focus on nonprice competition, such as product features, customer service, or promotional efforts.

Monopolistic Competition

The other leading type of market structure is monopolistic competition. Here, there are a large number of competitors for a particular product category, but firms are able to successfully differentiate their products from one another. Each firm establishes price relatively independently of the others without concern for retaliatory action from competitors. Specifically, each establishes price to reflect its own differentiated product offering. Further, and perhaps of greater significance, monopolistically competitive industries have fairly low barriers to entry.

Pizza parlors represent an example. There are a large number of them, and each attempts to differentiate itself in some manner. If a particular competitor develops a new type of pizza in response to market needs, then that firm may be able to reap considerable profits. However, entry barriers are low, enabling other firms to copy (and slightly modify) the innovation. As a result, competition tends to be intense and there is constant pressure for continued innovation and differentiation.

Under such circumstances, the prices charged by the monopolistic competitor are likely to change as conditions change. For instance, when the company first develops its unique product offering, it is in virtually a monopoly position. As a result, higher margins can be charged. When competitors enter and claim their own shares of the profit opportunity, prices are typically driven down. Special price deals, promotions, or rebates may be offered, and the general level of price is reduced. Unlike oligopoly, however, there is little opportunity for cooperative pricing behavior. The large number of current and potential competitors make this unrealistic.

The effective competitor will recognize the very dynamic nature of monopolistic competition. Pricing decisions will be made with an eye toward the long term. The goal should be to set a price that takes advantage of the significant demand for the firm's innovative product offering but that also helps to build a loyal customer following before the competition makes inroads. Once customer loyalties are well established, competitors have a much more difficult time achieving successful differentiation.

Emerging Competitive Structures

The nature of industry structures is undergoing a metamorphosis in response to the rapid rates of change in technology, supply availability, government regulation, customer characteristics, the economy, and social trends. This turbulence has produced markets which are increasingly differentiated, segmented, and fragmented (Sheth, 1985).

Differentiated market structures are those in which the customer base is fairly homogeneous but several sellers with specialized technologies are present. Each offers fairly proprietary and unique products or services to this common market using very similar marketing programs. The pharmaceutical industry provides an example. Each competitor offers unique and proprietary drugs to the general hospital and physician market using very similar marketing programs.

Segmented market structures result when the prevailing technology is universally adopted and quite versatile in its applications, while market demand is heterogeneous. This means a number of distinct market segments exist with differing needs. Basic products are adapted and marketed to meet the particular needs and application requirements of these specialized segments. Computer technology provides an example, where applications are tailored to the specific needs of hotels, hospitals, retail stores, professional services, and any number of other business segments.

Fragmented market structures give rise to niching strategies. These can be found where both demand and supply are heterogeneous. That is, there are many segments and many opportunities for product differentiation. Firms specialize by providing unique product and service offerings tailored to distinct market segments. An example of such a product-market specialist might be the firm that manufactures customized cabinets sold only to mobile home manufacturers.

These emerging market structures have important pricing implications. Where markets are differentiated, the manager should focus on pricing to capture the product's unique capabilities relative to the offerings of competitors. In segmented markets, price should be set to reflect the unique features and capabilities provided by each firm's product. The fact that the market is fairly homogeneous should not lead to standardized prices among competitors. When markets are segmented, it is likely that price elasticity will differ for each segment. Where feasible, prices should be varied among target segments to reflect these differences. In fragmented markets, prices will be customized to the niche in which the firm positions itself. Competitor prices will be of little importance for any one firm's price policy. The fact that a unique offering is being made to a unique market suggests a need for consistent pricing across customers within a niche but considerable diversity in prices for a product category across niches.

PREVALENT COMPETITIVE PRICING BEHAVIORS

Within a given market structure, there will actually be a number of different pricing strategies operating. Individual firms are apt to employ different approaches based on market conditions and their own current position in the market. However, there are some broader categories that tend to capture the pricing behavior found in most industries (Nagle, 1987; Sultan, 1974). These include parallel, opportunistic, predatory, and contingency pricing. The pricing manager may be able to better understand and anticipate competitor pricing actions by applying these categories to the firms in his industry.

Parallel and Adaptive Pricing

When firms are reasonably satisfied with their current market positions and desire price stability within the market, a popular approach is parallel pricing. This is especially true for firms having sizable market shares (e.g., oligopolies), and those producing at or near full capacity. Parallel pricing is a cooperative pricing behavior. One firm makes price changes and the others adapt their prices in accordance with prevailing market conditions to maintain their respective market shares. This sometimes means making adjustments in both price and production volume. However, the firms do not formally collude or collectively agree on prices.

In the automobile industry, each of the major automobile manufacturers possesses a significant share of the market. Also, each manufacturer is well aware of its competitors' price and cost structures. Therefore, when one manufacturer decides to cut the price of one of its more popular models, the other manufacturers quickly follow suit, thereby reducing competitors' gains from the price reduction in the short run. Knowing this, automobile manufacturers prefer to avoid such price wars and instead manage their respective price levels so as to maintain current market shares. In this way, the automobile manufacturers are able to maintain parallel prices throughout the industry without explicit collusion.

With parallel pricing, firms within an industry that have smaller market shares also willingly participate, in part because of the possible repercussions from larger firms if they do not cooperate. A smaller firm may also participate because of a desire to maintain market share and profit margins in the short run while steadily increasing production capacity. Larger firms will try to ensure that the established price does not allow small firms the leeway to expand to the point where they encroach on existing market shares.

Another variation of parallel pricing that may be less cooperative in nature is called pressure pricing. A market leader maintains prices at reasonable levels even when demand is surging. Otherwise, the higher prices would be an incentive for new firms to enter the market. When prices are permitted to increase, they do so incrementally. The market leader is able to bring pressure on (or punish) those who do not maintain the market price by underbidding them on key jobs or by establishing market prices at levels that are uncomfortably low for these other firms.

Sometimes firms with smaller shares rely on a variation of parallel pricing in which they follow pricing actions of larger firms but are unconcerned with maintaining the current market structure. For example, if market demand is declining and market leaders are attempting to maintain current price levels, smaller firms will also keep prices steady. However, while larger firms reduce their own production levels so that the demand reduction is shared proportionately, smaller firms will maintain production levels. This sometimes leads to an increase in their market shares.

Opportunistic Pricing

An alternative and more aggressive competitive behavior is called opportunistic pricing. As the name implies, firms attempt to take advantage of the pricing moves of their competitors. For instance, in periods of uneven demand, an opportunistic firm holds the line on price when other firms initiate a price increase so as to gain sales. Alternatively, when demand is very strong, they are apt to raise price to the limit of customer goodwill.

Opportunistic firms will also pursue price cuts, especially when they believe other firms cannot afford or are otherwise unwilling to retaliate. They may have a cost advantage over their competitors, such as in the case of the firm that enters the market as a low-frills, low-cost provider. Or their incremental costs may be low due to low overhead. Alternatively, the price cut may be targeted for a particular market segment that is not sizable or significant enough to warrant a retaliatory response from other competitors. In other cases, the opportunist believes other firms will not match lower prices because of a concern that it will harm their image or be inconsistent with their overall pricing strategy.

Another tactic used by opportunistic firms is to charge prices equivalent to those of competitors but rely on an active program of special price deals to gain additional sales. Discounts, coupons, rebates, free gifts, cents-off offers, and other incentives are relied upon to effectively undercut the going market price.

Predatory Pricing

An overt attempt to harm or eliminate competitors with aggressive pricing actions can be termed predatory pricing. Usually, significant price cuts are implemented and targeted toward a particular competitor or group of competitors. The price reductions are not intended to be permanent, but will be kept in place until the desired effect is achieved or it is apparent there is no chance of success. Where these cuts are below the predator's own costs, there are serious antitrust implications (see chapter 9).

The goal of predatory behavior is sometimes educational, such as when a firm is attempting to warn competitors that their current actions in the pricing or some other area are unacceptable. In other instances, the predator is after market share gains. Even more aggressive are predatory efforts motivated by a desire to eliminate marginal competitors from the marketplace. Here, the predator is risking short-run profits in an attempt to achieve long-run market stability. This behavior is likely to be more prevalent in the latter part of the growth stage and early part of the maturity stage of the product life cycle. Where competitive intensity is high but market growth rates may be stabilizing, such as with personal computers in the mid- to late 1980s, the goal is often to drive out some of the more opportunistic and less competitive firms so as to stabilize market shares. In addition, the firm may seek to acquire the assets of competitors once they are driven from the market.

Predatory efforts are not necessarily implemented on an across-the-board basis. Especially when one firm is attempting to "educate" one or more competitors regarding how prices should be set, the predator is likely to focus efforts on particular markets or customer groups. These are the markets from which competitors receive the largest percentage of their revenues and/or the markets where competitors have the most to lose. Such tactics represent a form of potentially illegal price discrimination. however, as discussed in chapter 9.

Contingency Pricing

When competitors behave somewhat autonomously and base prices on aspects of the current buying situation, their behavior can be termed contingency pricing. Such an approach is extremely flexible and can be effective when an industry is experiencing dynamic change. It is more frequently relied upon by service providers and by those offering customized products. It is also found when there are large numbers of competitors with relatively small and/or unstable market shares.

Airlines provide one case in point. Since being deregulated, the industry has become very competitive, especially in the price area. The industry has been subject to aggressive new market entrants as well as significant changes in their costs, technology, relationships with middlemen (travel agents), and customer behavior. The response has been contingency pricing. Prices on routes are apt to vary from week to week, with any two carriers charging different prices for the same trip. Prices are also varied based on time of day, time of week, length of trip, when a ticket is purchased, and whether the sale is to an individual or group.

When prices are set by negotiation or competitive bid, the result is often a form of contingency pricing. This is because of the considerable uncertainty surrounding such situations, especially regarding the prices of competitors. However, where firms are reasonably familiar with the negotiation or bidding strategies of their competitors, any of the four types of pricing behaviors are possible.

There are two significant problems with contingency pricing. First, unless properly structured, contingency pricing lacks real strategic focus. The prices charged could conceivably generate widely divergent profit rates on each sale, and could effectively prove to be a penetration level in one case and a premium level in the next. This becomes an especially critical problem over time, particularly when contingencies change dramatically. The result may be inconsistency in terms of company image and market positioning and confusion on the part of customers. Aggressive competitors can take advantage of these circumstances.

The second problem concerns the administration of contingency prices. Charging a single, across-the-board price for an item can be much easier than tailoring prices to current contingencies. Not only is it more difficult to keep track of the prices charged over time, but the actual determination of price becomes an issue. Firms cannot afford to appear arbitrary in arriving at a final price to a given customer. Some standard methodology must be in place for taking into account customer and competitor considerations as well as any other contingencies.

DEFINING COMPETITIVE POSITIONS

To better understand and anticipate the pricing moves of competitors, a formal analysis of competitive positions should be conducted on an ongoing basis. The analysis has two major components. The first involves determining the strength of one's own competitive position, while the second is concerned with evaluating the positions of other firms.

The Firm's Position

How does a company define its own position in a particular market? The most common method is to determine the number of competitors and then compare their respective shares of the market to that of the firm. This approach represents a gross oversimplification, however, and can produce significant miscalculations regarding the firm's pricing leverage. That is, where the strength of a firm's competitive position is over- or underestimated, the firm is more likely to make pricing moves that produce unanticipated reactions from competitors and customers.

A more complete set of factors that should be taken into account in defining one's competitive position is identified in table 7.1. The factors are divided into those external to the firm and those specific to the firm. External factors include barriers to entry, effective substitutes, and the bargaining power of suppliers, buyers, and distributors. For example, where barriers to entry are high due to capital requirements, economies of scale, or government restrictions, the firm already in the market is in a stronger competitive position. On the other

Table 7.1
Defining the Competitive Position of a Particular Firm

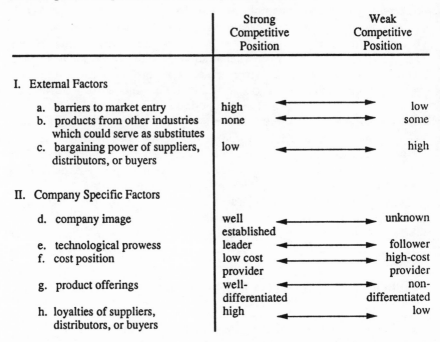

	Strong Competitive Position		Weak Competitive Position
I. External Factors			
a. barriers to market entry	high	⟵――――――⟶	low
b. products from other industries which could serve as substitutes	none	⟵――――――⟶	some
c. bargaining power of suppliers, distributors, or buyers	low	⟵――――⟶	high
II. Company Specific Factors			
d. company image	well established	⟵――――――⟶	unknown
e. technological prowess	leader	⟵――――⟶	follower
f. cost position	low cost provider	⟵――――――⟶	high-cost provider
g. product offerings	well-differentiated	⟵――――⟶	non-differentiated
h. loyalties of suppliers, distributors, or buyers	high	⟵――――⟶	low

hand, when substitute products that satisfy the same need are available (e.g., facsimile machines compete with providers of overnight express mail services), the firm is in a weaker competitive position. Further, if there is a single source of supply for a critical, purchased item or the firm must deal with a few large and powerful distributors or buyers, its competitive position is weakened.

Company-specific factors include image, technological prowess, cost structure, product differentiation, and established loyalties. Companies find their competitive position is enhanced when they have a well-established and clearly defined corporate image, are an industry leader in terms of developing and applying technology, or have a cost advantage over competitors. Similarly, competitive positions are weakened where different firms are unable to differentiate their respective products from one another, and where they have failed to establish and maintain loyal relationships with key suppliers, distributors and buyers.

Evaluating Competitors' Positions

Competitive analysis is concerned not only with determining the firm's own position, but also with estimating the likely pricing moves and responses of competitors. A number of high-quality books and articles have been written in recent years regarding how to evaluate competitors (e.g., L. Fuld, *Competitor Intelligence*, New York: John Wiley and Sons, 1985; K. Tyson, *Business Intelligence*, Lombard, Ill.: Leading Edge Publications, 1986). To be of value in the pricing area, this analysis must emphasize some particular pricing-related issues (see table 7.2).

First and foremost, the strategic orientation of competitors must be evaluated. The starting point is objectives. For instance, if a competitor is known to have minimum rate of return objectives, then this will provide a clue to its probable prices. Similarly, if it is committed to achieving or holding a certain market share, this will shed light on its likely price aggressiveness.

Beyond objectives, the pricing strategy of other firms is a source of insight. A competitor pursuing a premium price strategy is not in a strong position to match price cuts, and needs to compensate for any price increases so as to maintain a premium differential. Related to strategy is the question of target markets. If competitors are emphasizing target markets different from those of the firm, then they will be less concerned with attacking or retaliating to the firm's pricing moves. Alternatively, competitors that do not have clearly

Table 7.2
Ten Major Questions to Address Regarding Competitors before Making Price Decisions

1. How do the market objectives of our leading competitors differ from our own objectives?

2. Are there meaningful differences between the pricing strategies of leading competitors and our own strategy?

3. Which target markets are receiving priority from our competitors? Are these the same as ours?

4. What existing commitments do competitors have to production schedules for various products, to customer groups, to distributors, or to suppliers?

5. How much unused production capacity do competitors have?

6. Do competitors differ significantly in terms of their financial solvency?

7. What are the differences in the production costs and overhead positions of our leading competitors?

8. How quickly can competitors react to any pricing moves on our part, given their organizational structure, current product offerings, and their production techniques?

9. Are there differences in the depth and breadth of competitors product lines compared to our own? Are their prices for any one item less flexible because of overall product line considerations?

10. What situational factors exist for competitors which have implications for their pricing behavior (e.g. seasonability in a particular market, excess or obsolete inventory)?

defined target audiences may have a tendency to overreact to the firm's pricing moves. These competitors tend to view everyone as a customer, and so place undue emphasis on what other firms are doing.

A second area of focus concerns operating characteristics of competitors. Four of the most important characteristics are costs, product lines, production capacity, and financial resources. The extent to which a competitor is operating at an advantage or disadvantage either in production costs or in the amount of overhead that must be covered is directly related to its price responsiveness. Firms operating on a full-costing basis may be especially vulnerable in this regard.

Product line considerations have to do with the depth and breadth of a competitor's offerings. Given that the price of any one product must complement the other items in that product line, competitors may be less able to respond to pricing actions directed at that one product. Otherwise, the competitor would be creating inconsistencies and undermining product line strategy.

Pricing behavior is also driven by a competitor's available production capacity. The closer a firm is to 100 percent capacity utilization, the less concerned it will be with meeting any price reductions. However, the incentive to initiate or match price increases is strong among such firms. Similar to production capacity is the question of financial capacity. Competitors that are strapped in terms of financial resources are more apt to price for short-run profitability. They will be hesitant to risk revenues on price cuts, fearing lost margins will not be compensated by increased volume. Yet, they may tend to hold the line when other firms raise prices, in an attempt to capture sales from competitors.

The third major area of emphasis involves competitor flexibility in the pricing area. A major issue in this regard concerns how quickly competitors can react to the firm's pricing moves. Competitors with more bureaucratic structures and those in which pricing authority is either not clearly assigned or is maintained at the senior levels of the organizations tend to be slow to respond. Flexibility may also be hindered if price changes were made possible by changes in production techniques that will take competing firms time to adopt. An additional limitation on competitor price flexibility is the existing commitments to customer groups, suppliers, and production schedules for various products. Such commitments constrain firms in terms of what they are producing, how much, when, and for what price. Price changes can undermine the ability to fulfill those commitments.

The final set of competitor considerations include the situational factors that cause firms to engage in specific pricing actions, usually on a short-term basis. Some of these are predictable (e.g., seasonal sales patterns) while others are not (e.g., obsolete inventory). Predictable situational factors tend to produce consistent competitor behaviors over time, which can sometimes be capitalized upon. Alternatively, nontypical situational factors can be much more threatening, since competitors may be more experimental with prices under these circumstances.

PRICING FOR COMPETITIVE BIDS

Competitor considerations are especially critical when prices are determined through a process of formal bidding. In many cases, the winning bid is simply the lowest bid. In others, the customer will temper a given seller's bid by an evaluation of that bidder's ability to meet quality, design, and delivery requirements. Under either set of circumstances, the firm must identify its likely competitors, carefully evaluate the product or service offering of each competitor, and estimate the amount each is likely to bid.

As a generalization, bidding will either be sealed (closed) or open. With sealed bidding, each potential vendor is required to submit a sealed written proposal. Then, typically, all bids are opened, evaluated, and a decision rendered at a prespecified point in time. The lowest bid will usually win. With open (or negotiated) bidding, offers are formally made, sometimes verbally, after which the buyer may provide feedback that prompts a vendor to adjust its bid. This method is, in a sense, a combination of bidding and negotiation.

The first question to be addressed in competitive bidding concerns whether or not to submit a bid on a particular job. Managers should consider a number of key criteria in determining whether or not to bid on a project. Some of these include:

- Is the dollar value of the purchase large enough to warrant the expense involved in making a bid?
- Are the specifications of the product or service precise, and can the cost of producing the product or service be accurately estimated?
- How will getting the bid affect capacity utilization and our ability to serve other customers? Will it affect other products in our line?
- How many potential bidders are there likely to be, and how anxious are they to get this business?
- How much time is available to put together an adequate bid and to have it considered by the customer?

Once the decision has been made to make a bid, a bidding strategy must be developed. One of the more popular approaches to competitive bidding, and one with a proven record of success, is probabilistic bidding. This technique assumes the pricing objective to be profit maximization. Also, the assumption is made that customers will select the lowest bid submitted. Three variables are focused upon: the size of the bid, the expected profit if the bid wins, and the probability that the bid will win. A trade-off exists between bid amount or profit, on the one hand, and the probability of winning, on the other. With probabilistic bidding, the manager is objectively trying to identify the optimal trade-off.

The optimum bid, then, seeks to maximize the basic equation provided below (Morse, 1975).

$$E(X) = (P(X)) (Z(X))$$

where: X = dollar amount of the bid
$Z(X)$ = profit if the bid is accepted
$P(X)$ = probability of acceptance at this bid price
$E(X)$ = expected profit at this bid price

To see how this equation applies in the real world, consider the example of a computer manufacturer, Thompson Corporation, bidding on a job to provide computers to a chemical company for training new plant operations personnel. At least three other firms are expected to submit bids. All are qualified sources of supply, so the lowest bid should be the one selected. Thompson's costs to produce the computers have been estimated at $180,000. The marketing department, based on an evaluation of competitor positions and an assessment of historical bidding processes on similar jobs, has constructed a diagram relating the range of possible bid prices to the estimated probabilities of winning the bid. This is illustrated in table 7.3, which suggests that a bid of $140,000 has a 100 percent chance of winning, while a bid of $320,000 has zero chance of winning.

With these probabilities in hand, the marketer can now determine expected profit at each price using the basic equation described earlier. Table 7.3 first illustrates the actual profit at each bid price. These actual profit figures are then taken times the probability of being selected at that bid price, resulting in the

Table 7.3
An Application of the Probability Bidding Model to Thompson Corporation

Bid Price (X)	Cost	Cumulative Probability of Winning at this Bid P (X)	Profit Z (X)	Expected Profit E (X)
$320,000	$180,000	0.00	$140,000	$0
300,000	180,000	0.05	120,000	6,000
280,000	180,000	0.15	100,000	15,000
260,000	180,000	0.25	80,000	20,000
240,000	180,000	0.35	60,000	21,000
220,000	180,000	0.55	40,000	22,000
200,000	180,000	0.76	20,000	15,200
180,000	180,000	0.90	0	0
160,000	180,000	0.97	-20,000	-19,400
140,000	180,000	1.00	-40,000	-40,000

expected profit figures. The analysis indicates that $220,000 is the optimum bid price, for this is where expected profit is highest. To corroborate this optimum bid, calculate expected profit for intermediate bids of $215,000 and $225,000.

The most difficult task facing the marketer when using this approach is estimating the probability of a given bid being the lowest one submitted (the probability of winning). This probability is referred to as P(X) in the earlier equation. The ability to estimate P(X) is dependent upon the manager's experience in this market and with these competitors.

One creative solution that has proven to be fairly successful involves estimating data similar to that in table 7.4. This data can be used to determine actual probabilities by following the step-by-step procedure described below. For simplicity, assume the manager is only bidding against a single competitor.

Table 7.4
Estimating Probabilities for Use by the Manager in Competitive Bidding

	Competitor's Bid ($)	Marketer's Estimated Direct Costs ($)	Competitor's Bid as a Percentage of the Marketer's Direct Costs	Number of Times Competitor Submitted a Bid Higher Than This% of Direct Costs	Percent Higher (Probability of Underbidding if Marketer's Bid is Less Than This % of Direct Costs
Project 1	$ 39,600	$ 30,000	132	16	0.80
Project 2	176,000	130,000	136	12	0.60
Project 3	125,000	80,000	157	2	0.10
Project 4	67,500	50,000	135	13	0.65
Project 5	145,000	100,000	145	7	0.35
Project 6	22,200	20,000	111	19	0.95
Project 7	129,720	94,000	138	11	0.55
Project 8	24,160	16,000	151	4	0.20
Project 9	107,520	64,000	168	0	0.00
Project 10	198,800	140,000	142	10	0.50
Project 11	59,400	44,000	135	13	0.65
Project 12	121,800	84,000	145	7	0.35
Project 13	79,800	60,000	133	15	0.75
Project 14	59,600	40,000	149	5	0.25
Project 15	46,500	30,000	155	3	0.15
Project 16	68,880	42,000	164	1	0.05
Project 17	95,040	72,000	132	16	0.80
Project 18	86,400	60,000	144	8	0.40
Project 19	82,320	56,000	147	6	0.30
Project 20	147,500	118,000	125	18	0.90

Source: Adapted from W. J. Morse (1975), "Probabilistic Bidding Models: A Synthesis," *Business Horizons* 18 (April), 79-80

The first step is to determine how much the competitor bid in the past on projects similar to the one being bid on (column 1; table 7.4). Second, determine how much the manager's own direct costs would have been to complete each of those projects (column 2). Third, express the competitor's bid on each of those projects as a percentage of the marketer's direct costs (column 3). Fourth, for each of the bids submitted by the competitor, count the number of times the bid was higher than this percentage of the marketer's estimated direct costs on a project (column 4). Looking at project 14, the competitor's bid was 149 percent of the marketer's direct cost on that job. Only five times did the competitor submit bids that were a higher percentage of the marketer's direct costs. Finally, express this number as a proportion of all twenty bids (column 5). This proportion represents the probability of the marketer winning the bid if he or she bids less than a given percentage of his or her own direct costs.

So, let's say the marketer submitted a bid on Project X (a new product) that was equal to 149 percent of his or her company's estimated direct costs on the project. If, in total, the competitor had submitted bids on similar projects twenty times in the past and five of these were at a price exceeding 149 percent of the marketer's estimated direct costs on the project, then the marketer has a 25 percent probability of winning bids on projects similar to project X at this bid.

Unfortunately, the marketer frequently either has no experience in a particular product market area or is unable to obtain reasonably accurate data concerning the previous bids of competitors or their costs. As a result, probabilities are estimated in a subjective manner based on bidding and pricing experience, competitor analysis, market intelligence, management intuition, and related factors. Whether it is based on hard data regarding previous bids or upon more subjective estimates, the objective is to detail the relationships between winning the bid and the range of possible bid prices.

The approach described here represents a more basic bidding model. While this model and more complex ones do produce an ideal bid price, the decision maker must recognize that these are only tools to aid in the price decision. In practice, such bids are often further modified by managerial judgment. The models may be used simply to provide direction in bidding strategy.

Bids, once made, are also not always at a fixed price. When the supplier's costs are unstable and inflationary, a common approach to hedging risk is the use of escalator clauses. Here a fixed price bid is agreed upon, but the agreement allows for price increases if certain of the supplier's costs rise during the period of the contract. Such costs may be linked to economic indices, such as the wholesale price index. Changes in the index permit adjustments in certain cost estimates and the price charged.

SUMMARY

Pricing strategies, in the final analysis, are driven by market conditions. The forces of both supply and demand must be considered in establishing prices within a market environment. This chapter has focused on the supply side of the equation. Specifically, we have attempted to define the role of competitive considerations when determining a firm's prices.

In practice, the firms within an industry differ in terms of their goals, pricing strategies, pricing methods, and actual prices charged. However, a careful examination of these differences will reveal some general types of behaviors common to most industries. By recognizing and applying such commonalities to their major competitors, the pricing manager is in a much better position to make effective pricing moves.

This chapter provided an assessment of two of the more common competitive market structures, oligopoly and monopolistic competition, as well as a review of some newer, emerging structures. In the oligopolistic structure, the few firms competing in a particular market frequently follow a price leader when setting prices. Each firm is concerned with maintaining market share and finds its prices are highly interdependent with those of competitors. A firm facing a monopolistically competitive structure is more concerned with continually differentiating itself from the sizable number of existing and potential competitors. Price competition tends to be fairly aggressive. Emerging market structures include differentiated markets, segmented markets, and fragmented markets. Such structures are becoming more prevalent as industries confront growing environmental turbulence. They frequently produce pricing strategies tailored to the unique products and segments emphasized by individual firms.

In addition to common structures, the chapter examined some of the more prevalent competitive pricing behaviors relied upon within industries. These behaviors included parallel pricing, opportunistic pricing, predatory pricing, and contingency pricing. These differ in terms of degree of aggressiveness, extent of standardization versus customization, and nature of the focus, long-term or short-term.

The pricing behavior pursued by any one firm is constrained by its relative industry and market position. Competitive position is defined by a variety of factors, some of which are external to the firm and some of which are company-specific. These factors were identified, with an emphasis on how companies can enhance their competitive position and, correspondingly, their pricing leverage. Pricing decisions must also consider the positions of competitors and their likely response to pricing initiatives. Ten key considerations that can be helpful in predicting competitor response behavior were presented.

The chapter concluded with a discussion of competitive bidding. Managers are encouraged to improve their bid-winning performance by adopting a probabilistic approach. A practical method for estimating probabilities that focuses on direct costs was reviewed.

The competitive environment will only intensify in the years to come. Competition will come from completely unanticipated sources. At the same time, product differentiation will become increasingly difficult unless firms can produce a continuous flow of innovations. As a result, the price variable will receive renewed emphasis as a competitive weapon. New, creative approaches to setting and changing prices will prevail. Pricing managers will be forced to do more than react to the pricing actions of other firms. They must develop the insight necessary to anticipate and preempt the moves of competitors.

REFERENCES

Morse, W. J., "Probabilistic Bidding Models: A Synthesis." *Business Horizons* 18 (1975): 67-74.

Nagle, T. T., *The Strategy and Tactics of Pricing.* Englewood Cliffs, N.J.: Prentice-Hall, 1987. See chapter 4.

Porter, M., "How Competitive Forces Shape Strategy." *Harvard Business Review* 57 (1974).

Sheth, J., "New Determinants of Competitive Structures in Industrial Markets." In *A Strategic Approach to Business Marketing,* edited by R. Spekman and D. Wilson. Chicago: American Marketing Association, 1985.

Sultan, R. G., *Pricing in the Electrical Oligopoly.* Volume 1. Boston: Harvard Graduate School of Business Administration, 1974.

8

PRICING ACROSS THE PRODUCT LINE

While there are a number of "single product" companies, the more typical approach is to add new products and services as existing ones move through the stages of their life cycles. The firm that enters the market with an innovative tennis racket made out of a new lightweight material is apt to subsequently add high- and low-end versions of the racket, a variety of racket sizes, and related items such as tennis balls, gloves, and training equipment. Both the depth and breadth of the product line are expanded as companies attempt to tap new market segments, utilize their distribution channels more completely, and achieve greater economies in their production operations.

Product lines should be designed in a systematic and coordinated manner. Each item must fulfill a specific role. Each must be positioned in a way that complements the others. Profits should be maximized on the entire mix, not on individual products or services. This is the essence of strategic product line management.

The most important tool for achieving such coordination is the price variable. Prices delineate where products are positioned with respect to one another. They reinforce the relationships among products that management wishes to communicate to customers. If improperly designed, the product line pricing structure can send mixed messages to customers, items can receive an inappropriate amount of emphasis, and profits can be lost.

This chapter will address the role of price in product line management. We first investigate the issue of cross-elasticity, where the sales of one product in a line are either positively or negatively affected by the price of another product in the line. Related to cross-elasticity is the problem of cannibalism, where one product achieves sales at the direct expense of another. Following this is a discussion of the relationship between decisions within the product line and overall profitabilty. An approach for determining actual price differentials among the items in a line is then presented. In addition, an assessment of the strategic benefits of using price to bundle and unbundle items in a product line is provided. The chapter closes with a review of discounts and their role in product line management.

CROSS-ELASTICITY: COMPLEMENTS AND SUBSTITUTES

The elasticity concept was introduced in chapter 3. Elasticity measurement is an attempt to capture the relationships between changes in the price of a product and changes in the total revenue generated by that product. Sometimes, however, changes in the price of one product also affect the revenues generated by other products in the line. When this type of relationship exists, it is called cross-elasticity.

The basic formula for cross-elasticity is as follows:

$$\frac{\% \text{ Change in Quantity}_A}{\% \text{ Change in Price}_B}, \text{ or}$$

$$\frac{\text{Change in Quantity}_A}{\text{Quantity}_A} \times \frac{\text{Price}_B}{\text{Change in Price}_B}$$

The focus here is on the percentage change in the quantity of product A resulting from a 1 percent change in the price of product B, where A and B are two products within the product line. (It should be noted that cross-elasticity can also be measured between the products of two different companies). The coefficient of cross-elasticity is calculated by taking the change in the quantity of product A divided by the original quantity of product A and multiplying the result by the original price of product B divided by the change in the price of product B.

The closer this coefficient is to zero, the smaller the relationship of the two products to one another. A coefficient greater than zero means that increases in the price of product B lead to increases in the quantity sold of product A. Such positive relationships indicate that the market views the two products as substitutes. Alternatively, larger negative coefficients indicate that higher prices of product B discourage buyers not only from buying product B but also from buying product A. The two items are, in effect, complements in the minds of customers.

To consider an example, assume a theater decides to increase the price of its medium-sized box of popcorn from $2.50 to $2.75. Also sold is a small box for $1.85 and a large box for $3.95. A similar line of soft drinks is sold, at prices of $1.00, $1.50, and $2.35. Assume, in addition, that the 10 percent increase in the price of a medium-sized box of popcorn causes a reduction in the purchases of medium-sized soft drinks of 2.8 percent. This produces a coefficient of cross-elasticity of −.28, suggesting that the two goods are somewhat complementary. If, at the same time, sales of the small box of popcorn increase by 15 percent, a coefficient of +1.5 is produced between the two sizes of boxes. Customers clearly view the small box as an effective substitute for the medium box.

The biggest difficulty in estimating cross-elasticities involves controlling for any factors, other than the price of product B, that might be influencing sales of product A. This can sometimes be accomplished by tracking data for these other factors over time and using multivariate statistical techniques to isolate the effect of the price of product B. An alternative approach could involve the use of test markets. For instance, the firm could vary the price of product B in one market or store but not in others and compare the impact on sales of product A.

THE PROBLEM OF CANNIBALISM

When cross-elasticities are positive and customers are to some degree willing to substitute the products in a line for one another, the company is in danger of cannibalizing its own sales. Cannibalism can be defined as the negative effects on existing products or services that occur when the firm introduces new products (e.g., product line extension) or attempts to reposition existing products (Kerin, Harvey, and Rothe, 1978). More specifically, cannibalism occurs when two or more items from the same firm compete in the same market segment.

Pricing becomes a critical issue in determining the extent of cannibalism that results when products are introduced or repositioned. Table 8.1 presents an example. A company selling two products (A and B) is considering raising the price of one of them (product B) from $7 to $10 (42.8 percent). Projections have been made of expected revenues and total contribution both with and without the price increase. It appears that the price increase will reduce sales of product B by 350 units (19.4 percent) and increase sales of product A by 200 units (20 percent). The resulting coefficient of cross-elasticity is +.467. Apparently, the 150-unit difference in total unit sales represents customers lost to competitors or customers who simply choose not to buy. Upon further examination, it can be determined that the price increase is justified and the cannibalism worth enduring. In this case, total contribution increases not only for product A but also for product B. This is because the elasticity coefficient for B alone is −.4377, suggesting that demand for this product is inelastic.

As demonstrated in table 8.1, a product's sales in any operating period come from four potential sources. These include new customers who previously did not purchase this product type, customers of competitive brands, repeat customers who have purchased the brand in question previously, and cannibalized customers who previously bought an alternative brand within the same company's product line. It is not uncommon for firms to make significant mar-

Table 8.1
Example of Cannibalism Resulting from a Price Change

Scenario 1:
No Price Change

	Product A	Product B	Total
Forecasted unit volume	1,000	1,800	2,800
Sources of volume			
new customers	75	100	175
competitors customers	225	300	525
cannibalism			
current customers	700	1,400	2,100
Total	1,000	1,800	2,800
Unit Price	$5.00	$7.00	
Total Revenue	$5,000	$12,600	$17,600
Variable Cost/Unit	$3.25	$4.00	$10,450
Direct Fixed Costs	$600	$2,100	$2,700
Total Contribution	$1,150	$3,300	$4,450

Scenario 2:
Price Increase on Product B

	Product A	Product B	Total
Forecasted Unit Volume	1,200	1,450	2,650
Sources of volume			
new customers	100	50	150
competitors customers	175	150	325
cannibalism	200		200
current customers	725	1,250	1,975
Total	1,200	1,450	2,650
Unit Price	$5.00	$10.00	
Total Revenue	$60,000	$14,500	$20,500
Variable Cost/Unit	$3.25	$4.00	$9,700
Direct Fixed Costs	$600	$2,100	$2,700
Total Contribution	$1,150	$6,600	$8,100

Coefficient of Cross-Elasticity = +.467

keting decisions in an attempt to gain sales with little thought to the sources of these sales. Unnecessary cannibalism is often the result. It is important to note that the loss of potential profits from a cannibalized product is a real cost which must be factored into pricing decision analysis.

This is not say that cannibalism should be avoided, but that the incremental financial or competitive gains should outweigh the value of the lost sales from a particular product. The example in table 8.1 provides a case in point of net financial benefit. Net competitive benefit could derive from improving the firm's overall product line image, being perceived as having a more complete product line, or filling gaps in the product line in response to new competitor offerings. In terms of this last point, it may be worth cannibalizing one's own sales to keep a customer rather than losing that customer to a competitor, even if the customer is kept by offering a lower-margin product.

Cannibalism often results as a byproduct of the firm's attempt to open up or attract new market segments. New items are added or old ones repositioned to appeal to a previously unreached segment. Coca Cola managers were able to attract a significant number of male buyers with the introduction of Diet Coke. This more than offset the cannibalized unit volume from Tab, a product with significant appeal among women.

There is a tendency, however, to oversegment markets. Firms include more items in a line than there are homogeneous market segments. They try to be all things to all people. If a company attempts to offer six unique price-quality offerings, ranging from top-of-the-line to fairly cheap, but in reality finds there are only three unique market segments, unnecessary cannibalism will be the result.

Prices actually serve a dual role in cannibalism decisions. The price of an item effectively positions it relative to all the other items within a given line. Prices make a statement regarding the relative quality levels of each item. At the same time, prices determine the relative margins on each item in the line. A price change on one item that causes cannibalism must be evaluated within the context of the new and old margins on that item as well as the margins on any other items in the line losing or gaining sales because of the price change. Consider again the example in table 8.1. The margin on product B was much higher than on product A, suggesting that cannibalism will make the firm worse off in terms of total revenue. However, demand was sufficiently inelastic for product B to generate enough net revenue with the price increase to offset the cost of cannibalism.

RELATING PRODUCT LINE DECISIONS TO OVERALL PROFITABILITY

An important consideration in product line management is the need to ensure that overall profitability is maximized as opposed to the profitability of each individual item. The ability to do so requires a careful analysis of differences in the costs, volume, and prices for the items in the line. An illustration of such data for a line consisting of four products is presented in table 8.2.

In order to evaluate overall product line profitability, it is necessary to calculate a PV ratio for the entire line. As discussed in chapter 6, the PV ratio for any product is determined by subtracting the variable cost per unit for an item from the price and then dividing the result by the price. In table 8.2, the PV

Table 8.2
Hypothetical Costs, Volume, Prices and Weighted PV Ratio for a Product
Line

Product	Unit Cost	Price	PV Ratio	Proportion of Total Volume	Weighted PV Ratio
A	$3.25	$5.00	.35	.20	.07
B	$4.00	$7.00	.43	.25	.11
C	$5.15	$11.00	.53	.25	.13
D	$6.45	$16.00	.60	.20	.12
					.43

Common Fixed Costs for Product Line = $1,000,000 (given)

Weighted PV Ratio for Product Line = .43 (calculated from above)

Breakeven for Product Line = $1,000,000/.43 = $2,325,581

Source: Adapted from K. Monroe (1979), Pricing: Making Profitable Decisions (New York: McGraw-Hill), 149.

ratios are calculated for each of the four items in the line. These ratios are then weighted by determining the proportion of total product line unit volume represented by each product. For instance, product C has a PV ratio of .53, and it accounts for 25 percent of product line volume. Multiplying these two figures produces a weighted PV ratio for product C of .13. These weighted PVs for the four items are then added together, producing an overall ratio of .43.

This overall PV ratio is a useful tool for making product line management decisions. Assuming that the product line has shared fixed costs of $1,000,000, break even can be calculated by dividing this figure by the PV ratio. In this case, the line will achieve break even with sales of $2,325,581.

Similarly, if the manager desires to achieve a profit level of $3,000,000, the required level of product line sales is arrived at by dividing .43 into the sum of $3,000,000 plus $1,000,000, or $9,302,326. Also, if actual projected sales are $15,000,000, the manager can now calculate product line profitability. This is determined by taking expected sales times the PV ratio and subtracting fixed costs. In this case, the product line would generate profits of $5,450,000.

Using the basic framework presented in table 8.2, the manager can perform sensitivity analysis in terms of product line decisions. Assume, for instance, an across-the-board price increase of 10 percent was being considered. With such an increase, it is expected that some cannibalism will occur, leading the lower-end products (A and B) to account for larger proportion of total volume. This set of circumstances is illustrated in table 8.3.

Table 8.3
Evaluating the Effect of Changes in Price and Volume on PV Ratio for a Product Line

Product	Unit Costs	Price	PV Ratio	Proportion of Total Volume	Weighted PV Ratio
A	$3.25	$5.50	.41	.35	.14
B	$4.00	$7.70	.48	.30	.14
C	$5.15	$12.10	.57	.20	.11
D	$6.45	$17.60	.63	.15	.09
					.48

Common Fixed Costs for Product Line = $1,000,000 (given)

Weighted PV Ratio for Product Line = .48 (calculated from above)

Breakeven for Product Line = $1,000,000/.48 = $2,083,333

Source: Adapted from K. Monroe (1979), *Pricing: Making Profitable Decisions* (New York: McGraw-Hill), 149.

The overall PV ratio rises to .48 with the price increase. Break-even sales now fall to $2,083,333. The necessary level of sales to achieve a profit of $3,000,000 declines to $8,333,333. And to achieve the profit level of $5,450,000 expected before the price increase, only $13,437,500 must be sold, a reduction of 10.42 percent. If projected sales of $15,000,000 were still achieved, the firm's profits would increase to $6,200,000. Of course, the firm may need to adjust this projected sales figure to reflect the elasticity of demand for the total product line. For revenue to stay at $15,000,000, the firm would be facing unitary elasticity of demand. That is, the price increase of 10 percent would have to produce an equal percentage reduction in quantity demanded.

These two scenarios are presented graphically in figure 8.1. Separate lines are drawn to represent the two different product line PV ratios. The break-even points are also noted. The slope of the PV line is dependent, then, on the relative prices charged and the relative volume mix for the items in the product line. Overall profitability depends on the slope of the PV line and the total volume sold for the entire product line.

In the final analysis, profitability is best served by moving away from across-the-board product line pricing decisions such as the 10 percent increase discussed above. Instead, the manager should attempt to adjust the weighted-average PV ratio. By working to increase volume of items with higher relative

Figure 8.1
A Graphical Illustration of Break-Even Points for Product Line Using Overall PV Ratios of .43 and .48

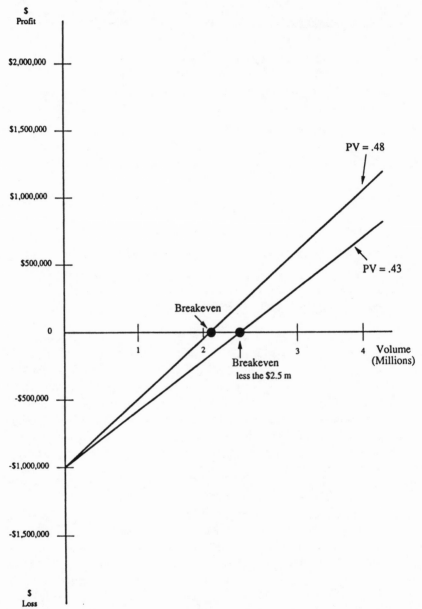

Source: Adapted from K. Monroe (1979), *Pricing: Making Profitable Decisions* (New York: McGraw-Hill), 148.

PV ratios and decrease volume of lower-PV items, the firm is able to extract greater profits from the line.

MAXIMIZING PRODUCT LINE PROFITABILITY: A CASE STUDY

The benefits of focusing on profitability across the product line are exemplified by considering the experiences of Wonder Business Systems (disguised), a fifteen-year-old office equipment dealer based in Georgia. The firm has ten branches, and achieved 1989 sales of $44 million. Wonder is a supplier of facsimile machines, word processors, typewriters, and copiers as well as service and supplies for the equipment it sells. The biggest percentage of Wonder's business has historically been generated through the sale of office copiers, supplies, and services. In fact, the company is the nation's largest dealer of one of the leading brands of copiers.

The office equipment industry has experienced both dramatic growth and significant change over the past five years. This is especially the case in the area of copiers. New technology has produced improvements both in durability and quality, extending average copier life from 25 months to nearly 48 months. As such, the replacement rate has dropped considerably. Customers increasingly view copiers as a commodity, perceiving little difference among brands and often confusing the dealer with the brand. The tendency is to take the product for granted, only taking notice when a machine is not working properly.

For some time, management at Wonder has recognized that the longer customers keep their equipment, the more heavily they will depend upon service and supplies to maintain that equipment. As the number of satisfied customers who keep current equipment has risen, the firm has experienced a steady increase in the proportion of revenues generated from service contracts and supplies. In recent operating periods, the proportion has exceeded 55 percent despite the fact that Wonder's customer base continues to grow at a steady rate.

While hesitant to take actions that might interfere with what has been a highly successful operation, management decided about a year ago to restructure prices to reflect current conditions. An example of these changes can be found by examining the firm's pricing approach to the Wilson 2000 SDR (also disguised), the firm's top-selling copier. This is a midranged machine which goes for roughly $9,000.

Historically, Wonder sold the machine at close to the manufacturer's suggested price. The manufacturer would recommend a percentage-above-cost (PAC) price, which provided a basic margin of profit for Wonder. To this, Wonder added a subsequent margin and then permitted the sales force to negotiate a price somewhere between the PAC price and this additional margin. Service and supplies were priced at three levels: a full-service contract price, which included supplies; a maintenance service agreement price, which excluded supplies; and a per-hour service rate for those not willing to sign a longer-term service agreement. All three prices were set based on a combination of the manufacturer's suggested service price on a particular machine and Wonder's own experience in terms of the number of copies produced and the amount of supplies consumed by a particular model over a given time period. The full-service contract price for one year on the Wilson 2000 SDR model was in the neighborhood of $550. For marketing purposes, these figures were reduced to an average cost per copy figure.

Wonder's revamped pricing strategy focuses on physical products and support services as complementary items within the larger product line. The PV ratio for equipment has tended to average about 19 percent, while for service the ratio is closer to 70 percent. These relative ratios, combined with the aforementioned marketplace trends regarding service relative to equipment, have led to a strategy of using equipment volume to generate service revenues. The Wilson 2000 SDR is now sold at a discount of 15 to 20 percent below the PAC price in an attempt to more aggressively place machines. Service prices have been increased an average of 10 percent in terms of the overall cost per copy, with specific increases in supplies (toner, paper) and in hourly labor charges. The net result has been an increase in the firm's overall profit rate of 22 percent in the past year, more than double the average annual increase in recent years.

DETERMINING PRICE DIFFERENTIALS WITHIN THE PRODUCT LINE

Establishing actual price levels of each item in a product line is a difficult task that requires considerable judgment. There are, however, some general guidelines which can be quite helpful in making such decisions. These guidelines are based on the work of Alfred Oxenfeldt and of Kent Monroe, two pioneers in the area of product line pricing. Key suggestions include the following:

- Prices in a line must convey noticeable differences among the particular product or service offerings. If items are too close in price, they fail to present customers with clear and distinct alternatives from which to choose. A customer asked to do too much work is likely to become alienated.

- If two items are so similar that price differentials are not justified, then the same price should be charged for both.

- Sales tend to cluster around a number of price points in a line. Products or services must be positioned and priced at those specific points.

- Price differentials or gaps between items tend to become larger as more features and capabilities are included with particular items. That is, the gaps become relatively larger in moving from the low end to the high end of the line.

- Customers evaluate the size of a price gap relative to the base price. A gap of $10 is seen as much more significant in moving from a base price of $40 to a price of $50 than in moving from a base price of $200 to $210.

- If price gaps are too large, not only will competitors likely take advantage, but customers may perceive that the firm has a limited set of offerings.

- Customers generally do not evaluate a price as being low or high based on the absolute level of the price or based on the price of the next closest substitute. Rather, the evaluation of any one price is influenced by the entire range of prices for all the items in the line.

Determining actual price levels involves two related sets of decisions. The first concerns establishing end prices, while the second focuses on the amount of differential or distance between the price of each item in the line. As will be seen, the ability to determine differentials becomes much easier once end prices are set.

End prices refer to the lowest- and highest-priced items in the line. Not surprisingly, these tend to be the prices most noticed and remembered of all those within a product line. In fact, Monroe (1971) has found evidence that the lowest-priced item in a line has a greater impact on the overall quantity sold for the entire line than does any other item. For instance, reductions in this price are likely to stimulate sales much more than reductions in prices of in-between items. Next in impact is the highest-priced item, which also tends to be the most significant conveyor of product line quality.

A useful concept for establishing end prices is the notion of threshold values, introduced in chapter 4. These are the upper and lower limits of what a person or market segment is willing to pay for a product, and can also be applied to a general product category or line. Threshold values will likely differ from customer to customer within a given market segment. The task of the pricing manager is to estimate the distribution of threshold values at the high and low end for a segment, and to then calculate the mean and variance. Survey research can be helpful in this regard.

End prices should reflect these threshold values as well as competitive considerations. While they tend to be interdependent, threshold values can differ significantly from the end prices charged by competitors. Moreover, competitors are especially responsive to pricing actions that involve the firm's end items. Also, the high visibility of end prices makes them a key factor in attracting or discouraging new market entrants, and especially niche firms.

Once end prices are determined, differentials between each item in the line can be decided upon. To accomplish this, it is helpful to revisit the Weber-Fechner law introduced in chapter 4. This law suggests that a logarithmic relationship exists between a price and a buyer's response to that price. Applied to product line pricing decisions, the law indicates that a constant proportion should be maintained between prices of items in a line. For instance, if the prices of the low-end price and the next lowest are $20 and $26, which represents a 30 percent difference, then the next item up in the line should be priced at $33.80. This will maintain the constant proportion because the difference between $33.80 and $26 is also 30 percent. In this manner, just-noticeable differences can be conveyed among the items.

This approach can be summarized with the following formula, proposed by Monroe (1979):

$$P_j = P_{min}K^{j-1}$$

where: P_j = the price of the jth product in the line
j = the jth product in the line
P_{min} = the low-end price in the line
K = the constant proportion

The formula states that the price of an item is equal to a constant proportion (K) added to the price of the preceding item in the line. This assumes that the items in line have been prearranged in order from bottom to top and that the low-end price has been predetermined.

The problem, then, is to estimate a value for the constant K. Monroe (1979) suggests the formula below for this purpose:

$$K = \left[\frac{P_{max}}{P_{min}}\right]^{[1/(n-1)]}$$

where: K = the constant proportion
P_{min} = the low-end price in the line
P_{max} = the high-end price in the line
n = number of items in the line

To apply this formula, consider a line of stereo speakers being marketed to a particular customer segment. The line has seven different speakers ranging in quality from relatively low to well above average. Preliminary research has suggested price thresholds of $70 (low end) and $600 (high end) for this market segment. The formula produces a constant of 1.43057. Taking this times the low-end price produces a price of $100.14 for the second item in the line, $143.26 for the third, and so forth. Table 8.4 provides a summary.

The approach is based on the assumption that this company offers a line of products covering the entire quality range captured by the lower and upper price thresholds, and that its offerings are fairly equally distributed across this range (i.e., the quality gaps are about the same). Also, this implies that there are no "blank spaces" in the line, although the firm could insert hypothetical offerings into any blank spaces for the purpose of calculating prices for their actual offerings.

CREATIVITY IN PRODUCT LINE MANAGEMENT

Product lines also lend themselves to considerable flexibility and creativity when it comes to pricing. Although a number of creative approaches are

Table 8.4
Determining Prices for a Line of Stereo Speakers

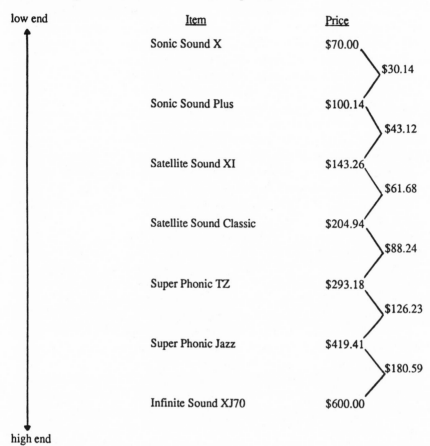

low end	Item	Price	
	Sonic Sound X	$70.00	
			$30.14
	Sonic Sound Plus	$100.14	
			$43.12
	Satellite Sound XI	$143.26	
			$61.68
	Satellite Sound Classic	$204.94	
			$88.24
	Super Phonic TZ	$293.18	
			$126.23
	Super Phonic Jazz	$419.41	
			$180.59
	Infinite Sound XJ70	$600.00	

high end

where:
$$k=(600/70)1/6 = 1.43057$$

possible, this discussion will focus on four particular strategies. These include the use of bundling, loss leaders, cross-benefit pricing, and anchors.

Product bundling is a tactic used to enhance value by combining different products and/or services and pricing them as one. The approach is generally to charge a combined price that is lower than that charged if each product or service is sold separately. Bundling may be indivisible (pure), where the buyer purchasing a product or service must accept the product or service in bundled form. Indivisible bundling is a seller-oriented tactic to the extent that the buyer is limited in his purchase alternatives and the seller is maximizing income by requiring the buyer to conform to a product offering in a form he or she might not otherwise have elected to purchase. Optional bundling is a more buyer-oriented approach where the purchaser has the option to buy the product or service either combined or separately. Absent monopoly considerations, bundling implies a price discount to the buyer. A variation of optional bundling is value-added bundling. Here, a value appeal is made to a particularly price-sensitive buyer by enhancing the product in a form or quality that is of less interest to the relatively price-insensitive buyer. The price-conscious buyer is attracted by this bundle, while the less sensitive buyer is retained with the normal offering.

Bundling is a prevalent tactic for a variety of reasons. First of all, meaningful cost savings can be realized by combining items. This includes costs of production, sales, and information provision. By getting customers to consume complementary items at one time, significant duplication of effort is eliminated.

Bundling also encourages purchases a buyer might not otherwise be willing to make. For instance, a person in the market for a boat may be hesitant to purchase accompanying sonar equipment either now or in the future. By bundling it with the boat and charging an intermediate price, the sonar equipment suddenly looks much more attractive. This reasoning also works when the customer is not seeking any of the products in the bundle. A woman shopping for lipstick finds that an exclusive cosmetic manufacturer has bundled a purse-sized mirror with an eyeliner and eyeshadow combination. Not a typical patron of this line, and not in the market for these items, the woman nonetheless finds this an attractive bundle.

The complementary nature of the items in most product lines is especially apparent when firms successfully use a loss leader strategy. With a loss leader, a product is priced below its own variable costs as a means of attracting customers to the rest of the product line. The firm is willing to take a loss on one item if revenues are earned on the others beyond what they normally would have made. Further, loss leaders are highly visible and can help encourage buyers unfamiliar with a manufacturer or retailer.

When using a loss leader strategy, the difficulty comes in deciding which item to highlight. Nagle and Novak (1988) have identified two criteria for making such selections: First, items within the line that are purchased more often make good loss leaders. This is because customers tend to remember the prices of relatively few items, and the ones most remembered are those purchased most frequently. As a result, customers associate the price of a commonly purchased item with the general level of prices charged by a vendor for all of its products. Second, products purchased more heavily by price-sensitive buyers are good candidates for loss leader strategies. By pricing this type of product very low, the vendor will achieve immediate visibility among the price-sensitive segment, attracting these buyers to the entire line. At the same time, these are products

PRICING ACROSS THE PRODUCT LINE / 139

not purchased as heavily by other segments, and so the vendor is able to maintain normal revenues from these other segments.

The strategy of cross-benefit pricing applies to situations where the firm sells two products, neither one of which is completely useful without the other. Such strict complementary relationships can be found between certain types of razors and razor blades, cameras and film, and personal computers and printers, among other products. A common strategy is to price the core product (i.e., the razor, camera, or computer) at or near cost, so as to create a sizable embedded base of customers. These customers then become captive and are charged a premium price for products offering the cross-benefit (i.e., blades, film, or printers).

A very creative twist on this strategy is that used with Cross pens. The firm charges a premium price for its pens and a relatively low price for its refills. In this case, the primary benefit sought by customers may well be the image of the pen itself as opposed to its writing qualities, justifying such a strategy. If refill cartridges were too expensive, it might simply provide a reason to no longer use the pen.

Cross-benefit pricing can also be used to stimulate existing demand. For instance, a bar will give away its pretzels free, not just as a friendly gesture, but to encourage greater consumption of beer. The buyer may well perceive that consumption of one naturally requires the other.

Anchoring is a less common product line strategy. Here, the firm adds an item to a line that is priced out of the normal range of prices in the line. The purpose of this is to affect customer perceptions of the remaining items in the line. For instance, a firm with a five-product line finds that customers are not purchasing its high-end products. An additional premium version is added and priced at a level higher than the items in the line and high relative to prices that the market is accustomed to paying. While this new item may not sell very well, it serves as an anchor. Purchases of the formerly high-end items go up, as they now look like a better buy.

THE ROLE OF DISCOUNTS IN THE PRODUCT LINE

The product line manager also has at his or her disposal a variety of price concessions that can be offered to customers. These include prepaid freight, drop-shipping privileges, installment financing, postdating, liberal return allowances, rebate programs, and others. Chief among these, at least in terms of use, is the structure of discounts provided to customers.

Three types of discounts are provided to customers or to middlemen: cash, quantity, and trade. Cash discounts are given to encourage speedy payment of invoices. A cash discount might be quoted as 3/10, n 30, indicating the buyer will receive a 3 percent discount if the invoice is paid within 10 days. Otherwise, the credit period until full payment is due extends for thirty days. Additional

Table 8.5
Application of Manufacturer's Discount Structure to the Hospital Distributor Company

The Hospital Distributor Company Order:

10 extinguishers at $45.00 each	....	$450.00
15 extinguishers at $24.00 each	....	$360.00
10 extinguishers at $60.00 each	....	$600.00
5 extinguishers at $90.00 each	....	$450.00
Total	....	$1860.00

Step 1: Apply quantity discount

Total order amount	$1860.00
Discount($1860.00 x .10)	186.00
Net order amount	$1674.00

Step 2: Apply trade discount

Net order amount	$1674.00
Discount($1674.00 x .30)	502.20
Amount due manufacturer	$1171.80

Step 3: Apply cash discount

Amount due Manufacturer	$1171.80
Discount($1171.80 x .02)	23.44
Actual (net) remittance	$1148.36

Source: M. H. Morris (1988), *Industrial and Organizational Marketing* (Columbus, Ohio: Merrill Publishing).

price incentives may be given for payment prior to receipt of goods or upon delivery.

Quantity discounts are quite common in industrial markets, providing an incentive to buy in large dollar amounts or large unit amounts. The discount can also be cumulative or noncumulative. Cumulative quantity discounts allow the buyer to include a series of purchases over some prespecified time period in determining the size of the discount for which he or she qualifies. Noncumulative discounts apply only to a single purchase. These discounts frequently are applied not just to a single item, but also to a set of products within the company's line.

Trade (or functional) discounts are provided to middlemen (wholesalers or retailers) to encourage distributor support for the firm's product line. Discounts frequently are used to encourage the performance of specific functions, such as storage or warehousing, selling activities, transportation, and promotional efforts.

Discounts can result in significant saving off the list price. Consider the case of a manufacturer selling a line of fire extinguishers to commercial firms and institutions through industrial distributors. Assume the discount structure includes terms of 2/10 n 30, plus a 10 percent incentive for orders of $500 or more and a trade discount of 30 percent. One of the manufacturer's middlemen, Hospital Distributors, Inc., has placed an order for four different types of extinguishers. The distributor will, in turn, sell them to hospitals and health care facilities. The list price for the total order comes to $1,860, as illustrated in table 8.5.

If the customer qualifies for all three discounts, the actual remittance comes to $1,148.36. This represents a 38 percent saving off the list price. Table 8.5 also illustrates the logical order in which the discounts would be taken. Those charged with setting price should recognize, then, the potential price flexibility that a competitive discount structure provides to both the marketer and the purchase decision maker.

SUMMARY

Most firms do not sell a single product, but offer instead broad product lines and mixes. Pricing these lines is a much more complicated process than pricing individual items. This chapter has attempted to identify the major strategic issues in product line pricing and to introduce some of the more salient approaches to addressing these issues.

The beginning point involved determining the nature of the relationships among the various items in a line. Items differ in the extent to which they are substitutes and complements for one another, or the degree to which they are completely independent. Prices can serve to reinforce these relationships, but can also create conflicts within the line.

The concept of cross-elasticity was introduced to better explain the relationships among items in a line. Of special concern was positive cross-elasticity, situations in which ill-designed pricing programs can create unwanted cannibalism. Prices not only help determine the margins on products, but also help identify their positions relative to one another. If these positions are not distinct or clearly established, customers are likely to purchase the cheaper of two items.

Once the relationships among items are understood, the items that constitute the line must be managed as a group. This means maximizing profit on the line, not on individual items. Contribution analysis was presented as a tool for evaluating product line profitability and ensuring that overall profit is considered in individual pricing decisions. The manager was encouraged to assess differences in costs, volume, and prices on each item before establishing pricing policies for the line.

Setting price levels that maximize overall profitability depends, further, on customer considerations. The more specific problem concerns determining end prices for a product line and then determining the size of the gap, or differential, in prices between individual items. To address this problem, concepts such as price thresholds and the Weber-Fechner law from the psychology of pricing discussion (chapter 4) were reintroduced and applied to line decisions.

Lines must also be managed flexibly and creatively. Examples of four creative product line strategies were provided. These included bundling, use of loss leaders, cross-benefit pricing, and anchoring. The chapter then concluded with an assessment of the price discount structure as a tool for managing product lines.

Unless close attention is paid to issues such as those presented in this chapter, managers can find themselves losing control of their product lines. The turbulence in competitive environments and corporate pressure for bottom-line performance can cause managers to focus too narrowly on individual products. Costs are arbitrarily allocated, and profitability on each item is artificially determined. Some products fall through the cracks, receiving too little emphasis. Others are stressed even though they do not represent the greatest source of opportunity.

REFERENCES

Kerin, R. A., M. G. Harvey, and J. T. Rothe, "Cannibalism and New Product Development." *Business Horizons* (October 1978): 25-31.

Monroe, K. B., *Pricing: Making Profitable Decisions.* New York: McGraw-Hill, 1979.

_____, "The Information Content of Prices: A Preliminary Model for Estimating Buyer Response." *Management Science* 17 (April 1971): B519-B532.

Nagle, T., and K. Novak, "The Roles of Segmentation and Awareness in Explaining Variations in Price Markups." In *Issues in Pricing: Theory and Research*, edited by T. Devinney. Lexington, Mass.: Lexington Books, 1988.

9

LEGAL AND ETHICAL ASPECTS OF PRICING DECISIONS

Throughout this text, considerable emphasis is placed on the need to view price as a creative marketing variable. Managers are encouraged to move away from standard, formula-based pricing methods and instead adopt a flexible, customer-based approach. Yet most firms continue to rely heavily on arbitrary techniques, simplistic rules of thumb, and reactive thinking when it comes to managing prices.

One possible explanation is that managers are comfortable with the status quo and are hesitant to change something that has worked in the past. In addition, market-based pricing requires more time and effort than do more traditional approaches. An alternative explanation, however, involves a concern on the part of managers with the legal and ethical implications of market-based pricing practices.

Price represents one of the more visible decisions a company must make. Prices are frequently quoted on contracts and bids, printed in catalogs, posted on supermarket shelves, cited in trade journals, and published in advertisements and promotional materials. Buyers not only are apt to compare the prices of different competitors, but frequently share their price perceptions and experiences with one another.

For these reasons, managers must be concerned about how the firm's image is projected through its prices and the extent to which they and their firms are legally liable for specific pricing actions. These concerns are the focus of this chapter. We begin by examining the principal legal mechanisms regulating pricing decisions, and then review a number of the price tactics that raise legal questions. Following this is an evaluation of the significant ethical considerations that come into play when pricing.

LEGISLATION GOVERNING PRICING ACTIVITIES

The legislation dealing with pricing behavior falls into the general area of antitrust law. The principal pieces of legislation include the Sherman Act of 1890, the Federal Trade Commission Act of 1914, the Clayton Act of 1914, the Robinson-Patman Act of 1936, the Miller-Tydings Act of 1937, the McGuire-Keough Fair Trade Enabling Act of 1952, and the Consumer Goods Pricing Act of 1975.

The Sherman Act explicitly forbids any contract, combination or conspiracy to restrain trade or commerce. Moreover, any person who monopolizes, attempts to monopolize, or conspires to monopolize a market is subject to prosecution. The act is fairly vague, and so has not produced an agreed-upon and clearly specified understanding regarding individual pricing practices. In fact, a literal reading and enforcement of the statutory language would serve to prohibit almost all competitive practices. As a result, the courts tend to interpret this legislation in a more normative fashion.

Owing in part to the vagueness of the Sherman Act and judicial reluctance to liberally interpret its provisions regarding specific business practices, Congress created the Federal Trade Commission Act in 1914. The commission was empowered to prohibit practices that might be unfair or injurious to competition even absent a showing that an actual injury had occurred. In the same year, the Clayton Act was passed to expressly forbid price discrimination that might substantially lessen competition (Section 2) and to limit tie-in and exclusive dealing contracts that require buyers to purchase separate products from the same seller (Section 3). Subsequent judicial decisions interpreting Section 2 held that secondary-line discrimination (which is at the buyer level, as discussed later in this chapter) was permissible and price differentials for quantity discounts were outside the scope of the act.

The depression of the 1930s witnessed an acute downward spiraling of prices. During this same time period, chain stores proliferated rapidly. Their flexibility in capital management, distribution, and pricing placed small independent stores under intense competitive pressures. In response, Congress passed the Robinson-Patman Act in 1936. Section 2 of the Clayton Act was amended to become subsection 2(a) of an expanded Section 2. The new subsection 2(a) eased the burden of a plaintiff having to prove that a competitive injury had occurred, closed the quantity discount exemption, tightened the cost justification defense, and narrowed the meeting competition defense. In addition, subsections c through f were added to circumscribe specified brokerage payments, advertising allowances, and the deliberate inducement of illegal discrimination by the buyer. Also, Section 3 was included to forbid predatory selling at low prices (below cost) with the intent of damaging competition.

The Miller-Tydings Act, McGuire-Keough Fair Trade Enabling Act, and Consumer Goods Pricing Act all dealt with resale price maintenance. The Miller-Tydings Act amended the Sherman Act to permit manufacturers who signed resale agreements to set minimum resale prices in states passing "fair trade laws." The McGuire-Keough Act extended price maintenance coverage to nonsigners. The Consumer Goods Pricing Act subsequently made resale pricing agreement illegal per se.

Of these pieces of legislation, by far the most significant to the pricing manager is the Robinson-Patman Act. For this reason, its provisions are elaborated upon below.

KEY ASPECTS OF THE ROBINSON-PATMAN ACT

The primary focus of the Robinson-Patman Act is illegal price discrimination, or situations in which two customers are charged different prices for the same item and the firm's competitors are subsequently damaged by the pricing practice. The act is one of the most confusing and complex laws ever enacted by Congress, and has been criticized by some as anticompetitive. Its key provisions include the following:

Sections 2(a) and 2(b) specify that price discrimination exists where a seller engaged in interstate commerce charges different prices for commodities of like grade or quality in at least two sales to different buyers within a reasonable period of time of one another and within the confines of the United States or its territories.

Section 2(c) states that it is unlawful for any person engaged in commerce to offer or receive anything of value (commissions, brokerage, or allowances) to an agent of the opposite party to the sale except for services rendered in connection with the sale if a service has not actually been performed.

Section 2(d) prohibits the furnishing of anything of value, most typically advertising allowances, to buyers unless such allowances are available on a proportionate basis to other buyers.

Section 2(e) governs payments for promotional assistance and advertising materials.

Section 2(f) makes it illegal for a buyer to knowingly induce or to receive an illegal discrimination in price.

If any of the conditions of Section 2(a) are not met or a seller can demonstrate that no competitive injury has resulted from the price discrimination, then the defendant can argue that the provisions of the Robinson-Patman Act do not apply. Assuming that the act does apply, there are three general defenses available: (1) the cost defense, which involves demonstrating that customers were charged different prices in direct proportion to differences in the seller's costs of serving those customers (e.g., due to the quantity they purchased or their geographic location); (2) the matching competition defense, which involves demonstrating that a lower price was used in a particular market in an attempt to respond to and meet a competitor's low (and lawful) price; and (3) the changing market conditions defense, which involves demonstrating that the goods for which a lower price was charged were subject to unique developments in terms of supply and demand conditions, necessitating their sale at a price different than that typically charged.

To better understand the Robinson-Patman Act, let us review these statutory conditions, the nature of "competitive injury," and the available defenses to an alleged violation.

Different Purchasers

There must be at least two or more sales involving different purchasers for the act to apply. A seller may sell the same product at different prices to the same buyer. If, for example, two separate divisions of a purchasing firm are charged different prices, no violation exists.

Products of Like Grade and Quality

Products are considered of like grade and quality if they are functional equivalents. In the Borden Company vs. the Federal Trade Commission case of 1967, the Supreme Court held that the perception of a product as different from another is insufficient as a defense. Borden had sold privately labeled milk at a lower price to retail foodstores while selling milk under its own label at higher prices. However, a subsequent decision by an appellate court found that no competitive injury had occurred if the price difference between a premium and nonpremium brand reflects a consumer preference for the premium brand. In a sense, the customer is paying for enhanced image and visibility created through the advertising and promotion of the premium brand. Further, when a functionally similar product is put to different uses, a price differential is permitted.

Substantial Lessening of Competition

A plaintiff must demonstrate that the pricing action serves to substantially harm competition at the primary, secondary, or tertiary level of distribution. Primary injury is to a competitor, and results when the marketer charges a lower price in the competitor's markets than it charges in other markets. Secondary injury is to a customer's competitor, such as where a lower price is charged to one customer than to another and these two customers are competitors (e.g., in industrial markets). The one paying the higher price finds itself at a significant disadvantage in its own markets. Tertiary injury involves a customer's customer, usually wholesalers or retailers. The manufacturer with two distribution channels, one involving wholesalers and retailers, and the other direct to retailers, may end up placing one set of retailers at a significant disadvantage with customers by charging them a higher price. Further, the primary, secondary, or tertiary injury must be to a buyer who is in actual competition with the favored competitor (i.e., the competitor receiving a lower price), and in the same geographic market.

The statute recognizes three types of damage to competition: (1) a tendency toward monopoly; (2) a substantial lessening of competition; and (3) injury, destruction, or prevention of any competition with any person (i.e., legal entity). Any of these types of damage may occur in the primary, secondary, or tertiary line of commerce. Therefore, there are nine possibilities where a tendency to damage competition may render the price discrimination illegal. The penalties for any of the nine situations are the same.

Injury may be found even where the benefits only lessen the disadvantage the favored buyer otherwise is under or where a price differential only lessens the advantages the disfavored buyer otherwise enjoys. For many years the courts found the existence of injury where the price discrimination did not actually hurt competition. The possibility rather than the reality that such a result might occur was sufficient to establish injury. Recently, however, the rulings have required the plaintiff to show which sales it has lost and how specifically it was harmed. Moreover, when a price differential on an intermediate or component product represents only a small portion of the final price of the buyer's end product, the courts have increasingly found that price differentials for products that represent only a component of the final price of the buyer's end product are not violations of law.

Brokerage

The brokerage provision has been interpreted by the courts to prohibit cost differentials paid by the seller to the buyer in the form of broker's fees or commissions. Under this section, buyers are forbidden to establish dummy or phony brokerages through which to receive payments from the seller. Such payments to the dummy brokerage would constitute a type of price discount, as no real service has been rendered and no cost incurred to earn the fee.

The Cost Defense

If the defendant seller can demonstrate that the discrimination results from a difference in costs incurred due to the quantity sold, conditions of manufacture, or delivery terms, then liability can be avoided. This defense is difficult to implement, however, as the seller must have maintained meticulous records documenting the different variable or marginal costs.

While the courts have permitted discounts on the basis of quantities purchased, such sales must involve a cost justification. It is important to emphasize that the cost defense is not available where the cost difference is attributable to manufacturing costs alone. That is, the manufacturer cannot simply claim that it happened to produce the goods sold to one customer more efficiently than the goods sold to another customer. The seller must demonstrate that the difference in manufacturing costs results from either differing selling methods or differences in the quantity of sales to customers. Similarly, only differences in sales costs and delivery costs resulting directly from these differing methods or quantities thereof are relevant to the cost defense. A seller may establish a cost differential relative to serving broad categories, groups, or segments.

The "Meeting Competition" Defense

The defense of pricing to meet the competition is only valid when the seller changes price to battle his own competitors. According to the statute, a seller is not permitted to establish prices that enable a buyer to meet competition by offering a price differential to that buyer. Here too, the Supreme Court in recent decisions has eased the burden of defendants.

In *The Great Atlantic and Pacific Tea Company v. Federal Trade Commission* (1979), the Court held that the seller, Borden, had satisfied the Section 2(b) meeting competition defense when it had substantially undercut a competitor's bid for A & P's private label milk business. Borden's initial offer was declined by A & P, which informed Borden that it must lower its offer by at least $50,000. Borden responded by substantially lowering its price and won the account. The Court used the standards of reasonableness and good faith in ruling that Borden's reliance on the buyers statements was prudent.

More recently (the Falls City case discussed later in this chapter), the Court has held that the Section 2(b) defense applies to competition met on an area-wide basis as well as on a customer-to-customer basis, and that the burden of proof is on the plaintiff to establish that the competitive price the seller is meeting is illegal. Also, under this defense new customers may be sought while existing accounts are preserved. The Court held that the defense applies even if the seller unintentionally beats the competitor's price and if prices are kept low in one market area while they are raised in others.

The "Changing Market Conditions" Defense

Although rarely used, this defense argues that prices can be varied because of changes in the market or the marketability of a product. Examples include a product that has become or is in danger of spoiling, becoming obsolete, or being sold by a company either under court-sanctioned bankruptcy or a legitimate going out of business sale. To use this defense, a defendant must show that the change in markets or marketability is a meaningful departure from typical conditions and that the change was not caused by the specific actions of the defendant or a competitor. Also, only those products marketed by the firm that are directly affected by obsolescence or changing preferences of buyers are covered by this defense.

PENALTIES UNDER THE LAW

While legal remedies to violations of these laws are made on a case-by-case basis, there are some specific limits to these penalties. For example, restraint of trade violations under the Sherman Act, Clayton Act, or Robinson-Patman Act make a corporation liable for up to one million dollars in fines. A culpable individual is subject to $250,000 in fines, three years in prison, or both. After 1974, Sherman Act violations were changed from misdemeanors to felonies.

These corporate and individual penalties are for felony prosecutions initiated by the Justice Department. For suits initiated by competitors or customers, a firm is liable for triple damages and attorneys' fees. Plaintiffs have up to four years to initiate a suit after the allegedly illegal action occurred. In addition, the Federal Trade Commission has the power to administratively issue cease and desist orders for practices it deems improper. If a company has not appealed the ruling to the U.S. Court of Appeals within sixty days, then the firm is thereafter subject to $10,000 per day in fines for each violation. The amount of Federal Trade Commission penalties is based on the size of a firm, its ability to pay, and its culpability in the particular violation.

PRICE BEHAVIORS THAT RAISE LEGAL QUESTIONS

The legislation governing competitive pricing has implications for a variety of behaviors. These behaviors can be grouped into four general categories: price fixing, resale price maintenance, forms of price discrimination, and deceptive price promotions. The specific pricing actions that constitute each group tend to have many different forms, and the question of legality tends to be situational. Moreover, a general trend has been toward a more permissive legal and regulatory environment.

Price Fixing

Price fixing represents an attempt by one or more business entities singly or in collusion to create an artificial level of prices such that actual or potential rivals (i.e., those not participating in the price fixing arrangement) will be inhibited from competing effectively or customers will be forced to pay prices which differ from those which would occur in the absence of price fixing. Collusion refers to a cooperative agreement or partnership among competitors in such areas as production quotas, price levels, and bidding strategies.

Since price fixing is a formal attempt to restrain trade, it comes under the province of the Sherman Act. In the landmark *Socuny Vacuum Oil v. United States* case (1940), the U.S. Supreme Court held that actual price fixing as well as any attempt to fix prices is illegal per se. That is, this is a practice that is conclusively presumed to be illegal. Neither the economic rationality nor the positive impact of this particular price-fixing action was admissible as a defense. This broad ruling encompasses a range of price behaviors, including attempts to lower market prices, indirectly raising prices by removing excess supplies of merchandise from competing channels, splitting markets by rotating proposers of the lowest bid on contracts (i.e., different competitors take turns submitting the "lowest" bid, which turns out to be a higher price than would otherwise have been the case), and maintaining price uniformity by sharing price lists with competitors. More recently, the medical and law professions have come under attack for attempting to enforce minimum fee schedules and opposing the advertising of professional services and fees.

Price fixing can be horizontal or vertical. Horizontal price fixing involves competitors at the same level in the distribution channel; for instance, two competing manufacturers may collude. Vertical price fixing involves organizations at different levels of the channel; for example, a manufacturer may work with a wholesaler or retailer to effect higher (or lower) prices to end users than normal competitive conditions might produce.

Parallel Pricing

A unique method of pricing which has price-fixing implications is called parallel pricing. Parallel or uniform pricing policies may exist in the absence of any formal agreements among competitors to set prices. For instance, company A announces a price increase, and within a few days all its major competitors follow suit with virtually the same increase. In oligopolistic markets (e.g., automobiles, steel, oil, computer hardware, banking), such price uniformity may be inevitable. With few competitors it is relatively easy for a firm to know what its rivals are doing and to respond quickly. This is particularly true where industry costs are well understood and where products are essentially undifferentiated. The courts have viewed parallel pricing as an acceptable practice except where a firm is in a monopoly position or has demonstrated that its behavior amounts to collusion with competitors. While the presence of collusion is difficult to prove, the courts have held that pricing agreements may be tacit or informal and still amount to collusion. Circumstantial evidence is sufficient to establish that a pattern of business behavior exists in which the intent of competitors is to uniformly control market prices.

In a series of cases in which the Supreme Court has examined parallel pricing, a number of conditions have been identified that suggest that parallel pricing is actually illegal collusion (i.e., the existence of a proposal by one or more competitors for joint pricing action). Further, collusion can be implied if the competitors engaged in a complex, yet identifiable, pattern of responses to an initial price change. Also, if direct communication among competitors took place, or the opportunity for direct communication clearly existed, then the parallel prices may be illegal. In addition, problems can arise where the participants failed to deny an agreement existed. Finally, when the circumstances suggest that a competitor who did participate in the parallel pricing behavior gained if all cooperated but suffered if others did not cooperate, the behavior may be interpreted as price fixing.

Exchanges of Price Information

Also related to the practice of price fixing is the question of whether competitors are allowed to exchange information about their prices. That is, does an exchange of information among competitors by itself demonstrate an intention to fix prices? In an open society, business information tends to be readily available. Numerous company documents and industry-related publications exist from which assessment can be made of business practices. However, when competitors in an industry exchange information either directly or, more commonly, through joint membership in a trade association, the courts have used the rule of reason in finding anticompetitive behavior.

In the *American Column and Lumber v. the United States* case (1921), the Supreme Court held that an association of hardwood manufacturers whose members exchanged industry information relating to sales, delivery, production, and inventories was engaged in an attempt to stabilize prices. Even though no explicit agreement existed to set prices, the arrangement which had been established among companies belonging to the association for reporting such information served the same purpose. The courts have paid close attention in many cases to the reasonableness of prevailing prices. In *Maple Flooring Manufacturers Association v. the United States* (1925), the manufacturers of hardwood flooring exchanged among themselves information relating to the average member's costs for all dimensions and grades of flooring and established freight rates from a base point to various end-user designations. The Supreme Court found that market prices were not uniform and were actually lower than those of manufacturers that were not members of the association.

Broadly, an agreement to exchange information may be found legal when there is not an agreement to set prices, when the actual prices prevailing in the marketplace are not uniform, and when a competitive situation exists in the industry. More specifically, information exchanges are permitted providing (a) they limit price reports to past transactions, (b) they preserve the anonymity of the individual seller, (c) data is made available to buyers as well as sellers, and (d) it is not implied or stated that the prices shared will be made mandatory. Conversely, price exchanges may be unlawful when (a) future prices are reported, (b) competitors are identified, (c) information is withheld from buyers, and (d) discussions are held and recommendations are made with respect to price and production policies.

An example of the legal controversies that continue to surround information sharing can be found in the practice of advisory pricing used by the insurance industry. Advisory pricing is based on extensive information sharing among companies regarding accident risk probabilities for different age and gender categories, statistics for illness and death rates, average costs of different types of policies, claims handling losses, marketing expenditures, and so forth. Using such information, the Insurance Services Office, which serves a substantial number of firms within the industry, proposes advisory rates for different types of insurance policies. These rates are eventually adopted by many companies.

The industry was exempted from restrictions on the sharing of price and cost information by the McCarran-Ferguson Act of 1945. Critics argue that the ability to share such information allows firms to set rates artificially high and that the advisory rate system discourages open competition. While the industry claims no price fixing is taking place, political pressures have grown. Perhaps in response to a recent decision by the state of California to eliminate McCarran-Ferguson exemptions for insurers within that state, the industry has recently decided to stop using advisory rates and to limit the types of information shared.

RESALE PRICE MAINTENANCE AND PRICE ADMINISTRATION

The second major category of regulated price behaviors involves resale price maintenance agreements. These agreements are attempts by manufacturers to control the prices at which their products are resold by wholesalers and/or retailers. They represent a potential form of vertical price fixing. Congress made such agreements legal in 1937, and in 1951 extended coverage to firms that did not sign formal resale agreements (i.e., those that were not voluntary parties to price uniformity within their markets).

Over the years, studies of various industries have produced evidence that laws permitting resale price maintenance had the effect of inhibiting the growth of small retail stores and contributed to the rate of business failure. State courts began striking down fair trade laws (laws passed in individual states permitting resale price maintenance) as unconstitutional. By 1975 the percentage of retail sales covered by fair trade laws had declined to 4 percent from a high of 10 percent in 1960. In that year, Congress made resale price maintenance agreements illegal per se. More recently, in the Monsanto v. Spray-Rite Service Corporation case (1984), the Supreme Court declined to reverse a lower court judgment against Monsanto for having dropped a distributor that had cut prices below those dictated by Monsanto.

Although firms do not have complete control over the prices that middlemen charge for their products, there are ways in which they can influence their distributors to be cooperative in the pricing area. Such attempts at influence are called price administration. Some general guidelines for administering prices should be kept in mind (Dawson, Mayer, and Keith, 1986). Manufacturers are well advised to announce the pricing policies and conditions under which they will and will not sell their products prior to formalizing distributor agreements. If a manufacturer seeks to terminate a distributor for failure to abide by agreed-on conditions, it should do so unilaterally and not at the real or apparent urging of a competing distributor. Beyond refusing to sell to a distributor that will not follow the recommended pricing policies, the manufacturer should avoid coercing the distributor into compliance. Further, nonprice considerations should accompany a decision to terminate a distributor. For instance, the manufacturer might clearly communicate the importance of the distributor providing advertising, promotion, postsale service, and related product support, all of which were presumed when the suggested price was determined. Dropping the distributor can then be explained as a response to the distributor's failure to provide the necessary support services. Alternatively, the distributor is encouraged to charge the suggested price in order to cover the costs of the support services provided. In addition, discounts and rebates should not be made contingent on a distributor complying with the manufacturer's specified price schedule. Also, manufacturers can advertise suggested retail selling prices provided that dealers are not required to comply with the advertised prices and that the advertisements do not significantly misrepresent actual retail selling prices. At the same time, it is permissible to specify resale prices in an agency relationship, such as where the firm is using sales agents to handle its products.

PRICE DISCRIMINATION

One of the most flexible approaches to market-based pricing involves the use of price discrimination, or charging various customers different prices for the same product or service. Also referred to as using price differentials, this represents the third category of price issues that raises legal questions. Because value is subjectively perceived by customers, individual buyers are apt to perceive different amounts of value from a given product. Such perceptual differences provide a rationale for price differentials. While buyers sometimes take the lead by coercing price breaks out of the seller, the greater concern here is with seller-initiated discrimination.

Ideally, a firm would charge each of its customers a different price based on the value perceptions of that customer. Unfortunately, precise assessments of how much value each individual customer receives from a product are difficult to make. A more realistic approach is to make such assessments for larger groups or segments of users, such as senior citizens, business travelers, members of the military, or companies of a particular size. Even here, though, the manager may be hesitant to charge differential prices due to concerns about legal issues.

The Robinson-Patman Act is the principal legislation governing the use of price differentials, and its provisions were discussed earlier. As those provisions suggest, most forms of price discrimination are legal. Examples of types of price discrimination that are generally legal are provided in table 9.1.

As a generalization, price discrimination restrictions do not apply to services,

Table 9.1
Categories and Types of Legal Price Discrimination

Class	Basis of discrimination	Examples
Personal	Buyer's income or earning power	Doctor's fees, royalties paid for use of patented machines, ·professional association dues
Group	Age, sex, military status or student status of buyer	Children's haircuts, ladies days, airline tickets, magazine subscription rates, theater admission charges, senior citizen rates
	Location of buyers	Zone prices ("prices slightly higher west of the Rockies"), in-state vs. out-of-state tuition
	Status of buyers	New magazine subscriptions, quantity discounts to large volume buyers
	Use of product	Railroad rates, public utility rates
Product	Qualities of products Labels of products Product size Peak-off peak services	Deluxe vs. regular models National, private, or unbranded Family, economy, giant size Off-season resort rates, airline excursion rates, evening and holiday telephone rates

Source: D. Watson (1963), *Price Theory* (Boston: Houghton Miffin), 312.

and apply only to those commodities involved in interstate commerce, sold in the same market, and not representing different levels of perceived quality (e.g., premium vs. nonpremium). Even in these cases, the practice must have a negative impact on competitive conditions. In practice, most price differentials actually serve to intensify competition and make markets more efficient. It is quite common, then, to see senior citizens pay less at a restaurant, females pay less at a nightclub, poor people pay less for medical care, and large-volume buyers pay less for purchases of industrial goods. Further, today's legal and regulatory climate is such that a firm should at least consider the merits of charging virtually any distinguishable group of customers a unique price based on their elasticity of demand.

The Justice Department and the Federal Trade Commission, the principal federal statutory bodies charged with enforcing the Robinson-Patman Act, have effectively abstained from initiating price discrimination suits in recent years. As of 1988, the Justice Department had not brought suit under the act since 1963, and the Federal Trade Commission had not since 1980. The suits brought since 1980 have been initiated by business enterprises. Further, the burden of proof is increasingly on the party bringing suit. Of the Robinson-Patman–related suits actually adjudicated, the overwhelming percentage (85.8 percent) were claims of injury under the price discrimination provision. Table 9.2 provides statistics on Robinson-Patman cases and outcomes over the past few decades.

Table 9.2
Legal Actions Brought under the Robinson-Patman Act and Resulting Decisions, 1961-1986

Plaintiff Action Under Robinson-Patman	Frequency	Percent
Price Discrimination (Section 2A)	332	85.8
Illegal Brokerage (Section 2C)	19	4.9
Paid for Services or Facilities (Section 2D)	3	0.8
Provided Services or Facilities (Section 2E)	12	3.1
Induced or Received a Discriminatory Price (Section 2F)	6	1.6
Other	15	3.9
Totals	387	100.0
Not Classifiable	133	

Court Decisions	Frequency	Percent
Won by Plaintiff	71	18.3
Not in Interstate Commerce	32	8.3
Good Faith Defense	20	5.2
No Competition	22	5.7
No Harm to Competition	36	9.3
Unlike Grade and Quality	8	2.1
Frivolous Complaint	5	1.3
Failure to Establish Action	129	33.3
Other	64	16.5
Totals	387	100.0

Source: N. E. Marks and N. S. Inlow (1988), "Price Discrimination and Its Impact on Small Business," Journal of Consumer Marketing (Winter), 34.

During this time period, defendants have been acquitted in over 80 percent of the cases brought. A third of these acquittals occurred because the plaintiffs were unable to establish a cause of action (i.e. insufficient evidence as to matters of fact). It is unclear how many price discrimination claims have been settled out of court. Similarly, the extent to which businesses have altered their pricing policies in view of potential suits cannot be established.

Example of a Price Discrimination Case

Falls City Industries, Inc., is a brewery based in Lousiville, Kentucky, supplying beer to a number of markets. A few years ago, however, its pricing policies came under fire when one of its wholesale distributors charged the company with price discrimination.

Falls City's distribution channels include wholesalers in both Henderson County, Kentucky, and Vanderburgh County, Indiana, which are separated only by a state line. The two cities of Henderson, Kentucky, and Evansville, Indiana, are less than ten miles apart and connected by a four-lane interstate highway. They are considered to be part of the same metropolitan area and geographic market.

At the time, Henderson County's sole distributor of Falls City products was Dawson Springs, Inc., while Vanco Beverage, Inc., was the sole distributor in Vanderburgh. However, Falls City charged Vanco and other Indiana distributors 10 to 30 percent more for its beer than it charged Dawson and other Kentucky distributors. As a result, both retailers and consumers in Indiana were forced to pay higher prices.

Although Falls City's pricing policies had left it open to suit under the Robinson-Patman Act, the brewery felt it was faced with little choice. Indiana state law required that brewers sell their products to all Indiana wholesalers at the same price, so Falls City could not simply charge Vanco the lower Kentucky price. Similarly, if the brewery charged all its Indiana wholesalers the same low price, it would lose gross dollar volume in that state to its competitors.

Raising Kentucky's prices statewide to match those in Indiana would amount to lost sales in Kentucky. If the brewery chose to raise prices only in Kentucky's Henderson County, then Dawson Springs would undoubtedly raise Robinson-Patman claims. In short, Falls City was stuck between a rock and a hard place.

Vanco eventually filed a price discrimination suit against Falls City, charging that the company was using unfair pricing practices. Falls City argued that its pricing structure was a necessary response to market conditions in the two states. The case went to the Supreme Court, which in 1983 ruled in favor of Falls City. The decision stated that charging different prices for the same product was permissible in this case because it was meeting competition in good faith.

Predatory Pricing

An alternative form of price discrimination (and potentially of price fixing) is predatory pricing. This involves setting prices so low as to either force competitors into line with the predator's preferred price or drive competitors out of the market altogether. Such policies assume that whatever profits the predatory firm foregoes will ultimately be compensated by the higher profits attending a less competitive market. Ordinarily predatory pricing occurs when a firm reduces prices in one selected geographic area and offsets these revenue losses with the higher prices and margins charged in other market areas.

The Supreme Court case of the *Standard Oil Company of New Jersey v. the United States* (1911) found that Standard Oil had violated the Sherman Act when the oil trust slashed prices in geographic areas with the intent of damaging its rivals and inducing them to accept a merger with Standard. In the *United States v. American Tobacco Company* (1911) case, the Court held that American Tobacco acted with monopolistic intent when it priced established brands at levels below cost, in fact sometimes charging a price close to zero (plus the tax on cigarettes).

In recent years, most cases of predatory pricing have involved companies whose superior efficiencies and management performance have prompted their less successful rivals to claim injury. When the courts have examined such claims, they have sought to establish the existence of predatory intent and a demonstration that the disputed prices yield returns below average variable or marginal cost.

Geographic Pricing

A related practice that touches on both price discrimination and price fixing is called geographic pricing. This usually involves single-point pricing schedules based on the buyer's geographic location. Generally, a seller will establish a base point from which products are shipped and then assign a delivery cost to selected destinations. Some customers will pay relatively more and others relatively less than the actual costs of transporting the products to them. However, at the point of purchase, there is no price differential and thus no discrimination. Multiple zone pricing schedules may be suspect when there is evidence that competing firms have colluded in establishing the zones. The issue of collusion would bring such pricing systems into violation of Section 1 of the Sherman Act (conspiracy in restraint of trade) and Section 5 of the Federal Trade Commission Act (unfair competition). The courts have not addressed the legality of base-point systems per se. It is the collective establishment and enforcement of such systems that has warranted attention. In *Federal Trade Commission v. Cement Institute* (1948), the Supreme Court held that the institute had attempted to enforce a pricing scheme among cement producers by firing employees, driving down prices in the markets of price cutters, and distributing freight schedule books. Even in the absence of such visible indications of collusion, the courts may find that a firm-specific pricing policy that consciously parallels those of rivals constitutes unfair competition.

DECEPTIVE PRACTICES AND PRICE

The fourth category of price-related actions that raise legal or regulatory concerns falls under the heading of deceptive practices. A mainstay in the area of product advertising is the use of price promotions. Under the regulations of the Fair Packaging and Labeling Act (1982), sellers must be careful to truthfully represent the various aspects of their price promotions. For example, price surveys that favorably compare a seller's prices to those of competitors must accurately detail the actual product prices compared. The seller may not use such surveys to create the inference that the survey applies to his entire, store-wide range of products.

When using cents-off price labeling (to imply the product is "on sale"), the Federal Trade Commission has specified that (1) the product must have been sold at the regular price recently, (2) the price reduction must be genuine, (3) the regular price must be prominently displayed on the shelf or on the package, (4) the frequency of the promotion must not exceed three months in a twelve month period, and (5) sales must not exceed more than fifty percent of the year's volume.

Further, "introductory offers" must involve products that are in fact new to the market. Such offers cannot exceed six months in duration, and the seller must intend to price the product at a more customary price for an ongoing period after the introduction. Also, if a product is advertised under an economy package label, the product must be available in at least one other size, the savings must be confined to that package size, and they must represent a real savings of at least 5 percent relative to other same-brand packages.

In general, price savings must be real. They must involve a savings relative to the standard price or, if already discounted, the most recent price at which the product has been sold.

ETHICAL ASPECTS OF PRICING

Should a pharmaceutical company charge an elderly person a higher price for a particular drug than is charged all other age groups, assuming the elderly person has a greater need for the drug? Many people would find such a practice distasteful, if not unconscionable. And yet free enterprise economies operate most efficiently when customers compete amongst themselves for goods and pay prices that reflect their willingness and ability to buy. Prices ultimately determine how the resources of a society will be allocated.

As a result, pricing practices that are perfectly legal often raise complex ethical questions for the concerned manager. Unethical actions are those that appear to be inconsistent with what one feels to be right. Unfortunately, there tends to be little agreement among those in the business community as to just what is and what is not beyond the pale when determining pricing policy. What agreement exists seems to be confined to below-cost predatory pricing practices, price fixing, and exploiting buyers who are in a particularly vulnerable position.

A major study in this area identified twenty key practices that raise ethical issues in pricing (Kehoe, 1985). Among these were (a) price discrimination with smaller accounts; (b) having less competitive prices for those buyers who use a firm as their only supplier; (c) providing gifts, prizes, or purchase volume incentives to some customers and not others; (d) using a firm's economic power to force premium prices on a buyer; and (e) adding higher markups to products sold by a franchisor or a franchisee. All of these represent potential forms of price discrimination that could be legal (see also table 9.3).

In a separate series of research projects (Dubinsky, Berkowitz, and Rudelius, 1980; Dubinsky and Gwin, 1981), the researchers found evidence of extensive disagreement regarding the acceptability of tactics such as those in table 9.3. A survey of sales managers and salespeople found a large minority of respondents concerned with the ethics of these tactics, while a comparison of salespeople and purchasing personnel indicated the two groups differed significantly in their assessment of the ethical nature of every one of eleven business practices.

Certain conditions tend to foster ethically difficult pricing behavior (Kehoe, 1985). For instance, when an industry has considerable excess production capacity and has an oligopolistic structure, pressure is strong to take advantage of questionable pricing opportunities. The same is true when the offerings of competitors are fairly homogeneous, or undifferentiated, and when prices are determined on an individual job basis. In terms of company operations, practices that raise ethical concerns are more likely when profit considerations are paramount in a firm's competitive posture, when management is perceived as indifferent to pricing ethics, when employees come into regular contact with their counterparts in competing firms, and when ethical rules are not well specified and their compliance provisions are lax.

At the root of many of these ethical dilemmas is the fundamental nature of price competition. The idea that customers pay in accord with the value they receive goes part and parcel with the efficient operation of a free enterprise system. The open bazaar from times past and the flea market of today provide cases in point. In these competitive markets, every transaction is negotiated, sometimes resulting in considerable differences in the final prices paid.

However, modern times find a strong egalitarian impulse among many managers. That is, they feel all customers should be treated equally and charged a uniform price. In so doing, managers perceive themselves to be acting fairly and believe customers will share that perception. Others counter that two customers paying the same price but receiving differing amounts of gain or benefit are not being treated equally. Ultimately, then, decisions regarding

Table 9.3
Twenty Pricing Practices That Raise Ethical Questions

1. determining a fair price that meets corporate objectives while not taking advantage of consumers
2. altering the quality and/or quantity of merchandise without changing the price
3. practicing price discrimination with smaller accounts
4. using multiple pricing deals at the retail level
5. excessively marking up products that are given as premiums
6. using lower quality merchandise for end-of-month sales
7. adding high markups to products sold by a franchisor to a franchisee
8. engaging in price fixing
9. having less competitive prices or terms of sale for those buyers who use a firm as their only supplier
10. providing gifts, prizes, or purchase volume incentive bonuses to some customers and not to others
11. obtaining information on a competitor's price quotation in order to requote or rebid
12. using a firm's economic power to force premium prices on a buyer
13. using reciprocity practices
14. the situation of a manufacturer printing a suggested retail price (list price) on a product or its package with the knowledge the retailer does not intend to sell at the suggested retail price but intends to mark over the price to give the impression the item has been marked down - the list price should be the price at which an item is usually and customarily sold according to the FTC in a case examining the meaning of list
15. the practice of pricing branded products higher than generic products - notes that "no ethic has been determined" regarding the pricing practices of branded versus generic products
16. using special price codes (as in automobile dealerships with used cars) so that the consumer cannot easily compare prices
17. failing to put the price on the product or to post it at the point of purchase, as is often done in the case of retailer's use of UPCs
18. bribery of purchasers to cause them to accept higher prices on items in the purchase order
19. failure of retailers to pass on to consumers discounts to which they are entitled
20. the practice of psychological pricing (e.g. intending that the consumer will perceive $299 as being closer to $200 rather than $300)

Source: W. J. Kehoe (1985), "Ethics, Price Fixing, and the Management of Price Strategy," inM arketing Ethics: Guidelines for Managers, ed. G. Laczniak and P. Murphy (Lexington, Mass: Lexington Books), 71-84.

whether a pricing practice is ethical or not will rarely be simple or clear-cut, depending instead on the value system of individual managers.

SUMMARY

The legal environment in which firms do business has important implications for pricing decisions. While managers must be careful to observe the current legislation in the area, considerable pricing flexibility is possible. The Sherman Act, Clayton Act, Federal Trade Commission Act, and Robinson-Patman Act contain both explicit and ambiguous provisions. While some actions are illegal per se, such as formal agreements to restrain trade, the vast majority of creative pricing practices available to managers tend to be legal.

The chapter identified four major categories of pricing activities that raise legal concerns. These included (a) price fixing and the related issues of parallel pricing and exchange of price information; (b) resale price maintenance and the related practice of price administration; (c) price discrimination and the related behaviors of predatory pricing and geographic pricing; and (d) deceptive price promotions, including misleading price advertisements, cents-off deals, and introductory offers. Of these, the areas offering the greatest regulatory leeway as well as the most room for creativity are price administration and the use of price differentials.

Most important, a review of the current legislation suggests that most attempts at value-based pricing are not illegal and may serve to improve rather than damage the competitive environment. Recent years have actually witnessed a liberalization in the regulatory climate. There has been a significant decline in the suits brought under the Robinson-Patman Act, and in the great majority of cases adjudicated, the defendant firm has been acquitted. Moreover, the burden of proof seems to be increasingly shifting from the defendant to the plaintiff.

The chapter also examined the ethical aspects of pricing decisions. Many apparently legal tactics are avoided because of their ethical implications. A variety of ethically controversial tactics were identified, with evidence suggesting widespread disagreement regarding how acceptable each was in practice. It is unlikely that most of the ethical questions in pricing will ever be resolved, at least as long as managers operate in a competitive, free-enterprise environment.

REFERENCES

Dawson, L. E., M. L. Mayer, and J. Keith, "Resale Price Maintenance: Changing Perspectives and Future Directions." *Journal of Consumer Marketing* (Fall 1986).

Dubinsky, A. J., and J. M. Gwin, "Business Ethics: Buyers and Sellers." *Journal of Purchasing and Materials Management* 17 (Winter 1986): 9-16.

Dubinsky, A. J., E. N. Berkowitz, and W. Rudelius, "Ethical Problems of Field Sales Personnel." *MSU Business Topics* (Summer 1980): 11-16.

Kehoe, W. J., "Ethics, Price Fixing, and the Management of Price Strategy." In *Marketing Ethics: Guidelines for Managers*, edited by G. R. Laczniak and P. E. Murphy. Lexington, Mass.: Lexington Books, 1985, 71-84.

Marks, N. E., and N. S. Inlow, "Price Discrimination and Its Impact on Small Business." *Journal of Consumer Marketing* (Winter 1988).

Posch, R. J., *What Every Manager Needs to Know About Marketing and the Law.* New York: McGraw-Hill, 1984.

Stern, L. W., and T. L. Eovaldi. *Legal Aspects of Marketing Strategy.* Englewood Cliffs, N.J.: Prentice-Hall, 1984.

10

COMPUTERS AS AN AID IN PRICING

CAPABILITIES OF ELECTRONIC DATA PROCESSING

Information is the essence of the price management function in organizations. Effective pricing programs depend on a timely flow of data regarding customer elasticity, product profitability, market trends, competitor pricing, discounts taken, distributor margins, and a variety of other strategic areas. These information requirements become more critical and complex as organizations confront faster rates of change, more hostility, and increasing complexity in their competitive environments.

The manager's ability to recognize and satisfy information needs has been considerably enhanced through advances in electronic data processing (EDP) technology. As a result, the pricing function is able to serve a more proactive and strategic role in the marketing programs of firms than has historically been the case. Those charged with making pricing decisions can help the firm more quickly identify and capitalize on new marketplace opportunities while rapidly adjusting to changing threats.

Unfortunately, computer technology is often resisted by those managers lacking either the technical literacy or analytical marketing skills necessary to appreciate the computer's potential. Also, the rapid rate of change and obsolescence in this technology has been an incentive to move slowly in its adoption. Further, concerns about computers replacing or dominating managerial judgment may inhibit the willingness of some managers to purchase available hardware and software products and services.

The purpose of this chapter is to evaluate how computers are being used and can be used by those responsible for price management. The primary focus will be on the personal computer (PC), as it provides virtually all of the capabilities the manager requires. Computer hardware and software are approached not as a source of pricing decisions, but rather as fairly simple yet powerful tools for helping managers make more intelligent and creative use of the price variable.

THE LIMITED COMPUTER SKILLS OF MANAGERS

The development and acceptance of the personal computer offers the pricing manager immediate electronic data processing capabilities. The ability of computers to store, retrieve, and manipulate vast quantities of data at the touch of a key makes it possible for a manager to run multiple iterations and evaluate a variety of scenarios instantly, spending the balance of time reviewing the results. The profit and revenue implications of new product prices, price changes, and the relationships between items in a line (cross-product elasticity) may be analyzed and the quality of decisions enhanced with the use of a personal computer.

Yet the evidence suggests that application of the computer to marketing-related decisions is happening fairly slowly. The results of a study of marketing managers performed by one of the authors (Morris, Burns, and Avila, 1989) found that these managers were open-minded toward computer technology, but also that they were not a proactive force pushing for innovative approaches to integrating the technology. Further, managers typically were not well acquainted with currently available computer technology. Spreadsheets and word processing packages were identified as far and away the areas of greatest familiarity. Even in these areas, however, less than one-fourth indicated that they had extensive knowledge. The computer skills managers do possess are often gained informally. Three-quarters of the managers were self-taught, half received lessons from colleagues or friends, and approximately 40 percent received formal on-the-job training and training from computer vendors.

Marketers' decidedly limited familiarity with and adoption of available computer technology exists despite the belief by almost three-quarters of the respondents that computers have become a necessity in marketing management. In addition, 70 percent indicated that computer competency is a key consideration when recruiting and selecting a new college graduate for a staff position in marketing. It would seem that the increasing importance of computer usage combined with the limited computer expertise of marketers offers savvy pricing managers a significant opportunity.

BUILDING A PRICING DATA BASE

In years past, if a manager wanted pricing data this usually meant submitting a formal request to the finance, accounting, or MIS (management information systems) departments. Several problems are inherent in such an arrangement. The information requested is often not the information received; it may arrive in an incomprehensible form or in the wrong units of analysis; it may be placed last in the queue, receiving attention several weeks after the request. Other departments may resent sharing "their" information or may not consider other departments' requests as legitimate. In many instances, information needed for pricing is simply not maintained by any of these departments in part or in full.

The value of the personal computer is that it allows the manager to timely receive desired information in a personally specified format. The development of a well-designed pricing data base is the first step in taking advantage of the potential of the personal computer. The most critical inputs are monthly or quarterly figures for sales, price levels, and competitor prices covering the past three to five years. A more comprehensive list of items useful to include in the pricing data base is available in table 10.1. Some of this information may already be available from internal company records, although a system must be put in place for regularly collecting, adjusting, and storing the numbers.

Consider the case of the marketer at an international plastics company who wishes to track something as seemingly basic as average price paid per unit per customer by sales representative in five territories on a quarterly basis. Where does such information originate? The office of the controller might be a logical

Table 10.1
Items to Be Included in a Pricing Data Base

> Product
> Date
> List Price
> Sale Price
> Units Sold
> Units Returned
> Customer Name
> Sales Representative
> Territory
> Quantity Discount Allowed
> Trade Discount Allowed
> Cash Discount Allowed
> Cost of Goods Sold
> Direct Fixed Annual Product Costs
> Quantity Discount Taken
> Trade Discount Taken
> Cash Discount Taken
> Trade-In Allowances
> Sales Commissions
> Other Variable Costs
> Gross Margins
> Rebates Allowed
> Rebates Taken
> Coupons Allowed
> Coupons Accepted
> Competitor's Name
> Competitor's Product's Name
> Competitor's Product's List Price
> Competitor's Product's Sale Price
> Competitor's Units Sold

first step, as the controller function is concerned with all information that has an impact on the company's financial statements. However, for financial statement purposes, the information must be summarized. For pricing purposes, the data needs to be in its basic form. Data such as unit price, order size, and customer name, delineated on an original invoice, may only be available from the controller on a divisional level. Unless the controller can provide the data found on the invoices summarized in its basic form, copies of the invoices may have to be obtained from the accounting or shipping departments, and the data reentered to fit the format of the pricing data base.

The office of the controller may also provide information on commissions paid. Again, however, the data would probably be on an aggregate basis. For sales per representative, the payroll department may be of some assistance, assuming the commission records are not lumped with salary payments. Another concern involves the assignment of territories. What if the sales representative generated sales in more than one territory? Or what if the buying company has offices in more than one territory? Neither the office of the controller nor the payroll department would necessarily maintain this data. The sales department may have to be contacted for records of this sort.

Unfortunately, no one source within the company is likely to have all the desired information. In this example, the information necessary to determine the average price paid per unit per customer by sales representative in five territories on a quarterly basis requires information from the office of the controller, the accounting department, the payroll department, and the sales department. Pricing data bases are adaptations of a wide range of informaton from sources both within and outside the company.

Common software packages for personal computer database management include the Ashton-Tate series of dBase II, dBase III, and dBase III Plus and Microrim's R:BASE. Lotus's Symphony and 1-2-3 also offer some database management capabilities. Before purchasing software, each package's interface

Table 10.2
Pricing Data Base Example

Product Number	Date MM DD YY	List Price	Sales Price	Quantity Ordered	Customer ID	Quantity Discounts Allowed %	Trade Discounts Allowed %
700241	11 06 89	9.00	9.00	500	52492	0	30
220300	11 06 89	13.26	13.01	2300	84319	10	30
944091	11 06 89	4.50	4.33	150	67903	0	20
700241	11 06 89	9.00	8.97	750	15967	10	0
243016	11 06 89	257.60	235.00	970	43904	15	0
464199	11 06 89	26.50	26.50	1500	26594	·10	15

*Total for Product

capabilities must be considered. The spreadsheet and database software should have translation compatibility. Lotus 1-2-3, the spreadsheet software illustrated in this chapter, offers the ability to transfer data between Lotus's 1-2-3 and Symphony and Ashton-Tate's dBase II, dBase III, and dBase III Plus, among other packages.

The information to be included, as well as the format and setup of the data base, must be determined before the first record is entered. Time invested on the front end organizing the data base will be returned many times over once the system is implemented. The database effort does not end with the initial design and setup, however. Once established, the data base must be updated with relevant information on a timely basis. Responsibility for implementing the scheduled updates must be assigned and changes monitored. Care must be taken to ensure that new information is in a format comparable to the installed data. Also, the information must be continually tested to ensure that the data included in the data base is that necessary for good pricing decisions. Has a competitor changed company focus and left a market? Should sales data for this company still be maintained?

A sample data base is shown in table 10.2. Data is maintained on the product's list and sale prices, the data and quantity ordered, the customer, the sales representative and territory, and discounts allowed and taken. Cost information, including unit variable costs and the direct annual fixed costs for the product, is also incorporated. Information drawn from this data base can be manipulated to answer questions regarding a product's unit sales, price effectiveness, customer price sensitivity, contribution margin analysis, or other pertinent areas. Standard managerial reports can be generated on a periodic basis from the data base program to summarize information in such areas and illustrate trends.

It is important to note that the information included in the data base is in raw form; little is available in terms of formulas or quantitative features from

Cash Discounts Allowed %	Sales Rep	Territory	Quantity Discounts Taken %	Trade Discounts Taken %	Cash Discounts Taken %	Variable Costs Per Unit	Direct* Annual Fixed
2	2920	17	0	30	0	6	1500000
2	7937	26	10	30	2	4.27	14600000
2	7937	26	0	30	2	1.35	1200000
2	1601	3	10	0	0	6	1500000
2	4418	51	15	0	2	166	7680000
2	3502	35	10	15	2	7.35	2750000

most database software. Rather, this software is most efficient in organizing and managing raw data. However, with an efficiently organized data base upon which to draw, the pricing manager can extract specific pieces of information and use alternative software for more sophisticated analysis. Also, when creating a pricing data base, it is helpful to enter raw data in numeric form. Alternatively, the use of words creates the possibility of variability in spelling, plurals, and capitals, which may affect the usefulness of the data base. For instance, the same product could be entered as light bulb, light bulbs, Light bulb, and Lite bulb and mistakenly be considered as four different products. Assigning a product number eliminates many of these problems.

USING ELECTRONIC SPREADSHEETS

Much of the data manipulation necessary for price analysis can be accomplished with electronic spreadsheets. In fact, data bases can be completely created on spreadsheets. Alternatively, information can be "downloaded" from a database program (such as dBase) and input into a spreadsheet program.

A computer spreadsheet is nothing more than a matrix worksheet consisting of lettered columns and numbered rows. Columns and/or rows of data may be added, subtracted, multiplied, and divided. Also, the manager can display only those columns or rows of data important to his or her analysis, and effectively "hide" the rest. Spreadsheet packages of value to the pricing manager include Lotus 1-2-3, Lotus Symphony, Microsoft Excel, Microsoft Multiplan, and Lotus Visicalc. As Lotus 1-2-3 is currently the industry standard, it is used in the examples presented in this chapter.

Lotus 1-2-3's release 2 offers a worksheet which includes 8,192 numbered rows and 256 columns designated by a letter beginning with A in the leftmost column and ending with IV to the right. An example of a blank worksheet is shown in table 10.3. Data can be entered into cells, which are defined by the intersection of the column letter and the row number. This intersection is called an address. For example, the cell in the top left corner of the worksheet has an address of A1. The manager may move around the worksheet using the arrow keys found on the computer's keyboard. Information can be manually entered as labels for descriptive purposes, numbers for use in calculations, or formulas for manipulation of the numbers. For those unfamiliar with the software, documentation is included with the software that describes the functions available in 1-2-3. In addition, supplemental texts, such as the series published by Que Corporation, are available in most bookstores and offer more comprehensive explanation.

An example of a spreadsheet with actual pricing data can be found in table 10.4. In this worksheet, the average price per unit charged has been determined for a particular product for all sales, by territory, by sales representative, and by customer. The information necessary for these calculations was taken from a data base similar to that illustrated in table 10.2, and is found at the top of the

Table 10.3
Example of a Blank Spreadsheet

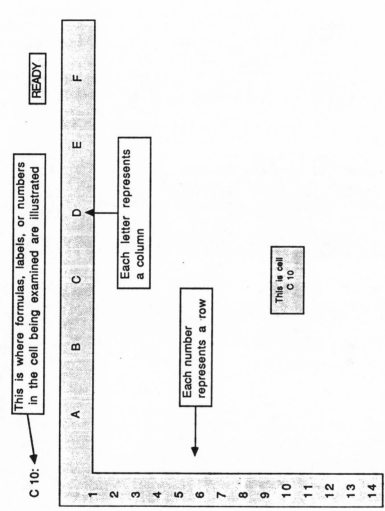

Table 10.4
Sample Spreadsheet with Pricing Data

	A	B	C	D	E	F
1	Simple Average Price Worksheet					
2						
3						
4						
5						
6	PRODUCT	SALES	QUANTITY	CUSTOMER	SALES	TERRITORY
7	NUMBER	PRICE	ORDERED	ID	REP	
8	-------	-----	--------	--------	-----	-------
9	700241	8.97	750	15967	1601	3
10	700241	8.97	1500	15967	1601	3
11	700241	8.99	750	24607	1943	3
12	700241	9.00	500	52492	2920	17
13	700241	9.00	500	52492	2920	17
14						
15						
16						
17	AVERAGE PRICE PER UNIT					
18	CHARGED FOR PRODUCT NUMBER 700241					
19	------------------------------					
20	OVERALL		$8.9813			
21	TERRITORY 3		$8.9750			
22	TERRITORY 17		$9.0000			
23	SALES REP 1601		$8.9700			
24	SALES REP 1943		$8.9900			
25	SALES REP 2920		$9.0000			
26	CUSTOMER 15967		$8.9700			
27	CUSTOMER 24607		$8.9900			
28	CUSTOMER 52492		$9.0000			
29						
30						
31						
32						
33						
34						
35						
36						
37						
38						
39						
40						

worksheet, in rows 6 through 13, columns A through F. Such a rectangle may be described in Lotus 1-2-3 by listing the top left cell and bottom right cell in the matrix, with two periods between them, or A6..F13. Based on this data, the spreadsheet has been programmed to make a number of useful calculations. The calculation titles and formulas are found below the data in cells A17..B28.

To determine the average price per unit overall (which turns out to be $8.9813), a formula was entered into cell B20. This formula calculates the total sales in dollars by the total amount of units sold, and appears as $(+B9*C9+B10*C10+B11*C11+B12*C12+B13*C13)/@sum(C9..C13)$. Note that the cell address in which each number is found replaces the actual number in the formula. This enables the formula to dynamically calculate correctly as the data changes. Therefore, as new information becomes available, only the data must be updated. The formulas will automatically reflect the numbers entered into the referenced cells. The formulas for the average price per unit by territory, sales representative, and customer follow the same pattern, but include only the cells with relevant data. Individual cell entries are delineated in table 10.5.

Once the spreadsheet is created, the real power of a software program such as Lotus 1-2-3 becomes apparent. The drudgery of generating countless numbers of calculations is removed. More importantly, the manager can evaluate an

Table 10.5
Cell Entries for a Sample Spreadsheet with Pricing Data

A1: 'Simple Average Price Worksheet
A2:
A6: PRODUCT
B6: SALES
C6: QUANTITY
D6: CUSTOMER
E6: SALES
F6: TERRITORY
A7: NUMBER
B7: PRICE
C7: ORDERED
D7: ID
E7: REP
A8: \-
B8: \-
C8: \-
D8: \-
E8: \-
F8: \-
A9: 700241
B9: 8.97
C9: 750
D9: 15967
E9: 1601
F9: 3
A10: 700241
B10: 8.97
C10: 1500
D10: 15967
E10: 1601
F10: 3
A11: 700241
B11: 8.99
C11: 750
D11: 24607
E11: 1943
F11: 3

A12: 700241
B12: 9
C12: 500
D12: 52492
E12: 2920
F12: 17
A13: 700241
B13: 9
C13: 500
D13: 52492
E13: 2920
F13: 17
A17: 'AVERAGE PRICE PER UNIT
A18: 'CHARGED FOR PRODUCT #700241
A19: \-
B19: \-
C19:
A20: 'OVERALL
B20: (+B9*C9+B10*C10+B11*C11
     +B12*C12+B13*C13)/@SUM(C9..C13)
A21: 'TERRITORY 3
B21: (+B9*C9+B10*C10+B11*C11)/@SUM
     (C9..C11)
A22: 'TERRITORY 17
B22: (+B12*C12+B13*C13)/@SUM
     (C12..C13)
A23: 'SALES REP 1601
B23: (+B9*C9+B10*C10)/@SUM
     (C9..C10)
A24: 'SALES REP 2920
B24: (+B11*C11)/C11
A25: 'SALES REP 2920
     (+B12*C12+B13*C13)/@SUM
     (C12//C13)
A26: 'CUSTOMER 15967
B26: (+B9*C9+B10*C10)/@SUM
     (C9..C10)
A27: 'CUSTOMER 24607
B27: (+B11*C11)/C11
A28: 'CUSTOMER 52492
B28: (+B12*C12+B13*C13)/@SUM
     (C12..C13)

endless number of scenarios virtually on command. Depending on the spreadsheet in question, managers can instantaneously evaluate such everyday pricing questions as

What if our variable costs were 5 percent lower?

What if we raise price 5 percent?

What if our customers are assumed to be somewhat more price sensitive?

This capability will be demonstrated later in the chapter.

BUILDING MODELS

The manager's ability to understand price and its relationship to other decision variables is facilitated through the use of models. Model building represents an attempt by the manager to reduce the complex world into more simplified relationships. It is not uncommon for managers to intuitively formulate hypotheses or "best guesses" regarding how two variables are related, typically based on their previous experiences. Models are more formalized attempts to specify those relationships, often in terms of cause and effect.

As an example of a simpler pricing model, one might propose that monthly sales of product X are a function of the average price charged for it over the past four weeks. Or, sales of product X may be a function of the difference between the price of product X and the price of product Y (possibly another product in the line or a competitor's product). The percentage of customers taking advantage of a particular quantity discount might be a function of current economic conditions, such as the rate of inflation.

More complex pricing models include those proposing nonlinear relationships between variables and those involving more than two variables. For instance, the impact of price rebates on unit sales might be hypothesized to increase exponentially with the size of the rebate. Or the impact of a particular price cut on unit sales might be significantly greater than it would be if accompanied by an increase in advertising expenditures.

Computers have revolutionized the ability of managers to formulate and test models. Again, in the pricing area much of this can be accomplished with a personal computer. Simple models using electronic spreadsheets can be specified. The formula function available with spreadsheets permits the analyst to calculate averages, indexes, percentage changes, and similar calculations involving relationships between or among variables. More sophisticated analysis generally necessitates the use of statistical packages, a number of which are available for use with the PC.

PERFORMING PRICE ANALYSIS WITH COMPUTERS

To better appreciate the value of computers in pricing, four applications are described in the following pages. Each of these brings together a data base, a spreadsheet, and a simple model. A fundamental knowledge of Lotus 1-2-3 is assumed. In addition to a description of the models involved, each spreadsheet will be shown as it would appear on the computer screen, and the information entered in each cell is delineated.

The first application demonstrates the impact that various prices will have on the sales of a newly designed product and what percentage of the market must be captured to break even at each possible price. The second application calculates customer price sensitivity and the impact that price changes may have on sales. The third application examines volume changes that must result from a given change in price. The final application is more comprehensive, and builds on Applications Two and Three. Cost-volume-profit analysis is performed to determine if the price change proposed in Application Three is desirable.

Application One: Break-Even Analysis

The Everlight Corporation, a manufacturer of fluorescent light bulbs, was first introduced in chapter 6. Management was concerned with setting an initial price for the firm's new 72-inch fluorescent lamp that burns 50 usage hours longer and uses 10 percent less energy than available lamps. One of the key questions confronting the firm concerns the minimum price that must be charged to achieve break even.

The information provided in chapter 6 included Everlight's variable and fixed costs, the competitor's price, and the total size of the market. Using Lotus 1-2-3, this information can be entered into a spreadsheet for use in calculating contribution margin, break-even units, and required market share to achieve break even. Table 10.6 provides an illustration of the spreadsheet, while table 10.7 provides a listing of the actual cell inputs necessary to produce the desired calculations.

As the underlying purpose of this spreadsheet is to assess the viability of different unit prices, the various prices should be specified in the top row. The proposed prices do not need to be inserted manually; 1-2-3 has the ability to enter them. This may be accomplished by delineating an incremental price change to be added to a base value. Assuming that the price charged will be no less than the total variable cost figure, the variable cost may be considered the base value. Therefore, a formula that adds the incremental price change (see cell D13) to the variable cost figure may be entered in cell C5, the first cell to be used in the row for proposed prices. Moving one cell to the right to cell D5, a formula can be entered that adds the incremental price change to the amount in the cell immediately to the left (C5). This formula may then be copied from D5 to D6, D7, and beyond.

Please note that the formula must recognize that the incremental price change will always be found in cell D13 (an absolute reference), but the amount to which the incremental price change will be added will be found in the cell to the left of the current cell, which is a relative reference. 1-2-3's default is a relative reference. That is, unless specified, 1-2-3 will assume that the formula addresses should be automatically adjusted to correspond to the address into which it was copied. The command to tell 1-2-3 to reference absolutely is a dollar sign ($) inserted before the cell address. A relative reference requires no additional command. Therefore, a dollar sign should be inserted in front of both the D and the 13 in the formula, and the other cell referenced in the

Table 10.6
Computer Worksheet, Everlight Corporation, Implications of Various Prices

	A	B	C	D	E	F
1						
2						
3	Everlight Corporation					
4						
5	Unit Price		$7.00	$8.00	$9.00	$10.00
6						
7	Unit Contribution Margin		$1.00	$2.00	$3.00	$4.00
8						
9	Breakeven Units		1,500,000	750,000	500,000	375,000
10						
11	BE Market Share %		30.00	15.00	10.00	7.50
12						
13	Incremental Price Change			$1.00		
14						
15	Variable Costs:					
16	Manufacturing		$6			
17			- - -			
18	Total Variable Costs:			$6		
19				===		
20	Annual Fixed Costs:					
21	Plant	1,000,000				
22	Administrative OH	200,000				
23	Sales/Distribution OH	300,000				
24		- - - - - - - - -				
25	Total Annual Fixed Costs:		$1,500,000			
26						
27	Market Size (Units)		5,000,000			
28						
29						
30						
31						
32						
33						
34						
35						
36						
37						

Table 10.7
Cell Entries, Everlight Corporation, Implications of Various Prices

```
A1:
A2:
A3:    'Everlight Corporation
A5:    'Unit Price
C5:    +$D$18+$D$13
D5:    +C5+$D$13
E5:    +D5+$D$13
F5:    +E5+$D$13
G5:    +F5+$D$13
H5:    +G5+$D$13
A7:    'Unit Contribution Margin
C7:    +C5-$D$18
D7:    +D5-$D$18
E7:    +E5-$D$18
F7:    +F5-$D$18
G7:    +G5-$D$18
H7:    +H5-$D$18
A9:    'Breakeven Units
C9:    +$D$25/C7
D9:    +$D$25/D7
E9:    +$D$25/E7
F9:    +$D$25/F7
G9:    +$D$25/G7
H9:    +$D$25/H7
A11:   'BE Market Share %
C11:   (+C9/$D$27)*100
D11:   (+D9/$D$27)*100
E11:   (+E9/$D$27)*100
F11:   (+F9/$D$27)*100
G11:   (+G9/$D$27)*100
H11:   (+F9/$D$27)*100
A13:   'Incremental Price Change
D13:   U 1
A15:   ' Variable Costs:
A16:   ' Manufacturing
C16:   U 6
C17:   '      ---
A18:   ' Total Variable Costs:
D18:   +C16
D19:   '    ===
A20:   ' Annual Fixed Costs:
A21:   ' Plant
C21:   U  7000000/7
A22:   ' Administrative OH
C22:   U 200000
A23:   ' Sales/Distribution OH
C23:   U 300000
C24:   \ -
A25:   ' Total Annual Fixed Costs:
D25:   @SUM(C23..C21)
D26:   \ =
A27:   ' Market Size (Units)
D27:   U 5000000
```

formula should be entered plainly. For cell D5, then, the formula to be entered is +C5+$D$13.

The unit contribution margins found in row 7 may be calculated by a formula that subtracts the total variable costs summed in cell D18 from each individual price located in row 5. Again, cell D18 must be referenced absolutely and the individual prices relatively, resulting in an entry for cell C7 of +C5-$D$18, which may be copied across row 7.

To determine the units necessary to sell to break even, the total fixed costs summed in cell D25 must be divided by the contribution margin for each unit, found in row 7. These formulas are entered in row 9. For example, +$D$25/C7 is the formula placed in cell C9. The market share percentage that must be captured to break even may then be determined by dividing the break-even units for each price already calculated in row 11 by the total market size in units located in cell D29, and multiplying that quotient by 100. This formula is somewhat more complicated than those already entered, and requires the use of parentheses to ensure that the division function is completed before the multiplication. As a result, the formula (+C9/$D$27)*100 should be set in cell C11 and copied across row 11.

The marketer now has the ability to manipulate countless iterations and analyze the implications of various prices. The worksheet as designed is interactive. By simply changing the incremental price change in cell D13, the marketer can generate and critique different prices. As may be seen in table 10.6, by pricing at $8 per unit to match the competition, 15 percent of the market must be captured just to break even. With a price cut of $1 below the competition, or $7 per unit, a 30 percent share would be required. Similarly, at a price of $9, only 10 percent of the market must be captured to break even.

The computer is useful in this example in that after the relatively short spreadsheet development time, several price scenarios may be evaluated almost instantly. The marketer can gain important insights into what price should be charged within the context of the objectives management is trying to achieve.

Application Two: Price Elasticity

Elasticity calculations can also be simplified with the use of a 1-2-3 spreadsheet. Let's assume that Bigbulb Corporation is one of the top three lamp producers in competition with Everlight. Bigbulb had 24 percent of the 72-inch-long fluorescent lamp market in 1989, with unit sales of 1,200,000. In 1987, Bigbulb sold 1,252,000 units at $7.86 per unit. To match the competition, Bigbulb reduced its price in 1988 to $7.62 per unit, and sold 1,322,000 units. To reflect increased costs of production, Bigbulb raised its price to $8.00 per unit in 1989, as did its major competitors.

Let's begin with a qualitative assessment of elasticity. Assume that Bigbulb has targeted the industrial market, in which fluorescent lamps are a necessity. Substitutes are available to these customers, but fluorescent lamps are considered to be a relatively low-cost purchase, and buyers are averse to spending time and labor changing inferior bulbs. As a result, then, the demand for the product is likely to be only somewhat elastic.

A quantitative assessment of price elasticity using a Lotus 1-2-3 spreadsheet is provided in tables 10.8 and 10.9. Both point and arc elasticities can be calculated for 1989 and 1988; however, there is insufficient data available in the example to determine 1987 elasticity, because information for the 1986 average unit price and annual unit sales would be necessary.

Since the focus of the worksheet is price elasticity, the elasticity calculations should be placed in the top rows. These formulas are dependent upon manipulations of the annual unit sales and average unit price, entered in rows 20 and 22 respectively. This information does not require the insertion of formulas,

Table 10.8
Computer Worksheet, Bigbulb Elasticity Example

	A	B	C	D	E	F
1						
2						
3						
4						
5						
6	Year	1989		1988		1987
7						
8	Elasticity Coefficient (Point)	-1.851		-2.026		
9						
10	Elasticity Coefficient (Arc)	-1.988		-1.935		
11						
12	% change in Quantity	-9.288	%	6.185	%	
13						
14	Unit change in Quantity	(122,000)		77,000		
15						
16	% change in Price	4.987	%	-3.053	%	
17						
18	Dollar Change in Price	$0.38		($0.24)		
19						
20	Annual Unit Sales	1,200,000		1,322,000		1,245,000
21						
22	Average Unit Price	$8.00		$7.62		$7.86
23						
24						
25						
26						
27						
28						
29						
30						
31						
32						
33						
34						

Table 10.9
Cell Entries, Bigbulb Elasticity Example

A1:	
A2:	
A3:	
A4:	' Bigbulb Elasticity Example
A6:	' Year
B6:	1989
D6:	+B6-1
F6:	+D6-1
A8:	'Elasticity Coefficient (Point)
B8:	+B12/B16
D8:	+D12/D16
A10:	'Elasticity Coefficient (Arc)
B10:	(+B14/(0.5*(B20+D20)))*((0.5*(B22+D22))/+B18)
D10:	(+D14/(0.5*(D20+F20)))*((0.5*(+D22+F22))/+D18)
A12:	'% change in Quantity
B12:	(+B14/D20)*100
C12:	'%
D12:	(+D14/F20)*100
E12:	'%
A14:	' Unit Change in Quantity
B14:	+B20-D20
D14:	+D20-F20
A16:	'% change in price
B16:	(+B18/D22)*100
C16:	'%
D16:	(+D18/F22)*100
E16:	'%
A18:	'Dollar Change in Price
B18:	+B22-D22
D18:	+D22-F22
A20:	'Annual Unit Sales
B20:	1200000
D20:	1322000
F20:	1245000
A22:	'Average Unit Price
B22:	8
D22:	7.62
F22:	7.86

and may simply be entered. Point elasticity, as explained in chapter 3, is equal to the percentage change in quantity divided by the percentage change in price. Simple subtraction and division formulas can be used to solve the point elasticity equation.

To illustrate, the dollar change in price from one year to the next can be found by entering a formula that calculates the difference between the average unit prices located in row 22. For 1989, the dollar change in price is determined by the formula +B22−D22, which adds the 1989 average unit price (cell B22) and subtracts the 1988 average unit price (cell D22). The percentage change in price for each year may be calculated by dividing the dollar change in price for that year by the average unit price for the prior year and multiplying the result by 100. In cell B16, the percentage change in price for 1989 is a result of the formula (+B18/D22)*100, which divides the 1989 dollar change in price (cell B18) by the 1988 average unit price (cell D22), and multiplies the product by 100. Since this is a referent formula, it may be copied into cell D16, and the percentage change in price for 1988 will appear.

The change in quantity formulas, found in rows 12 and 14, are similar to those used for the changes in price, but are dependent upon the annual unit sales information. The 1989 unit change in quantity (cell B14) is achieved by taking the 1989 annual unit sales (cell B20) and subtracting the 1988 annual unit sales (cell D20). The percentage change in quantity divides the unit change in quantity for that year by the annual unit sales for the year before and multiplies the result by 100. For 1989, the percentage change in quantity formula located in cell B12 is (+B14/D20)*100.

Arc elasticity involves a more difficult formula. As explained in chapter 3, arc elasticity is found by (1) dividing the unit change in quantity by one-half (50 percent) of the sum of the annual unit sales for this year, (2) taking one-half (50 percent) of the sum of the average unit price for this year and the average unit price for last year and dividing this by the dollar change in price, and (3) multiplying the result of each calculation times one another. This rather complicated formula may be entered into a single cell by nesting the different multiplication and division results in parentheses. Multiple parentheses are necessary as 1-2-3's hierarchical calculation structure places multiplication and division ahead of subtraction and addition. The parentheses indicate to the software the order in which the formula must be calculated to achieve the desired result. The formula can be found in cell B10 of the spreadsheet illustrated in tables 10.8 and 10.9.

Point elasticity appears simpler to calculate because the numbers on which it depends have already been computed in the worksheet. Point elasticity can be determined by dividing the percentage change in quantity by the percentage change in price for the same year. For 1989, the point elasticity coefficient formula found in Cell B8 is +B12/B16. For 1988, it is +D12/D16.

The resulting point elasticity measurements of −1.851 for 1989 (cell B8) and −2.026 for 1988 (cell D8) and arc elasticities of −1.988 for 1989 (cell B10) and −1.935 for 1988 (cell D10) indicate that industrial consumers are somewhat price sensitive. For each 1 percent change in price, the quantity demanded will change in the opposite direction by approximately 2 percent. These numbers correspond with the qualitative judgment of price sensitivity discussed above.

The quantitative and qualitative assessments should reinforce one another. Both sets of results must make sense logically. If there is a sizable disparity between the two, this might serve as an indicator that the manager responsible for qualitative price sensitivity is out of touch with actual market conditions. Alternatively, the quantitative assessment may have an input error, incorrect data files may have been incorporated, or the spreadsheet may have been designed poorly.

Application Three: Evaluating a Price Change

Assume Bigbulb would like to evaluate a possible price change. Specifically, management is considering a specific percentage increase (or decrease) in price. Common questions that one might want to resolve before implementing any such change include

- Does the proposed price change contribute an amount at least equal to the amount currently being contributed to cover indirect costs?
- What level of volume will allow the firm to maintain the current level of contribution to indirect costs at the proposed price?
- How much is volume expected to change with the proposed price using the price elasticity coefficient?
- What is the market share necessary to break even at the proposed price? What is the market share currently?
- At the proposed price, how much difference is there between the units necessary to maintain the current level of contribution and the expected amount of units to be sold?
- What is the expected contribution to indirect costs at the proposed price?

Bigbulb must have certain data on hand to perform this analysis. Specifically, data is needed regarding current unit price, annual unit sales, unit variable costs, total direct fixed costs, and market size in units. In this example, the arc elasticity is input and not calculated, since its calculation was already demonstrated above. Otherwise, it would also have to be included in the calculations. The final piece of data that must be input is the proposed price change percentage. All other calculations are formulas driven from these pieces of information.

Tables 10.10 and 10.11 present a spreadsheet that answers the questions asked by Bigbulb's management. As before, the most important part of the worksheet, the proposed price change, is at the top. Cell B7 is the cell into which proposed price change percentages are entered as a whole number. It is important to add the correct sign for negative numbers. For example, a price change of 11 percent would be entered in cell B7 as 11; a price change of −7.5 percent would be entered as −7.5. Other cells requiring data input include the current price, found in cell B14, the current annual unit sales in cell B18, unit variable costs in cell B20, total direct fixed costs in cell B22, market size in units in cell B48, and the current arc elasticity in cell B39.

The pricing manager would like to know if the price change is viable at the present time; that is, does the proposed price change incorporate a contribution margin and sales estimate resulting in a contribution to indirect costs at least equal to that offered by the current price? If the estimated net revenue generated by the new price is less than the net revenue available with the current price, then the proposed price change should be discarded as inadequate. Alternatively, a proposed price that offers a greater contribution to indirect costs should be noted, and the new contribution should be calculated.

Table 10.10
Computer Worksheet, Bigbulb CVP Analysis

	A	B	C	D
1				
2				
3				
4	Bigbulb CVP Analysis			
5				
6				
7	Proposed price change %	11	Proposed price sales revenue	$8,325,746
8				
9	Does the proposed price change	Yes	Less:Variable costs	$5,391,108
10	contribute an amount at least			-----------
11	equal to the current level		Contribution margin	$2,934,638
12	of indirect costs?			
13			Less:Direct fixed costs	$2,000,000
14	Current price	$8.00		-----------
15			Contribution to	$ 934,638
16	Proposed price	$8.88	indirect costs	==========
17				
18	Current annual unit sales	1,200,000		
19				
20	Unit variable costs	$5.75		
21				
22	Total direct fixed costs	$2,000,000		
23				
24	Current profit-volume ratio	0.2813		
25				
26	Proposed profit-volume ratio	0.3525		
27				
28	% volume reduction allowable	-28.1150		
29	or increase necessary to			
30	maintain current level of			
31	contribution to indirect costs			
32				
33	Allowable or necessary units	862,620		
34	to maintain current level of			
35	contribution to indirect costs			
36				
37	Current arc elasticity	-1.9880		
38				
39	Estimated % change in volume			
40	using elasticity coefficient	-21.8680		
41				
42	Estimated unit sales after	937,584		
43	proposed price change using			
44	elasticity coefficient			
45				
46	Proposed price breakeven units	638,978		
47				
48	Market size in units	5,000,000		
49				
50	Market share % needed to	12.78		
51	breakeven at proposed price			
52				

Table 10.10 (continued)

	A	B	C	D
53	Current market share %	24		
54				
55	Spread (in units) between	298,606		
56	estimated and breakeven			
57	unit sales			
58				
59	Spread (in units) between	74,964		
60	estimated and necessary			
61	or allowable unit sales			
62				
63	% difference between	6.25		
64	estimated and necessary			
65	or allowable unit sales			

Such answers depend upon other calculations. First, the proposed price must be determined. This calculation, found in cell B16, divides the percentage price change (cell B7) by 100 and adds one; this result is then multiplied by the current price (cell B14). As demonstrated in Table 10.11, the proposed price formula located in cell B16 is +B14*(1+(B7/100)). Next, the profit-volume (PV) ratio (see chapter 6) for both the current and the proposed prices must be calculated. The current PV ratio, found in cell B24, is determined by subtracting the unit variable cost figure from the current price and dividing the result by the current price. The PV ratio under the proposed price (cell B26), is found by subtracting the unit variable costs (cell B20) from the proposed price (cell B16) and dividing the result by the proposed price. Therefore, the formula entered into cell B24 for the current PV ratio is (+B14−B20)/B14. The PV ratio under the proposed price (cell B26) is basically the same, except that cell B14 is replaced with cell B16 in both the numerator and the denominator.

The next formula is more difficult, and was discussed in the chapter on costs. This formula is concerned with determining the percentage change in volume necessary to maintain a desired level of profitability with a given price change. In this example, management wants to achieve a level of profitability equal to the total contribution (to indirect fixed costs and profits) being achieved under the current price. That is, they wish to maintain the status quo. Therefore, this formula calculates on a percentage basis how much unit sales can go down (or up) with a given percentage increase (or decrease) in price without any change in overall profitability. For example, with a price increase of 11 percent, volume may change by negative 28.115 percent before the contribution to indirect costs falls below that offered by the current price. Remember that this does not predict that volume will decrease by this amount, but, rather, that the volume has the freedom to change this much without affecting product profitability. The calculation of this volume change, located in cell B28, involves multiplying the proposed price change percentage (cell B7) by negative one (−1) and then dividing by 100; this result is then divided by the current profit-volume ratio

Table 10.11
Cell Entries, Bigbulb CVP Analysis

A7:	'Proposed Price Change %
B7:	11
D7:	'Proposed price sales revenue
E7:	@IF(B42<0,B42*0,B16*B42)
A9:	'Does the proposed price change
B9:	@IF(+B59<0," NO"," YES")
D9:	'Less: Variable Costs
E9:	@IF(B42<0,B42*0,B20*B42)
A10:	'contribute an amount at least
E10:	\ -
A11:	' equal to the current level
D11:	'Contribution Margin
E11:	+E7-E9
A12:	'of indirect costs?
D13:	'Less: Direct Fixed Costs
E13:	+B22
A14:	'Current Price
B14:	8
E14:	\ -
D15:	'Contribute to
E15:	+E11-E13
A16:	'Proposed Price
B16:	+B14*(1+(B7/100))
D16:	' Indirect Costs
E16:	\ =
A18:	'Current annual Unit Sales
B18:	1200000
A20:	'Unit Variable Costs
B20:	5.75
A22:	'Total Direct Fixed Costs
B22:	2000000
A24:	'Current Profit-Volume Ratio
B24:	(+B14-B20)/B14
A26:	'Proposed Profit-Volume Ratio
B26:	(+B16-B20)/B16
A28:	'% volume reduction allowable
B28:	(((-1*B7)/100)/(B24+(B7/100)))*100
C28:	'%
A29:	'or increase necessary to
A30:	'maintain current level of
A31:	'contribution to indirect costs
A33:	'Allowable or Necessary Units
B33:	(1+B28/100)*B18
A34:	'to maintain current level of
A35:	' contribution to indirect costs
A37:	'Current Arc Elasticity
B37:	'Estimated % change in volume
B39:	B37/B7
C39:	'%
A40:	'using elasticity coefficient
A42:	'Estimated Unit Sales after
B42:	(+1+B39/100)*B18
A43:	'proposed price change using
A44:	'elasticity coefficient

Table 10.11 (continued)

```
A46:  'Proposed Price Breakeven Units
B46:  +   B22/(+B16-B20)
A48:  'Market Size in Units
B48:  5000000
A50:  'Market Share % Needed to
B50:  (+B46/B48)*100
C50:  '%
A51:  'Breakeven at proposed price
A53:  'Current Market Share
B53:  (+B18/B48)*100
C53:  '%
A55:  'Spread (in units) between
B55:  +B42-B46
A56:  'estimated and breakeven
A57:  'unit sales
A59:  'spread (in units) between
B59:  +B42-B33
A60:  'estimated and necessary
A61:  'or allowable unit sales
A63:  '% difference between
B63:  +B59/B10*100
C63:  '%
A64:  'estimated and necessary
A65:  'or allowable unit sales
```

(cell B24) plus the proposed price change percentage (divided by 100). The entire result is then multiplied by 100. The actual cell entry for B28 is, then, $(((-1*B7)/100)/B24+(B7/100))*100$.

The result of this formula may be used to determine the number of units that must be sold at the proposed price to maintain the current level of contribution. Simply add one to the percentage volume change calculated in cell B28, divide by 100, and multiply the result by the current annual unit sales found in cell B18. The necessary formula is $(1+B28/100)*B18$, and is found in cell B33.

The number of units that must be sold to break even at the new price can also be calculated, and is located in cell B46. The total direct fixed costs found in cell B22 must be divided by the proposed price (cell B16) minus the unit variable costs (cell B20), or $+B22 (+B16-B20)$.

The market share percentage needed to break even at the proposed price and the current market share captured can be determined and compared. For the market share percentage needed to break even at the proposed price located in cell B50, the proposed price break-even units calculated in cell B46 are divided by the market size in units found in cell B48, and the result is multiplied by 100. The current market share percentage calculated in cell B53 is found by dividing the current annual unit sales (cell B18) by the market size in units (cell B48) and multiplying the result by 100. For cell B50, the formula is $(+B46/B48)*100$; for cell B53, $(+B18/B48)*100$.

Application Four: Cost-Volume-Profit Analysis

This application is a continuation of Application Three, but brings the analysis full circle. So far, the calculations have shown what can happen to sales before profitability is harmed, but the pricing manager still is unsure what effect the price change is expected to have on sales. The price elasticity coefficient, as calculated in an earlier application, is of use here. The estimated change in volume on a percentage basis may be calculated by multiplying the arc price elasticity coefficient found in cell B37 by the proposed price change percentage located in cell B7. The resulting percentage, calculated in cell B39, forecasts the percentage change in units expected to occur if the proposed price change is implemented.

Thus the number of expected units to be sold can be determined by adding one to the current arc elasticity (cell B37), dividing by 100, and multiplying the result by the current annual unit sales located in cell B18. Entered in cell B42, the formula is $(+1+B39/100)*B18$.

Three related calculations may be of interest to the pricing manager. First, the difference between the number of unit sales that management expects will be made at the new price, which was calculated using the price elasticity coefficient (cell B42), and the number of units necessary to break even at the proposed price (cell B46) defines the buffer zone of sales that the marketer has available before the new price will cause the product to become unprofitable. The formula for this calculation, located in cell B55, is $+B42-B46$. Second, the difference between the unit sales estimated at the new price (cell B42) and the unit sales that must be made before the current level of profitability is affected (cell B33) indicates to the manager how many units of leeway are available before the new price causes sales to negatively affect profitability. Again, this calculation is fairly straightforward ($+B42-B33$), and is found in cell B59. Third, by dividing the number just calculated in cell B59 into the current annual unit sales and multiplying the result by 100 (entered in cell B63 as $(+B59/B10)*100$), the firm's pricing leeway is expressed as a percentage of the current annual unit sales. This percentage delineates the size of the variance between the product's expected revenues and the chance of negatively affecting profitability. Comparisons can be drawn using this percentage at any number of possible price levels. A larger percentage indicates that the proposed price allows relatively more variability in sales before profitability shows a decline. A small percentage may raise a red flag, indicating that if sales do not meet expectations, there is little leeway before profitability is negatively affected.

A more comprehensive picture can be achieved by moving to columns D and E of the spreadsheet, in which total contribution is analyzed. Cell E7 calculates the total sales revenue using the estimated unit sales and the proposed price. So long as the estimated unit sales are greater than zero, then the estimated sales units are multiplied by the proposed price (cell B16), to result in gross sales revenue. Next, total variable costs are determined by multiplying estimated unit sales by the variable cost per unit found in cell B20. The total contribution margin is then calculated by subtracting the total variable costs from the estimated sales revenue generated using the proposed price. As calculated in cell E11, the formula is +E7−E9. The direct fixed costs are also easily incorporated in this pro forma; they have already been entered in cell B22, and may be remembered in cell E13 by entering +B22. Finally, the contribution to indirect costs may be calculated by subtracting the direct fixed costs (cell E13) from the contribution margin (cell E11). Therefore, +E11−E13 is entered in cell E15.

Now, all formulas are available and the spreadsheet is ready for manipulation and analysis. Keeping in mind that the pricing manager wants to know if the price change is feasible at the present time, Lotus 1-2-3 has a feature called an @IF statement that can address the question with no further work by the executive. This analysis assumes that a price change is viable only if the calculations indicate that the proposed price will contribute more to covering indirect costs and profits than the current price. If the difference between the expected unit sales and the necessary or allowable unit sales (already calculated in cell B59) is negative, then the contribution to indirect cost will be less than the current contribution to indirect cost. Therefore, if B59 is less than zero, the price change is not viable; if B59 is positive, then the price change is conceivable. Reduced to an @IF statement in cell B9, the formula would be @IF(+B59?0,"NO," "YES").

To begin manipulating and analyzing the spreadsheet, go to cell B7 and enter various proposed price changes. Start with zero. If zero is entered in cell B7, what is the contribution to indirect costs? Since a zero price change would mean that the current price is maintained, the minimum amount of contribution to indirect costs may be found. According to the worksheet, the current price contributes $700,000 to pay indirect costs. Therefore, the search is for a price change that results in the highest amount of contribution above $700,000. What is the result of a price reduction of 10 percent? Enter −10 in cell B7. A price reduction of 10 percent would contribute a positive $85,912 to indirect costs. However, cell B9 tells us immediately that although the contribution is positive, it is less than the amount contributed were price to be left alone. Therefore, the negative 10 percent price change must be removed from consideration. Go back to cell B7. Is a 5 percent increase in price valid? A quick glance at cell B9 produces an affirmative answer. The contribution to indirect costs is $863,908. If a 5 percent increase is good, then a 20 percent increase is probably better. Entering 20 in cell B7 shows that a 20 percent increase is also viable. However, the contribution to indirect costs is $783,088, less than that offered by a 5 percent increase. By entering different numbers into cell B7 and comparing the results, it soon becomes apparent that a price increase of 11 percent results in the highest contribution to indirect costs at $934,638.

A further review of the spreadsheet in table 10.10 reveals additional insights regarding a price change of +11 percent. First, a price change of positive 11 percent results in a proposed price of $8.88 per unit. The proposed PV ratio also increased, as the price went up and the variable costs per unit remained constant. Cells B28 and B33 show that sales can decline by 28.115 percent to 862,620 units before the contribution to indirect costs drops below the $700,000 barrier. Luckily, however, sales are estimated to drop only 21.868 per cent due to the price increase, and unit sales are estimated to be 937,584. The number of unit sales required to break even, 638,978, suggests that only 12.78 percent of the market must be maintained to break even, and the current market share is 24 percent. This translates into a comfort zone of 298,606 units between the estimated sales and break even, as shown by cell B55. However, the spread between the estimated unit sales and the number of units necessary to achieve a contribution to indirect costs of $700,000 is much smaller, at 74,964 units, or 6.25 per cent of current annual unit sales.

A final consideration in cost-volume-profit analysis involves verifying one's assumptions about costs. Specifically, the analysis up to this point has assumed that unit costs stay the same with changes in volume. However, it is quite possible that unit costs could go up or down if production volume changes, possibly due to capacity limitations or experience curve effects. Changes in unit costs will impact on the contribution margin and the PV ratio. This, in turn, will change the level of sales that must be achieved at a given price to achieve break even or some desired profit level. As a result, possible changes in the underlying cost structure should be evaluated, again with a spreadsheet.

Assume, in the example used throughout this application, that variable cost per unit will fall to $5.50 per unit from the current $5.75 per unit if volume exceeds 1,200,000 units. This assumption can be incorporated into the spreadsheet by changing the formula for variable costs (cell B20) into an @IF statement which says that if the estimated unit sales subsequent to the proposed price change calculated using the elasticity coefficient (cell B42) is 1,200,000 or less, then the unit variable cost per unit would be $5.75; if the volume is greater than 1,200,000, the variable costs per unit would be $5.50. Therefore, the formula in cell b20 would be @IF(B42 < 1200001,5.75,5.50).

Price increases would not be pertinent in this analysis, as they produce lower volume levels, which would have no impact on unit costs. Consider, however, a price decrease of 1 percent. If demand remains relatively elastic, volume will now exceed 1,200,000 units, unit costs would fall to $5.50, and contribution to indirect fixed costs and profits would now be $961,732 compared to $655,768 if the unit costs had remained constant at $5.75. This new level of contribution also exceeds that projected both under the current price and under the 11 percent price increase.

ADDITIONAL STATISTICAL ANALYSIS FOR PRICING

A major drawback of spreadsheet and database programs when performing price analysis involves their limited statistical capabilities. The manager interested in more sophisticated analysis may need to consider downloading data into a statistical software package. There are a number of fairly powerful packages available for use with the personal computer. Examples include SPSS/PC+, PC–SAS, SYSTAT, MicroTSP, and Statgraphics.

As an example of a pricing problem requiring such analysis, again consider Everlight and Bigbulb, the two competing lightbulb manufacturers. Everlight may want to know how its own sales are affected by the price levels charged by Bigbulb. Alternatively, Everlight might wish to examine how sales are affected by the difference between its prices and those of Bigbulb.

Data would have to be maintained on Bigbulb's price schedule over time (e.g., monthly). This data plus that for Everlight's sales and prices on a monthly basis would then be input into a computer file using one of the available statistical software packages. While packages differ, some permit the downloading and/or merging of data from existing data bases or spreadsheets into the statistical program. Alternatively, one can enter data on a case-by-case (month-by-month in this example) basis for each variable.

Most programs are menu driven. As a result, the analysis becomes fairly straightforward. To determine whether or not relationships exist between Everlight's monthly sales and (a) Bigbulb's average monthly prices and (b) the difference between Everlight's average monthly prices and those for Bigbulb, a correlation analysis might be run in each case. The program will produce the desired correlation coefficients plus supporting statistics. Once the data is in place, it is a simple matter of selecting any other procedure from the menu to run additional analyses.

SUMMARY

This final chapter has attempted to demonstrate how a number of the tools and concepts introduced in earlier chapters can be applied using personal computers. The computer was presented as a tool for helping managers more quickly identify and capitalize on marketplace opportunities in the pricing area. Yet many managers have been slow to take advantage of this potential, largely because of limited familiarity with the available hardware and software.

An effective computerized price management system consists of four interacting components; a pricing data base, spreadsheets, models, and statistical capability. The database component is most critical, and is typically dependent on a timely stream of inputs from other functional areas within the firm as well as external sources. Spreadsheets are helpful frameworks both for storing data and performing basic data manipulation. Moreover, spreadsheets are capable of generating a variety of useful managerial reports. Models represent attempts to mathematically describe relationships between or among variables. Models of pricing relationships can often be formulated as part of a spreadsheet. Models are applied to the pricing data base through the use of statistics. Many of the required statistics involve little more than adding or dividing rows and columns by one another, which can again be accomplished using spreadsheets.

More advanced manipulations, such as correlation or regression, require an investment in a statistical software package.

The ease with which pricing analysis can be accomplished on a personal computer was demonstrated with a series of applications. These included break-even analysis, calculations of elasticity, assessment of a price change, and an evaluation of cost-volume-profit relationships. Further, once any particular analysis is in place, an endless number of scenarios can be evaluated wherein the manager varies his or her underlying assumptions and/or decision criteria.

The future will find opportunities for computer applications in the pricing area continually expanding. As this occurs, the pricing function will begin to serve a more proactive and strategic role in the marketing programs of firms. The vital ingredient will be the pricing manager. The manager's vision in recognizing how computer technology can be used as a strategic pricing weapon and the manager's skills in building data bases, designing models, and drawing creative insights from data analysis are the keys to taking advantage of this powerful resource.

REFERENCES

Morris, M., A. Burns, and R. Avila, "Computer Awareness and Usage by Industrial Marketers," *Industrial Marketing Management*, 18 (August 1989), 197-204.

Suggested Readings

Abratt, R. and L. F. Pitt (1985), "Pricing Practices in Two Industries," *Industrial Marketing Management* 14: 301-6.

Alcaly, R. E. (1979), "Information and Food Prices," *Bell Journal of Economics* 7 (Autumn): 658-71.

Bailey, E. L. (1982), *Pricing Practices and Strategies*. New York: The Conference Board, Inc.

Barkman, A. I. and J. D. Jolley (1986), "Cost Defenses for Antitrust Cases," *Management Accounting* (April): 37-40.

Barnes, James G. (1975), "Factors Influencing Consumer Reaction to Retail Newspaper 'Sale' Advertising," *Proceedings*, Fall Educators' Conference, Chicago: American Marketing Association, 471-77.

Berkowitz, Eric N. and John R. Walton (1980), "Contextual Influences on Consumer Price Responses: An Experimental Analysis," *Journal of Marketing Research* (August): 349-50.

Berry, D. (1983), "How Marketers Use Microcomputers—Now and In the Future," *Business Marketing* (December): 44-53.

Blair, Edward A. and E. Laird Landon, Jr. (1981), "The Effects of Reference Prices in Retail Advertisements," *Journal of Marketing* 45 (Spring): 61-69.

Blattberg, Robert C., Gary D. Eppen, and Joshua Lieberman (1981), "A Theoretical and Empirical Evaluation of Price Deals for Consumer Nondurables," *Journal of Marketing* 45 (Winter): 116-29.

Business Week (1974), "Pricing Strategy in an Inflationary Economy" (April 6): 42-49.

Business Week (1977), "Why Price-cutting Backfires in the Airline Industry," (October 10): 116-18.

Business Week (1977), "Flexible Pricing" (December 12): 78-88.

Business Week (1982), "Why Detroit Can't Cut Prices," (March 1): 110-11.

Butcher, J. (1984), "Try the 'True Market' Test First," *Accountancy* (March): 136-39.

Butcher, J. (1985), "Pricing Technique: Is there a Price for Everything?" *Accountancy* (October): 103-6.

Byrnes, J. F. (1987), "Ten Guidelines for Effective Negotiating," *Business Horizons* (May-June): 7-12.

Curry, D. J. and P. C. Riesz (1988), "Prices and Price/Quality Relationships: A Longitudinal Analysis," *Journal of Marketing* 52 (January): 36-51.

Darden, B. R. (1986), "An Operational Approach to Product Pricing," *Journal of Marketing* 32 (April): 29-33.

Dawson, L. E., M. L. Mayer, and J. Keith (1986), "Resale Price Maintenance: Changing Perspectives and Future Directions," *Journal of Consumer Marketing* (Fall): 83-90.

Day, G. S. and A. B. Ryans (1988), "Using Price Discounts for a Competitive Advantage," *Industrial Marketing Management* 17: 1-14.

Dean, J. (1970), "Techniques for Pricing New Products and Services," *Handbook of Modern Marketing*, 5-51 – 5-61. New York: McGraw-Hill Book Company.

Devinney, T., ed. (1988), *Issues in Pricing: Theory and Research*, Lexington, Mass.: Lexington Books.

Dion, P. A. and P. M. Banting (1988), "Industrial Supplier-Buyer Negotiations," *Industrial Marketing Management* 17: 43-47.

Dodds, William B. and Kent B. Monroe (1985), "The Effect of Brand and Price Information on Subjective Product Evaluations," in Elizabeth Hirschman and Morris Holbrook, eds., *Advances in Consumer Research* 12, Provo, Utah: Association for Consumer Research, 85-90.

Dolan, R. J. (1980), "The Panic of the 1980's: It's Pricing," *Sales and Marketing Management* (June): 47-49.

_____. (1981), "Pricing Strategies that Adjust to Inflation," *Industrial Marketing Management* 66 (July): 151-56.

Dubinsky, A. J. and J. M. Gwin (1981), "Business Ethics: Buyers and Sellers," *Journal of Purchasing and Materials Management* 17 (Winter 1986): 9-16.

Dubinsky, A. J. and W. A. Staples (1981), "Are Industrial Salespeople Buyer Oriented?" *Journal of Purchasing and Materials Management* (Fall): 12-19.

Dubinsky, A. J., E. N. Berkowitz, and W. Rudelius (1980), "Ethical Problems of Field Sales Personnel," *MSU Business Topics* (Summer 1980): 11-16.

Emery, F. (1970), "Some Psychological Aspects of Price," in Bernard Taylor and Gordon Wills, eds., *Pricing Strategy*. Princeton, N.J.: Brandon/Systems Press, 98-111.

Enis, Ben and J. Stafford (1969), "The Price-Quality Relationship: An Extension," *Journal of Marketing Research* 6 (November): 256-68.

Fisher, Roger and William Ury (1981), *Getting to YES*. Boston: Houghton Mifflin.

Forbis, J. L. and N. T. Mehta (1981), "Value-Based Strategies for Industrial Products," *Business Horizons* 24 (May-June): 32-42.

Forgionne, G. A. (1984), "Economic Tools Used by Management in Large American Operated Corporations," *Business Economics* (April): 5-17.

Fry, Joseph and Gordon H. McDougall (1974), "Consumer Appraisal of Retail Price Advertising," *Journal of Marketing* 3 (July): 64-66.

Gabor, A. (1988), *Pricing Concepts and Methods for Effective Marketing*. Cambridge: University Press.

Gabor, A. and C. Granger (1961), "On the Price Consciousness of Consumers," *Applied Statistics* 10 (November): 170-88.

_____ (1965), "The Pricing of New Products," *Scientific Business* 3 (August): 141-50.

Gabor, A., C. Granger, and A. Sowter (1971), "Comments on Psychophysics of Pricing," *Journal of Marketing Research* 8 (May): 251-52.

Gardner, David (1971), "Is There a Generalized Price-Quality Relationship," *Journal of Marketing Research* 8 (May): 241-43.

Ghosh, A., S. A. Neslin, and R. Shoemaker (1983), "Are There Associations Between Price Elasticity and Brand Characteristics?" *Educator's Proceedings*, Chicago: American Marketing Association, 228-33.

Gibson, Paul (1979), "De Beers: Can a Cartel Be Forever?" *Forbes* (May 28): 45.

Graham, J. L. (1986), "Negotiations in Industrial Marketing," *Journal of Business Research* 14: 549-66.

Groocock, J. M. (1986), *The Chain of Quality*. New York: John Wiley and Sons.

Gultinan, J. P. (1976), "Risk-Aversive Pricing Policies: Problems and Alternatives," *Journal of Marketing* 40 (January): 10-15.

———— (1980), *Pricing Bank Services: A Planning Approach*. American Bankers Assoc., Washington, D.C.

Hall, R. L. and C. J. Hitch (1939), "Price Theory and Business Behavior," *Oxford Economic Papers* 2 (May): 12-45.

Hinkle, Charles (1965), "The Strategy of Price Deals," *Harvard Business Review* 43 (July-August): 75-85.

Jacoby, Jacob and Jerry C. Olson (1976), "Consumer Response to Price: An Attitudinal Information Processing Perspective," in Yoram Wind and Marshall Greenberg, eds., *Moving Ahead in Attitude Research*. Chicago: American Marketing Association.

Jensen, J. (1985), "Consumers Want Hospitals to Include Price of Services in Advertisement," *Modern Healthcare* (April 12): 48-50.

Jereski, L. K. (1984), "Computers in Marketing: Simplifying Chores," *Marketing and Media Decisions* (November): 136-40.

Johnson, James C. and Kenneth C. Schneider (1984), " 'Those Who Can, Do—Those Who Can't . . .' Marketing Professors and the Robinson-Patman Act," *Journal of the Academy of Marketing Science* 12: 123-38.

Jones, D. Frank (1975), "A Survey Technique to Measure Demand Under Various Pricing Strategies," *Journal of Marketing* 39 (July): 75-77.

Kamen, J. and R. Toman (1970), "Psychophysics of Prices," *Journal of Marketing Research* 7 (February): 27-35.

Karr, M. (1988), "The Case of the Pricing Predicament," *Harvard Business Review* (March-April): 10-20.

Karrass, Chester L. (1974), *Give & Take: The Complete Guide to Negotiating Strategies and Tactics*. New York: Thomas Y. Corwell Co.

Kehoe, W. J. (1985), "Ethics, Price Fixing, and the Management of Price Strategy," in G. R. Laczniak and P. E. Murphy, eds., *Marketing Ethics: Guidelines for Managers*. Lexington, Mass.: Lexington Books, 71-84.

Keiser, Stephen K. and James R. Krum (1976), "Consumer Perceptions of Retail Advertising with Overstated Price Savings," *Journal of Retailing* 52 (Fall): 27-36.

Keller, R. E. (1988), *SalesbNegotiating Handbook*. Englewood Cliffs, N.J.: Prentice-Hall.

Kerin, Roger A., Michael G. Harvey, and James T. Rothe (1978), "Cannibalism and New Product Development," *Business Horizons* (October): 25-31.

Kessel, Reuben (1958), "Price Discrimination in Medicine," *Journal of Law and Economics* 2 (October): 20-42.

Koch, James V. (1974), *Industrial Organization and Prices*. Englewood Cliffs, N.J.: Prentice-Hall.

Kortge, G. D. (1984), "Inverted Breakeven Analysis for Profitable Marketing Decisons," *Industrial Marketing Management* 13: 219-24.

Kottas, John F. and Basheer M. Khumawata (1973), "Contract Bid Development for the Small Businessman," *Sloan Management Review* 14 (Spring), 31-45.

Lambert, Z. V. (1975), "Perceived Prices as Related to Odd and Even Price Endings," *Journal of Retailing* 51 (Fall): 13-20.

Lamm, D. V. and L. C. Vose (1988), "Seller Pricing Strategies: A Buyer's Perspective," *Journal of Purchasing and Materials Management* (Fall): 9-13.

Liefeld, J. and L. A. Helsop (1985), "Reference Prices and Deception in Newspaper Advertising," *Journal of Consumer Research* 11 (March): 868-76.

McCann, J. M. (1987), "First Steps Toward the Expert Marketing Computer," *Marketing and Media Decisions* 22 (Fall): 136.

McFarlan, F. W. (1984), "Information Technology Changes the Way You Compete," *Harvard Business Review* (May-June): 98-103.

McFillen, J. M., R. R. Reck, and W. C. Benton (1983), "An Experiment in Purchasing Negotiations," *Journal of Purchasing and Materials Management* (Summer): 2-8.

Main, J. (1983), "How to be a Better Negotiator," *Fortune* (September): 141-46.

Marks, N. E. and N. S. Inlow (1988), "Price Discrimination and Its Impact on Small Business," *Journal of Consumer Marketing* (Winter): 31-38.

Meyerowitz, S. A. (1986), "Bearer of Price Discrimination Pitfalls," *Business Marketing* (June): 136-40.

———— (1986), "Tightening the Reins on Distributors' Prices," *Business Marketing* (May): 94-100.

Milmo, S. (1986), "Firms' Pricing, Service Deals Termed Unfair," *Business Marketing* (May): 32-33.

Milsap, C. R. (1985), "Wrestling with Consumer Price Resistance," *Business Marketing* (May): 120-26.

Monroe, K. B. (1971), "The Information Content of Prices: A Preliminary Model for Estimating Buyer Response," *Management Science* 17 (April): B519-B532.

———— (1971), "Psychophysics of Pricing: A Reappraisal," *Journal of Marketing Research* 8 (May): 248-50.

———— (1973), "Buyers Subjective Perceptions of Price," *Journal of Marketing Research* 10 (February): 70-80.

———— (1978), "Models for Pricing Decisions," *Journal of Marketing Research* 15 (August): 413-28.

———— (1979), *Pricing: Making Profitable Decisions*. New York: McGraw-Hill.

Monroe, K. B. and Susan Petroshius (1981), "Buyers Perception of Price: An Update of the Evidence," in Harold H. Kassarjian and Thomas S. Robertson, eds., *Perspectives in Consumer Behavior*. 3rd edition. Glenview, IL: Scott, Foresman and Company, 43-55.

Monroe, K. B. and William B. Dodds (1988), "A Research Program for Establishing the Validity of the Price-Quality Relationship," *Journal of the Academy of Marketing Science* 16 (Spring): 151-68.

Morris, Michael H. (1987), "Separate Prices as a Marketing Tool," *Industrial Marketing Management* 16: 79-86.

Morris, Michael H. and Donald Fuller (1989), "Pricing an Industrial Service," *Industrial Marketing Management* 18 (May): 139-46.

Morris, Michael H. and Mary Joyce (1988), "How Marketers Evaluate Price Sensitivity," *Industrial Marketing Management* 17: 1-8.

Morrissey, W. (1984), "What the Computer Can do for Marketers," *Marketing and Media Decision* (November): 102.

Morse, W. J. (1975), "Probabilistic Bidding Models: A Synthesis," *Business Horizons* 18: 67-74.

Morton, J. and M. E. Rys (1987), "Price Elasticity Prediction: New Research Tool for the Competitive '80's," *Marketing News* (January 2): 7-8.

Nagle, Thomas T. (1983), "Pricing as Creative Marketing," *Business Horizons* (July-August): 14-19.

_____. (1984), "Economic Foundations for Pricing," *Journal of Business* 57 (January): S3-S26.

_____ (1987), *The Strategy & Tactics of Pricing*. Englewood Cliffs, N.J.: Prentice-Hall.

Nagle, T. and K. Novak (1988), "The Roles of Segmentation and Awareness in Explaining Variations in Price Markups," in T. Devinney, ed., *Issues in Pricing: Theory and Research*. Lexington, Mass.: Lexington Books.

Narasimhan, C. (1984), "Coupons as Price Discrimination Devices—A Theoretical Perspective and Empirical Analysis," *Marketing Science* 3 (Spring): 128-47.

Narus, J. A. and T. Guimaraes (1987), "Computer Usage in Distributor Marketing," *Industrial Marketing Management* 16: 43-54.

Nielsen, R. P. (1986), "Piggybacking Strategies for Nonprofits: A Shared Costs Approach," *Strategic Management Journal* 7: 201-2.

Olson, Jerry C. (1977), "Price as an Information Cue: Effects on Product Evaluations," in Arch G. Woodside, Jagdish Sheth and Peter D. Bennett, eds., *Consumer and Industrial Buying Behavior*. New York: North Holland, 267-86.

Oxenfeldt, Alfred R. (1973), "A Decision-Making Structure for Price Decisions," *Journal of Marketing* 37 (January): 48-53.

Paranka (1971), "Competitive Bidding Strategy: A Procedure for Pre-bid Analysis," *Business Horizons* 14 (June): 39-43.

Perdue, B. C., R. L. Day and R. E. Michaels (1986) "Negotiation Styles of Industrial Buyers," Industrial Marketing Management 37 (August): 171-176.

Porter, M. (1974), "How Competitive Forces Shape Strategy," *Harvard Business Review* 57: 137-45.

Posch, R. J. (1984), *What Every Manager Needs to Know About Marketing and the Law*. New York: McGraw-Hill.

Posner, R. A. (1976), *The Robinson-Patman Act: Federal Regulation of Price Differences*. Washington, D.C.: American Enterprise Institute for Public Policy Research.

Prentice, R. M. and P. W. Farris (1987), "Point/Counterpoint/Poll-Promotion at What Price?" *Marketing and Media Decisions* 22 (September): 129.

Rao, V. R. (1984), "Pricing Research in Marketing: The State of the Art," *Journal of Business* 57 (January): 539-60.

Reibstein, D. J. and H. Gatignon (1984), "Optimal Product Line Pricing: The Influence of Elasticities and Cross-elasticities," *Journal of Marketing Research* 21 (August): 159-67.

Rowe, Debra and Christopher P. Puto (1987), "Do Consumers' Reference Points Affect Their Buying Decisions," in M. Wallendorf and P. Anderson, eds., *Advances in Consumer Research*, 14, Provo, Utah: Association for Consumer Research, 188-92.

Russo, E. J. (1977), "The Value of Unit Price Information," *Journal of Marketing Research* 14 (May): 193-201.

Schewe, C. D. and J. L. Wick (1977), "Innovative Strategies for Improving MIS Utilization," *Academy of Management Review* (January): 138-42.

Schewe, C. D. and W. R. Dillon (1978), "Marketing Information System Utilization: an Application of Self-Concept Theory," *Journal of Business Research* 6 (January): 67-79.

Schindler, R. M. (1984), "Consumer Recognition of Increases in Odd and Even Prices," *Advances in Consumer Research* 10: 459-61.

Shapiro, B. P. and B. B. Jackson (1978), "Industrial Pricing to Meet Customer Needs," *Harvard Business Review* 56 (November-December): 119-27.

Sheth, J. (1985), "New Determinants of Competitive Structures in Industrial Markets," in R. Spekman and D. Wilson, eds., *A Strategic Approach to Business Marketing.* Chicago: American Marketing Association.

Simon (1979), "Dynamics of Price Elasticity and Brand Life Cycles: An Empirical Study," *Journal of Marketing Research* 16 (November): 439-52.

Smith, H. B. (1988), "How to Concede—Strategically," *Sales and Marketing Management* (May): 79-80.

Stern, Andrew A. (1986), "The Strategic Value of Price Structure," *The Journal of Business Strategy* 7: 22-31.

Stern, Louis W. and Thomas L. Eovaldi (1984), *Legal Aspects of Marketing Strategy.* Englewood Cliffs, N.J.: Prentice-Hall.

Sultan, R. G. (1974), *Pricing in the Electrical Oligopoly.* Volume 1. Boston, Mass.: Harvard Graduate School of Business Administration.

Teplitz, C. J. (1988), "Negotiating Quantity Discounts Using a 'Learning Curve Style' Analysis," *Journal of Purchasing and Materials Management* (Summer): 33-43.

Thaler, Richard (1985), "Mental Accounting and Consumer Choice," *Marketing Science* 4 (Summer): 199-214.

Wall Street Journal (1981), "Prices: How They Get Set," Wall Street Journal Series, New York: Dow Jones and Co.

Weiner, Joshua L., James W. Gentry, and Ronald K. Miller (1986), "The Framing of the Insurance Purchase Decision," in Richard Lutz, ed., *Advances in Consumer Research* 13, 251-56.

Wilcox, J. B., R. D. Howell, P. Kuzdrall, and R. Britney (1987), "Price Quantity Discounts: Some Implications for Buyers and Sellers," *Journal of Marketing* 51 (July): 60-70.

Williams, Monci J. (1983), "The No-Win Game of Price Promotion," *Fortune* (July 11): 93-102.

Willis, E. (1986), "Using Modern Business Computers as a Marketing Tool," *Industrial Management and Data Systems* (July-August): 25-26.

Wisniewski, K. and R. C. Blattberg (1983), "Response Function Estimation Using UPC Scanner Data," in *Advances and Practices of Marketing Science*, ed., F. Zufryden, 300-11.

Zeithaml, V. A. (1987), "Defining and Relating Price, Perceived Quality, and Perceived Value," Report No. 87-101, Cambridge, Mass.: Marketing Science Institute (June).

———— (1988), "Consumer Perceptions of Price, quality, and Value: A Means-End Model and Synthesis of Evidence," *Journal of Marketing* 52 (July): 2-22.

Zicha, M. A. and R. A. Roy (1986), "Conjoint Analysis: One Way to Answer Pricing Questions," *Marketing News* (September 12): 16-23.

INDEX

ABOUT THE AUTHORS

Michael H. Morris is a member of the faculty in marketing at the University of Central Florida. Dr. Morris has published extensively on pricing and other marketing-related topics in *Business Horizons, Industrial Marketing Management,* the *International Journal of Research in Marketing,* the *American Journal of Economics and Sociology,* the *Journal of the Academy of Marketing Science,* and the *Journal of Business Research.* He also has authored a textbook entitled *Industrial and Organizational Marketing* (1988).

Dr. Morris has been recognized for both his reasearch and teaching efforts. In addition, he regularly consults with a number of corporations and other organizations, and is active in the American Marketing Association and the Academy of Marketing Science.

Gene Morris is a marketing consultant, currently residing in the Washington, D.C. area. He previously worked as a financial manager for an investment partnership.